THE POLITICAL ECONOMY OF DOWRY

The Political Economy of Dowry

Institutionalization and Expansion in North India

RANJANA SHEEL

MANOHAR
2025

First published 1999
Reprinted 2025
First eBook edition 2025

ISBN 978-81-7304-264-5 (hardbound)
ISBN 978-93-6080-180-9 (eBook)

Published by
Ajay Kumar Jain for
Manohar Publishers & Distributors
4753/23 Ansari Road, Daryaganj
New Delhi 110 002

Printed and bound in India

To
my parents
and
my parents-in-law
with love and gratitude

Contents

Foreword

Talking to a group of village men and women a few days ago, I asked those who had daughters, whether they had any regrets on this count. Almost all of them answered 'yes'. 'When a girl is born,' they said, 'our main worry is dowry and that is why we are unhappy.' This is a constant refrain—a search for a suitable boy and the anxiety of huge dowries and consequent indebtedness. The scourge of dowry and the maltreatment and burning of brides has led to the revival of female infanticide and foeticide in several parts of the country. It was, therefore, very appropriate that Dr Ranjana Sheel should have taken up the subject for her doctoral dissertation and I am happy that this thesis is now being published.

Dr Sheel traces the historical origin of the system of dowry as an integral part of marriage among Hindus of north India in recent times. She attempts to show how the practice of dowry is the product of modern political, economic and cultural processes. In pre-modern India, there were eight forms of marriage sanctioned and legitimized by the Dharmashastras. These eight practised forms were *Brāhma*, *Daiva*, *Prajāpatya*, *Ārsha*, *Asura*, *Gandharva*, *Rākshasa* and *Pishacha*. Of these, the first four were approved as superior and practised by the high castes. Only *Brāhma* and *Asura* marriages required some form of marital payments and transfer of property either in kind as gifts of jewellery and costly garments or in money. They respectively provided the basis for dowry and brideprice. The most respected form of marriage was the *Brāhma*, one which required the gift of a daughter, *kanyādāna*, together with presents or dowry. Till the medieval period, dowry seems to have been prevalent more among the high castes which practised the *Brāhma* form of marriage. Many lower castes had brideprice.

Dr Sheel shows how before the establishment of British rule, there was a great deal of fluidity in marriage forms in India. New interpretations of Hindu tradition, rituals and customs within a broad and rigid framework by the colonial rulers led to the gradual creation of a single form of Hindu marriage. She describes how the codification of Hindu laws led to the 'Brahmanization' and 'Sanskritization' of society and established the *Brāhma* form of marriage with dowry as its integral part as the only legally accepted form. This led to the adoption of the dowry system by all social groups and castes. In colonial India, the legally prima facie assumption was to consider all marriages in the *Brāhma* form and the courts did not consider the solemnization of a marriage in *Brāhma* form if no transaction of gifts from the bride's side to the other took place along with the *kanyādāna.* The colonial state thus not only legitimised dowry but also supported its expansion.

In the first phase of the women's movement, the national women's organizations such as the Women's Indian Association, All India Women's Conference, National Council of Women and others took up issue of child marriage, women's education, votes for women, legal rights for women but curiously dowry was not prominent on their agenda. However, women's journals in the vernacular languages in this period contain innumerable articles against dowry. In the women's movement since the mid-1970s, the issue of dowry has been of central concern. This was partly the result of the Status for Women's Committee Report which revealed the widespread and increasing practice of dowry. A large number of 'accidental' deaths of young married women were discovered by women's groups to be 'dowry murders' and an anti-dowry campaign was launched. A Dowry Prohibition Act was passed in 1961 which has been subsequently amended in 1984 and 1986. The giving and taking of dowry is prohibited by law but the law is totally ineffective and is flouted with impunity every day. Parents give dowry to raise their status and that of their daughters and with growing consumerism, there is no end to the greed of the bridegroom's side whose demands keep on increasing. Laws alone cannot bring about social change. They need to be given massive publicity and an awareness needs to be created about the value and worth of the girl child to bring about a change of attitudes.

Dowry is thus an issue of great contemporary relevance and Dr Sheel's book should be of interest both to specialists as well as to the general readers. It is an important contribution to the field of gender studies and offers insights and perceptions of our society.

APARNA BASU

Preface

Dowry, an integral part of the modern marriage system in India, has closely and crucially affected the status of women in contemporary Indian society. It has expanded all over India and its wider ramifications are visible in the spate of cases of bride-burning, suicides, and harassments. Professor M.N. Srinivas (1984: 29) thus aptly comments, 'it is necessary to remember that dowry is the suttee of the twentieth century'. How had this happened? The need and urgency to comprehend this problem led me to take up this subject for my Ph.D. research. The present study is the revised version of my Ph.D. dissertation.

When I began my study on the political economy of dowry, I thought of dowry as synonymous with bride-burning, people's greed, callousness and inhuman behaviour. The initial statistical counting of dowry deaths and individual incidents of harassment as reported in the newspapers, journals, and other print media as well as personal investigation of the amount and nature of dowry demanded in marriages across castes and classes failed to provide satisfactory answers—except engulfing me with a lot of anger and emotion. Yet, it indicated the complexity of the phenomenon and the need of linking and locating of dowry within a broad historical and social framework. It led me to pose questions such as: how does dowry interface with the issues of caste, class, property, etc., and how these themselves have changed over time to impact upon dowry. The present study therefore attempts to analyse how and why the form and practice of dowry encountered in the present times is itself the product of social, political, economic and cultural processes historically at work in society. In doing so, it links a number of wide ranging themes and issues on a variety of levels to comprehend not only the reasons for the expansion of dowry but also for failure at various levels to tackle the problem. The study in its present form is generally exploratory in nature and hopefully, more micro-level regional case studies along the lines would better substantiate the arguments put forward.

In completing the present work, my intellectual debts to Dr Aruna Sinha (History) and Professor Surinder Jetley (Sociology and Women's Studies) are immense. The study originally began under their guidance. They encouraged me to work on what appeared to me to be a subject with seemingly unending dimensions and scope. The canvas of my research was big and wide and it was their excellent intellectual support and innate patience that enabled me to traverse on it and draw a meaningful historical picture. I am especially thankful to Professor Surinder Jetley with whom I worked at the Centre for Women Studies, Banaras Hindu University. My association with her and my involvement with the activities of the Centre helped me to gain insights into women's studies.

Professors Aparna Basu (University of Delhi) and J.P. Sharma (University of Hawaii) offered valuable criticisms and suggestions to improve the work and encouraged me to present it for publication. I am thankful to them for their trust in my work. Professor Aparna Basu also very kindly wrote the Foreword in spite of her very busy schedule. I am also indebted to the faculty members of the Department of History, BHU, and especially to Professor J.P. Mishra, Dr J. Chaube and Dr K.S. Santha who evinced keen interest in my work and provided all possible help in both their academic and administrative capacities. Professors Uma Chakravarty, Leela Dube, Kumud Sharma, Kusum Kedia, Anjoo S. Upadhyaya, Govind Kelkar read/discussed some or whole of the manuscript and offered useful comments and suggestions. My colleagues at the Centre for Women's Studies, Sami Akhtar Khan, Kiron Bansal, Poonam Sinha and Sangeeta Krishna provided immense support in carrying out this work. I am also thankful to all at the CWDS, New Delhi, as well as the Law School, BHU, and Nagari Pracharini Sabha, Varanasi, for helping me locate necessary materials. Shri Ramesh Jain of the Manohar Publishers deserves special praise for not only agreeing to take up this study for publication but also for providing all the support.

I offer my sincerest gratitude to my father-in-law, Professor A.K. Narain and to my husband Professor Kamal Sheel who read the manuscript from beginning to end at various stages of its preparation. If the present work reflects imprints of their styles I am not at fault. For constant encouragement and appreciation of my work, I am thankful to my mother-in-law, Mrs Usha Narain. My parents, Mr N.P. Varma and Mrs Savitri Varma have provided unflinching support and strength in all my endeavours. I owe more to them than I can acknowledge. Manju and Avinash Varma and Krishna and Ameeta Saini always considered that I was doing some important work. I hope they are right. My two children, Siddharth and Aditi, lovingly bore the burden of their mother being seemingly endlessly involved in writing work. But their presence made writing a more pleasing exercise. Finally, needless to say, I alone am responsible for all the shortcoming and errors which may have occurred in the present work.

RANJANA SHEEL

Abbreviations

AIR	*All India Reporter*
AIDWA	All India Democratic Women's Association
AIWC	All India Women's Conference
AS	*Arthashāstra*
Bau. Dh. S.	*Baudhāyana Dharma Sūtra*
CAI	Constituent Assembly of India
CHI	*Cambridge History of India*
CrPC	Criminal Procedure Code
DVCM	Dahej Virodhi Chetna Manch
DPA	Dowry Prohibition Act
EWP	*Economic and Political Weekly*
FAOW	Forum Against Oppression of Women
IAWS	Indian Association of Women's Studies
ILR (Mad)	*Indian Law Review* (Madras)
ILR (Bom)	*Indian Law Review* (Bombay)
ISI	Indian Social Institute
IPC	Indian Penal Code
LSD	Lok Sabha Debates
NCWI	National Council of Women in India
NCWS	National Conference on Women's Studies
n.d.	No date
PIHS	*Proceedings of Indian History Congress*
RV	*Ṛgveda*
SC	Supreme Court
TE: CSWI	Towards Equality: Committee on the Status of Women in India
TOI	*Times of India*
VDS	*Vashishta Dharma Sūtra*
WIA	Women's Indian Association
YAJ.	Yajnavalkya

CHAPTER ONE

Introduction

> The dowry always signified much more than a transfer of funds; recent investigation of the dowry in various periods and places reveal its centrality to the history of women. . . . Through the dowry, the political, economic, and social determinants which limited women's agency are revealed. . . . Studies of the dowry address issues of the women's status, their roles in the family, the family economy, and the economy at large. Such studies force us to ask questions about women's power and autonomy . . . raise important issues of family history, from the foundation of the family economy to the reproduction of the family; from the power relations between genders and generations to the realm of affection among family members. . . Finally, political and economic changes affected the history of the dowry, but dowries were also used to alter political constellations and to build economic alliances. Therefore, a focus on dowries can also provide social historians the tools with which to approach the political and economic history. (Kaplan 1985: 2)

Historically, dowry has been an integral and institutionalized part of the Hindu marriage system.[1] It ideally and customarily denoted the gifts voluntarily presented to the bride, groom, and his family in marriage. The concept of *kanyādāna* with gifts ranging from ornaments, expensive clothes and other precious items finds references from the ancient to modern texts on customs and rituals. This social transfer of wealth within a cultural framework provided on the one hand the fulfilment of material obligation on the part of bride's family towards the bride, and on the other, served as a moral basis for the establishment of relationship between the two families.

The modern phenomenon of dowry however reflects a change in this customary system whereby the presentation of gifts has no longer remained a voluntary process. More often than not, the bride's family is coerced into providing dowry in the name of gift-giving. Also, gifts are evaluated in terms of their total cash value. Its amount is determined after negotiations between the bride and the bridegroom's families, often through a mediator. It is the bridegroom's family which settles the amount on the basis of its own socio-economic status. A better status fetches larger amount of dowry. The bride's family either reluctantly or eagerly complies with the 'gifts demands' primarily because of the socio-cultural stigma attached to keeping the girl in parental house beyond the marriageable age and to fulfil their own this-worldly obligations. If unable to fulfil all the demands at one time, gifts are promised in installments so as to eventually match the cash value demanded. Thus, two of the most distinct phenomena of modern dowry are discerned in the shift from voluntary to forced gift-giving or extortion by consent, and in the primary role of the bridegroom's family in determining the demand for gifts from the bride's family thus negating its connection with pre-mortem inheritance.

Repercussions of these shifts in the customary form of dowry are evident in the traumatic experiences of the bride's family and in the erosion of traditional moral ethos which provided a cohesive unity between families and community within the society. Marriages are increasingly becoming a source of financial strain for the bride's family. Increasing demands in cash or kind from the bridegroom's family make it difficult for daughters to be married off. Having large number of daughters in a family is viewed as a socio-religious curse, and for the girls themselves, it means a subordinate position in the family and society.

Inadequate dowry or the failure to meet the demands of the bridegroom's family often causes humiliation, trauma, and at the extreme end, the torture and death of brides. Reports of 'bride burning' or other dowry-related harassment abound in regional or national newspapers. Such incidents and the alarming proportion of dowry and its related harassment, have stirred the common people, scholars and women's organizations to start movements to stop the dowry system itself.

The shift in the system of dowry from a customary ritual to a modern socio-cultural evil is the subject of the present study. It aims to seek the historical roots of dowry as an institutionalized custom connected with marriage and its present peculiarities and characteristics. The dowry system cannot be viewed as a fast disappearing remnant of traditional society but rather, as a still expanding, if not strengthening, deep-rooted custom in modern Indian society. In this context, the study raises such questions as: What are the socio-political, economic and cultural forces which have contributed towards the perpetuation of dowry as a part of marriage system? How and why did its form change over the time? To what extent did it play a role in the growth of women's movement in India? And, finally, how was the problem of dowry perceived by the state and women's organizations and what constraints did they confront in the eradication of this custom? This study thus not only examines those socio-economic and cultural imperatives which provided the moral basis and legitimacy to the system of dowry but also attempts to identify forces which shifted its meaning and turned it into an alarming socio-cultural problem. Such a task requires the articulation of dowry within the rubric of political economy to analyze it in the context of a social structure with its distinct socio-economic, cultural and ideological forces.

Thus far no major study has attempted to provide a comprehensive historical picture of dowry and its various dimensions within the north Indian Hindu marriage system and society. Most of the recent studies focus on dowry's modern form and its present manifestations with specific reference to its traditionally legitimized practice of gift-giving. This often produces one-sided and incomplete analyses ignoring an investigation of social structures and caste/class dynamics in which the practice of dowry arose.

Much of the recent work on dowry have been produced by social scientists who have advanced various theories to explain the phenomena. One of the major trends in such studies focuses on the concepts of *dāna* and in this particular case, *kanyādāna,* and the attendant *dakshiṇā* as well as *strīdhana* as the moral basis for the practice of dowry (e.g. Van der Veen 1972; Madan 1975; Vatuk and Vatuk 1976; Paul 1986; Fruzzetti 1990, etc.). The '*dāna* and *dakshiṇā*' theory is based on the highest cultural and spiritual merit accorded to gift-givers and gift-giving in the traditional Hindu society. Dowry as such not only sanctifies material wealth but also enhances social status.

The ritual of marriage, this theory explains, involved *kanyādāna* or the gifting of daughter to the groom by the bride's father. The presentation of gifts accompanying the *kanyādāna* was the *dakshiṇā* which accorded sanctity to the marriage as well as enhanced the social status and prestige of the bride's family. In traditional society as evident from references in the Vedas and Smritis, no stigma was attached to the practice of gift-giving to the girl at the time of marriage. Such a practice was a part of the 'approved' forms of marriage. What was condemned was the price demanded by either side for consideration of marriage. The practice of bride-price was therefore highly 'disapproved'. Manu says, 'accepting the price out of greed, he (the father) becomes the seller of children' (III.51). While setting a price in marriage, or asking for gifts out of greed was strongly discouraged, dowry as a voluntary gift-giving, with its moral basis located in the superior spiritual and religious merit of the *dāna* and *dakshiṇā*, was heartily endorsed and extolled in the *shāstric* texts.

Dowry, not unlike *dāna*, as the voluntary gift-giving and as a means to earn spiritual and religious merit symbolized expression of love and affection of the giver towards the daughter. Explaining the growth of its present distorted form from the context of gift theory, Swarn Hooja (1968) posits that among aristocratic and royal families, huge gifts or dowry were traditionally offered to the bride and groom at the time of marriage by the bride's family as a mark of social prestige and honour. From about the mid-thirteenth and fourteenth centuries, this practice became rampant among the Rajputs. Associated with prestige and status, it gradually assumed a very rigid form whereby an element of competition and show predominated. After the mid-nineteenth century, several new factors combined with this and transformed dowry into a monstrous evil in the modern Indian society. Yet, for the non-aristocratic families, dowry has remained a mark of affection and love on the part of the family towards the daughter.

Similarly, Van der Veen (1972) puts forward the notion of an enhanced status for the giver of dowry as it was offered without expectation of any reciprocity. Following Louis Dumont (1959 and 1964), he considers dowry to be a *dakshiṇā* accompanying the *kanyādāna* which bestowed merit on the person who performed it selflessly with no thoughts of receiving any wealth in return. Moreover, describing dowry only as a part of the total process of Brahmanization, he explains that 'dowry marriage in itself is . . . not a realization of Brahman ideology, though the ideology provides a means for rationalizing the phenomenon. Dowry marriage is an ideological denial of reciprocity.' However, in practice, status is acquired in return for cash. 'Status increase' and 'status confirmation' are the aims for which dowries are now paid.

Vatuk and Vatuk (1976) however reject the notion of the enhanced status for the bride's family. They point out that the bride-giver always remains inferior in status to the bride-taker regardless of the offer of gift or dowry. Besides, they argue that dowry may have been a 'pure' gift in the ancient times but this is not true of the modern practice. In modern times, it may be, what Madan (1975) observes, the presentation as a means to ensure a daughter's well being in her in-laws' house. For girls, he argues, dowry provided acceptance and good will in their marital families on the one hand and compensation for the lack of inheritance rights on the other.[2] The giver in turn earned fame and social prestige. Dowry thus is

> a *sine qua non* of marriage and a substitute for women's lack of right of inheritance equivalent to those of men. . . . Sons inherit determinate shares by right. Daughters receive gifts at marriage and afterwards partly because it is a structural requirement—for without such gifts there can be no marriage and partly as a token of love (*pritidatta*). (Madan 1975: 237)

Fruzzetti (1990), in her recent study, *The Gift of a Virgin,* too concurs with the linkages of dowry with the gift of daughter. She however points out that while both dowry and the gift of daughter form part of the marriage rituals, they must be differentiated on lines of the sacred nature and the economic aspects of marriage. After all, if the gift of the virgin is the highest form of giving, why does the dowry then play such an important role in accepting or rejecting the girl? She traces its answers to the attitude towards women in the society which makes it imperative for a daughter to be married on grounds of purity and pollution. 'The purity of one's women has to be maintained, and the best way to ensure this is by giving them away in time'. As a result, 'elaborate rituals surround the gift of a virgin and seemingly unbalance the economics of dowry giving' (ibid: 31). Dowry 'physical' and 'changeable' thus reflects the economic status of the giver, while *kanyādāna* is dictated by caste and kinship principles and is 'unalterable and sacred'.

The '*dāna* and *dakshiṇā*' theory thus explores the moral basis of dowry by linking it either to symbols of love and affection or to religious and spiritual merit to gain social prestige and status. Thus institutionalized, the process of rigidification of dowry in the medieval period was aided by changes in the social set-up with pre-puberty marriages becoming the norm. This resulted in rising compulsion for the parents to arrange an early marriage for the girl at any cost. Dowry then served the purpose of luring desirable grooms and appropriating political benefits. This brought in distortion in the earlier character and purpose of the gift-giving or dowry.

Further twist in the meaning and practice of dowry is linked to socio-economic developments during the late nineteenth and early twentieth centuries. The monetization of economy during the colonial period provided impetus to 'acquisitionism' and consumerism. This altered the notion of both 'desirable' dowry as well as of 'desirable' grooms. 'Desirable' in the modern context came to be determined both by customs and usages like caste and *gotra* as well as by the parameters of 'success' in the new socio-economic set up. Traditional custom of gift-giving was now replaced by demands for cash, jewellery and other items. This is legitimated by the practice of customary ritual of *vara-dakshiṇā* before the marriage. Thus, in its modern manifestation, dowry connotes involuntary gift-giving with its amount determined by the bridegroom's family.

Without denying the contribution of the *dāna* and *dakshiṇā* theory in the comprehension of the historical shift in the meaning of dowry, its weakness lies in its obfuscation of the bride and her rights. It not only presumes love and affection giving fillip to gift-giving but also puts the onus of gaining social status and prestige through such *dāna* and *dakshiṇā* to the bride's family. It does not answer what made it imperative for the bride's family to perform such a ritual of gift-giving at the time of marriage. If in modern marriages, a great deal of pomp and show is displayed by the bride's family to demonstrate their social status and to gain prestige in the community, performance of rituals of all types and related to birth, death, and other social occasions in all historical periods, served the purpose of reaffirming the performer's linkages and status within the community. So, what was so special about gift-giving at the time of marriage, whether with or without love and affection? Alternatively, one may ask why did not the bridegroom's family indulge in gift-giving to the bride's family to enhance its status? Indeed, the origin of dowry thus cannot be specifically related to the desire for gift-giving out of love and affection or for enhancing one's status. The rights of the daughter within a family set-up which developed a sense of obligation towards her and expressed symbolically in gift-giving at the time of marriage, i.e. parting from her own family, need to be studied carefully in order to comprehend the system of dowry.

M.N. Srinivas (1984) in his short but illuminating article, 'Some Reflections on Dowry', traces the origin of dowry to the prevailing ideology of kinship structure, caste system, and hypergamous marriage. The combination of these factors shaped the economic behaviour of the people having daughters, brought about 'status asymmetry' between affinal groups and promoted the practice of dowry in north India.[3] To be more precise, dowry was synonymous with hypergamy. The bride's family gained status by establishing relationship with the higher ranked groom's kin by presenting a great deal of cash, jewellery, clothing and other goods. In weddings, gifts were thus rarely exchanged on an equal basis and flowed in a one-way direction even long after the actual marriage ceremony was over.

The 'modern' dowry, in contrast, is the product of such additional factors as the volatile money economy, increased agricultural prosperity, and the rise of 'organized sector' on the one hand, and the customary rules of caste endogamy and pre-puberty marriage on the other. Its rigid framework turned it into a 'social evil'. Thus, 'modern' dowry, according to Srinivas (1984: 12-13), should not be confused with 'ancient and respected custom' of *strīdhana* or *kanyādāna* which had a definite purpose. To equate the huge amount of goods, cash, jewellery with *dakshiṇā* is stretching the point too far to legitimize or explain 'a modern monstrosity', yet it is common enough among scholars.

What then lends the practice of dowry its legitimacy? How does it perpetuate in the social set-up of today? Srinivas points to the factor of the increasing emulation of higher caste by the lower castes for contributing to the legitimacy and spread of dowry. Even those hypergamous communities where the bride price was earlier practised subsequently shifted to the practice of dowry. Yet, this process of social mobility, he argues, cannot be termed as Sanskritization, as referred to by scholars like Epstein (1973) and others in their discussions of dowry. 'Dowry came to the Brahmins through the process of "Westernization" and it does not become Sanskritization when others take it over from Brahmins' (Srinivas 1984: 22). This distinction facilitates Srinivas to link the evils, rigidities, greed, etc., of dowry to the process of Westernization and the new socio-economic forces after World War II.

To a large extent, cultural anthropologists subscribe to articulation of linkages between dowry and hypergamy. Veena Das (1975) conforms to the theory of kinship with hypergamy as determinants for dowry. Arguing against purely economic explanations, she writes that stratification in status, wealth and power which determines the rank and lineage within a caste group, such as the Rajputs, gave impetus to hypergamous marriage to gain social prestige. 'The social cost' of such a marriage for the bride's family was met through either political support or money. Van der Veen (1972) too finds connection between societies practising hypergamous marriages and dowry.[4] When caste sets the limit from which the groom has to be sought, often escalation in dowry results. Within this framework, G.N. Ramu (1977) discusses other factors like class, occupation and education of the groom on the one hand and bride's personal appearance, merit, etc., on the other, as determinant to the amount of dowry. According to him, dowry in modern times thus acts as a preventive measure for a person from lower status from entering into marriage alliance with those in higher status. To be sure, in modern India, the practice of hypergamous marriages provided necessary social background to the prevalence of the dowry system. The process of Sanskritization or Westernization spread the practice of hypergamous marriages among the lower castes too, and dowry came to encompass the larger part of the society.

Indira Rajaraman's (1983) purely economic analysis of dowry as a 'negative bride-price in the organized sector' is yet another attempt to discuss the problem from a very different angle. She argues that the earlier bride price served as compensatory payment to the bride's family for the loss of a productive member by way of her economic contribution to the household. As women's participation in production declined, organized sectors arose and prosperity increased, dowry served as compensation for women's share of 'leisure' and her 'negative networth'. Only rising contribution of women to family income can inhibit the dowry demands.

Rajaraman's polemical and ahistorical exposition of dowry and reasons for its expansion elicited strong response from scholars.[5] Her interpretation appears to be rooted in Comaroff's (1980) 'cost-benefit ratio' type of analysis where marriage payments, dowry and bride-price, are observed as compensation for a dependent and productive member respectively. But this does not explain the historical pattern of change. Dowry continues to be given and demanded irrespective of the 'positive' or 'negative' worth of a woman. The increasing leisure for women from outside work may have, as Srinivas (1984) argues, resulted from growing prosperity. In fact, historically, prosperity led peasants turned landowners to keep their women secluded in keeping with the ideal observed by the Brahmin women. Moreover, the extension of dowry among the low castes, the women of which have historically continued to contribute to the work force in the earlier manner, negates the 'negative net worth' analysis. Ursula Sharma (1984) too does not find any large scale withdrawal of women especially of low caste from the work force in the Indian society and hence its causal relation to the shift to dowry is not discernible. What may however be seen as having some applicability to the question of dowry is a change in proportion and the nature of women's contribution in relation to men.

For a student of history, the gradual evolution of the patriarchal structure and the consequent subordinate position of women assume greater significance in raising questions which are confined not only to the current dimensions of dowry. First, why do the hypergamous marriages involve the question of status only for the bride's family? Why was it not historically necessary for the bridegroom's family to gain its own prestige by marrying their sons to daughters of superior families? While hypergamy helps to comprehend the modern distortion and manifestation of the dowry system, it does not provide an adequate analysis of the historical reasons for shifting the onus of gift-giving on the bride's family through the practice of hypergamous marriages. Second, the question of dowry also requires an analysis of the historical evolution of customary and traditional restriction on socio-economic rights of the woman over the property of her natal or marital families. Was not the gift given to the bride's family historically symbolic of the social transfer of that portion of wealth over which the bride had the right? Third, the system of dowry was not limited to Indian society. Such practices have been found to exist in such agriculturally dominant societies as the Chinese, South East Asian or even pre-modern European.[6] Can gift-giving or dowry in all these societies be linked to hypergamous marriages?

Goody and Tambiah (1973) provide a wider analytic perspective to comprehend the historical roots of dowry. This together with the theory of hypergamous marriages provide illuminating insights to the political economy of dowry. In a comparative study of the origin of bridewealth and dowry in Africa and Eurasia, Goody and Tambiah (1973: 64) relate dowry to 'a type of pre-mortem inheritance' to the bride. Dowry, they write,

> connotes female property or female right to property which is transferred at a woman's marriage as a sort of pre-mortem inheritance. Dowry also connotes, in complementary fashion that property is transferred together

with a daughter so that she is enabled to enter into marriage. In other words, a daughter and her dowry become vehicles for setting up a relation of affinity between the bride's family and the husband's family.

The origin and development of this practice, it is argued, was the result of a shift from tribal to agrarian and from matrilineal to patriarchal social structure. This consequently subordinated women's socio-economic position in society. Women's position in rural communities in two broad groups of society is thus distinguished as what Boserup (1970: 50) remarks:

> [T]he first type is found in regions where shifting cultivation predominates and the major part of agricultural work is done by women. In such communities, we can expect to find a high incidence of polygamy and bride-wealth. . . . The second group is found where plough cultivation predominates and where women do less agricultural work than men. In such communities we may expect to find that only a tiny minority of marriages, if any, are polygamous, that a dowry is usually by the girl's family; that a wife is entirely dependent upon her husband for economic support. . . .

She further mentions that the first type of rural community is seen in Africa, south of the Sahara, in many parts of South-East Asia and in tribal regions in many parts of the world. The second type predominates in regions influenced by Arab, 'Hindu' and Chinese cultures (ibid).

For our purposes, the important point to note is that the shift in the socio-economic basis of the society initiated and provided imperative to a process which had bearings on the evolution of the different institutions of marriage and the practice of gift-giving. While Goody views polygamy and monogamy as well as bride wealth and dowry as 'being related less directly to women's contribution to agriculture and more to the problem of "status placement" in societies with varying degrees of socio-economic differentiation' (1973: 46); the importance of the new socio-economic changes which created a framework for this cannot be undermined. In the ancient egalitarian tribal structure women's participation was equal to, if not more than, men. The establishment of agriculture-based society necessitated growth of private property and male domination in production process. Landholding thus became an important criteria for the social differentiation between members of the same village. It connoted 'status'. Social consequences of the agriculture-based production process manifested itself in the declining role of women, control over women's customary socio-economic rights, and the maintenance of status or upward social mobility either through the preservation or expansion of landed property. 'One way of maintaining one's status', as Goody (1973: 25) remarks,

> might be by limiting the number of heirs who would share in the heritable property. However, it was a matter of preserving the status of daughters as well as sons. Sons might inherit all the productive capacity but daughters had to be assured of a marriage that would provide them with the same (or better) standard of life to which they are accustomed. They had to be endowed with property to attract a husband of the same rank, though other factors such as beauty and lineage, and even the location of property entered into the match.

The endowment of a share of movable property to the bride may be viewed as pre-mortem inheritance provided as her right and also to maintain and forge relationship based on the status.

Goody and Tambiah's hypothesis about the equation of dowry with pre-mortem inheritance has received criticism from scholars who have attempted to relate it to the modern context alone. They argue that the contemporary shape of dowry more as a 'groom-price' (Billig 1991; Caplan 1984), with brides having no control over it and being only a vehicle for its transmission (Sharma 1984; Agarwal 1988; Madan 1975), stretches the meaning of inheritance too far. To be sure, dowry in its modern context may be different from its original intent and meaning. But this does not rob the concept of pre-mortem inheritance of its heuristic applicability to trace the origin of modern dowry. This being especially so when both the English etymology of the term 'dowry' and the Sanskrit origin of the term '*dahej, daeej*, etc.' appear to refer to nuptial presents or share of inheritance depending upon the root word to which the latter term is linked. Linkages between marriage, property and dowry, as we shall see later, has been evident from the ancient times.

Dowry, in its historical context, may thus be more appropriately viewed as arising from both compensation to a girl in lieu of the full right of inheritance and from hypergamy to maintain or provide a desired social status. The practice of dowry gets its specific colouring in the way it gets linked up with prevailing socio-cultural ideology and the politico-economic institutions. In Indian society, this act of gift-giving was performed through the socio-culturally prescribed channel of '*dāna*'. Dowry, thus, as Tambiah (1973) notes, lends itself to being dressed up as a 'gift' that accompanies the gift of virgin (*kanyādāna*). It is this facsimile of gift-giving that the proponents of '*dāna-dakshiṇā*' theory attribute to the origin and development of the practice of dowry. The specific *dāna* and *dakshiṇā* at the time of marriage, when viewed also in the context of its socio-economic and cultural meanings, makes the characteristic significance of dowry apparent.

The historical origin of dowry may thus be connected to the shift in social set-up marked by a gradual move from a relatively egalitarian to patriarchal structure and from a communal to private property/ plough cultivation economy. As this shift took place over a long span of time, several practices pertaining to the earlier social structure continued till they were rendered meaningless with the strengthening of the new system. The dowry with all its manifestation thus needs to be viewed within the larger patriarchal system and its attendant subordination of women.

In the above context, the present study pertains to an examination of the political economy of dowry with special reference to north India. It aims to trace the social and economic context to the historical origin and the phenomenal expansion of the system of dowry as an integral part of the north Indian Hindu marriage form during the modern times. It also attempts to analyse its history and growth in the context of the women's movement and the state's efforts to combat it. This study is therefore concerned less with the historical record of incidence of dowry from ancient to the present times or the discussion of its justification or denunciation by the earlier Dharmashāstras and its later interpretations in the books of conduct. It deals more with the extent to which the form and practice of dowry encountered in the present times is itself the product of modern social, political, economic and cultural processes. The persistence of a traditional custom or practice requires comprehension of those features of Indian society which make dowry an important aspect of the current marriage form.

Moreover, it may also be pointed out that the need to achieve aims outlined above and to present a conceptual framework for a broader study of dowry has resulted in our usage of diverse historical and contemporary sources. This has also transcended the scope of the study from specific regional and community confines and historical periods. It is hoped that the conceptual framework presented can be further tested in separate studies of different regions by employing local historical and contemprary sources including such oral history techniques as interviews and reminiscences.

Chapters two and three argue dowry's linkages with cultural tradition and pre-modern marriage forms as well as with such socio-economic factors as property and inheritance rights of women, overriding caste/class dimensions, and the colonial impact to facilitate the understanding of its pervasive impact on the marriage system in north India. The second chapter deals particularly with the historical background to the dowry drawing upon the standard texts on Hindu customs and rituals. It does not provide a textual study but attempts to highlight major features of social prescriptions presented therein. While these prescriptive texts may or may not provide the actual conditions, they at least help us learn the 'ideal-types' propagated in the early Indian situation.[7] They demonstrate that dowry was not part of all the eight forms of marriage sanctioned and legitimated by the Hindu Dharmashāstras. Besides, descriptions in Dharmashāstras and other relevant works on the position of women in ancient Hindu society emphasize the plurality and fluidity within marriage forms. Only two forms of marriage, namely *Brāhma* and *Asura*, have been described as requiring some distinct form of marital payments and transfer of property either in kind as gifts of jewellery and costly garments or in money. They respectively provided the basis for the practice of dowry and bride-price. The most respected form was designated to be the *Brāhma* marriage which required the gift of daughter with precious presents or dowry. It appears to have become an integral part of the social set-up marked by hypergamous marriage alliances. Till the medieval period, dowry seems to be prevalent more among high castes and classes which went through the *Brāhma* form of marriage. Yet, even among the higher castes, the non-dowry-giving forms of marriage, such as *Gandharva*, provided legitimate options without any obligatory payment. The larger section of society consisting of hierarchically lower castes seems to have indulged not in dowry but bride-price.

The third chapter is entitled 'The Institutionalization and Expansion of Dowry in the Colonial Period'. Based on such primary sources as census reports, travelogues, judicial records, and caste surveys, it discusses the colonial reinvention of tradition and law. It describes how the codification of Hindu laws by the British led to the Brahmanization or Sanskritization of society and established the *Brāhma* form of marriage with dowry as its integral part the only legally accepted form. The earlier fluid pattern thus melted away. It also details the impact of colonial restructuring of the socio-economic order on the class/caste patterns and the system of dowry. It emphasizes that the context in which myriad social changes took place during the colonial period was marked by incomplete modernization and the reinforcement of tradition from the above. Such developments promoted caste rigidities as well as Brahmanization of the socially mobile sub-caste groups.

The next two chapters are discussed in the light of the contemporary manifestations of dowry and the nature of the attention given to it by the women's movement (chapter four) and the state (chapter five). The major purpose is to demonstrate that large scale class/caste changes during the colonial period, which had distinct gender dimension as well as bearing on dowry (discussed in chapter three), were often ignored or inadequately presented in the contemporary focus on women. As a result, some social practices and their social, political, and legal redressals were highlighted as encompassing women's question. The early reform movement and the state's response to women's issue starkly reflect this failure. The women's movement's perception and responses to the problem of gender inequality, and specifically to the question of dowry, initially differed at the regional and national levels. The earlier phase was marked by a relatively limited yet consistent regional protest against dowry. For example, in the Hindi belt of north India, as discussed in chapter four, it was expressed primarily by the middle classes in local areas through caste *sabhās* and the vernacular press publishing women's journals and magazines. The main focus of the national level organizations of women remained on issues of child marriage, widow remarriage, etc., and later the varying strands were subsumed under the intensified struggle for independence from foreign rule. The rise of the second or post-Independence phase of the women's movement beginning from the late seventies has been attributed to the escalation in dowry practice and a large number of 'accidental' deaths of young married women revealed by women's groups as 'dowry murders'. On the basis of reports and journals of women's groups and writings of women activists, this chapter attempts to comprehend the nature of the women's movement and its perception about dowry. It also examines various forms of anti-dowry protests in the contemporary period.

The fifth chapter discusses the state measures to combat the problem of dowry. Focusing on the Constituent Assembly and the Lok Sabha Debates, it describes the nature of legislators' perception on the issue of dowry and its impact on the enactment of the Dowry Prohibition Act of 1961, its Amendments in 1984 and 1986, and on women's right to property. In the light of the above discussion, the chapter attempts to gauge the real intent and content of the state's programmes and its commitment to bring change in the existing state of affairs. The conclusion (chapter six) presents broad generalizations linking complex historical developments during the colonial and post-colonial period to the institutionalization and expansion of the system of dowry in modern India.

NOTES

1. It may be mentioned here that the dowry was an integral part of marriage in many societies. In the Indian context, one can find its existence and expansion to the marriage system of non-Hindus too. However, the present work focuses on the dowry's phenomenal and distinctive form based on an element of compulsion which, to a great extent, historically emerged as a specific characteristic of the Hindu marriage system. In the present work, our discussion is limited to its nature in north India.
2. Madan, however, does not equate dowry with inheritance rights for the bride because whatever she carries with her is a gift as the 'comprehensive notion' of *kanyādāna* is inclusive of both the girl and gifts. What she receives as gift is reflective of her family's socio-economic situation at the time of marriage only. It is in no way related to her shares in the ancestral property. Her exclusive property jurally remains the *strīdhana* which includes gift from her natal as well as marital families but over which her control may remain limited. Moreover, *strīdhana* constitutes only a part of the total dowry which also include separate gifts for groom and his families.
3. Srinivas (1984) distinguishes between the hypergamous and the non-hypergamous regions of India, the former giving rise to and inculcating dowry of the pre-British variety. In the non-hypergamous areas, bride price and exchange system are the dominant trend. The higher and richer castes practised dowry and the lower and poorer practised marriage by exchange or paid bride-price.
4. In a recent study discussing the case of the Marathas, Anavil Brahmins and the Rajputs, Ranjana Kumari (1989) also contends that hypergamous marriages are integral to dowry and *vice-versa.*
5. For the detailed criticism of Indira Rajaraman's 'cost-benefit ratio' type analysis, see Aziz (1983); Sambrani and Sambrani (1983); and Randeria and Visaria (1984). Ursula Sharma's (1984) critique of

Comaroff also makes several valid points which are applicable to the criticism of Rajaraman.

6. For a good analytic discussion of historical evolution and patterns of marriage bargains and dowry in European societies, see Kaplan (1985). It has been discussed that dowry in these societies developed to protect lineage and property and to consolidate the existing social relations. It varied in size and scope with vacillations in the economy during various stages of capitalism. The practice declined in the advanced capitalist society only with the entrance of a large number of women as paid workers. Similarly, in China, as Siu's (1990) study demonstrates, the revival and expansion of this old practice is related to the recent sudden economic spurts in a traditional society.
7. For the pitfalls of judging women's position in early Indian society only on the basis of these texts and the need for recreating an alternative analysis, see Chakravarty (1989 and 1993).

CHAPTER TWO

Historical Background of Dowry in India

The contemporary prevalence and expansion of the dowry system in India necessitates search for its historical background. This is not because dowry in its present form has been a part of the marriage forms in the long history of ancient Indian tradition but because its contemporary practice is often legitimized by indicating its socio-religious linkages with, and sanction by, ancient religious texts and numerous digests. So much so that dowry is either equated with, or legitimized by, religious traditions and social practices. For many, its contemporary dimension is linked with those anachronistic parts of tradition which have continued to survive and flourish in the same way as the caste system. For others, it is considered a necessary part of a vigorous and glorified 'Hindu' marriage tradition. Its contemporary defects are more or less linked with the changed outlook of its modern practitioners. There are indeed ample evidence which trace the origin and evolution of dowry to traditions. Yet, the prevalence of dowry and its pervasive impact on the marriage system of contemporary India raises the question: How integral was dowry to the marriage forms of pre-modern India? How, why and to what extent was it legitimized by a tradition or traditions? A comprehension of the position of dowry in pre-modern Indian marriage forms is thus imperative to analyse the nature of its linkages with tradition as well as its contemporary prevalence.

In a wider perspective, the custom of dowry raises yet another issue. Studies of other societies of the world indicate that the dowry was not unique to Indian society. It, as well as the bride-price, was practised in marriage forms found in as diverse societies as African and European or the tribal and the urban. The common factor which characterizes this widespread custom has been its intricate connection with patterns of inheritance and property within a patriarchal set-up. What were these linkages between property, dowry and marriage in pre-modern Indian society? How did these reinforce the custom of dowry? The relationship between property, women's inheritance rights, and marriage (with the exchange of payments in the form of either dowry or bride-price) needs to be explored to analyse modern dowry. In the above context, this chapter investigates the evolution and pattern of the dowry system in pre-modern India.

Property, Marriage and Women

The symbiotic relationship between property, women's inheritance rights and forms of marriage is generally traced to the shift from tribal to agricultural society. Not unlike other societies of the world, this lent impetus to the reconfiguration of the status and the position of women in Indian society. Historically, the sexual subordination of women, as Lerner (1986: 9) has pointed out, was effected through ideology, force, economic dependency on the male head of the family, and privileges conferred in order to gain the compliance of women of the upper classes. Within a patriarchal set-up, characteristic forms of inheritance and patterns of kinship developed. These perpetuated subordination of women. Property in all its forms came to be regarded 'as a crucial indicator of the balance of power between women and men' (Hirschon 1984: 1).

Accordingly, patriarchy has been defined to indicate that "men hold power in all the important institutions of society and that women are deprived of access to such power. It does not imply that women are either totally powerless or totally deprived of rights, influence and resources' (Lerner 1986: 239). These developments established the basis on which customs, rituals, religious and legal codes and prescriptions developed over a long period of history to institutionalize the process of women's subordination. The evolution of dowry thus must be seen not only in the cultural symbols and social practices of a particular society but also in the structural dimensions of property and gender hierarchy inherent in it. The basis for the growth and evolution of a particular set of customs, beliefs and rituals which institutionalized dowry needs careful observation.

The process of transformation to a patriarchal society was slow and gradual. In India, 'the historical picture', as Kosambi (1965: 50-1) writes, 'is of a slow expansion of food producing society in a virtually limitless environment very thinly populated by food gatherers'. Historians agree that the Rgvedic period was characterized by a pastoral society with the predominance of tribal elements. As R.S. Sharma (1983: 27; see also Altekar 1956) writes that 'in the *Ṛgveda,* people were organized not along *varṇa* lines or class lines but along tribal lines. . . . Women, the producers of fighters and cattle herders, were in great demand because men perished in perpetual tribal wars.' Besides the importance of women's reproductive role, the pastoral economy in which the household was an important unit ensured women's position in society. Suvira Jaiswal (1981: 55-6) maintains that although many warrior and priestly families had emerged as elites, and references to prayers for sons appear, yet the Ṛgvedic society was communal in functioning and no stratification on class or gender lines was apparent. On the other hand, Uma Chakravarty (1993: 579-81) finds both class stratification and gender hierarchy in an incipient form in this period. She demonstrates that patriarchal control through legitimate reproduction, patrilineal succession, *niyoga* and dominance over female slaves by men as well as women of the dominant class had become somewhat institutionalized. Such pictures of the Ṛgvedic society indicate the beginning of a process of social change affecting the position of women. Yet, the society appears in a transitory stage in which rituals and practices legitimizing subordination of women had still not been firmly rooted. The daughter's birth was still not a source of consternation and the marriage system, as we shall see later, was fluid.

The post-Vedic period witnessed withdrawal of women as a group from the production process as dependency on agriculture increased. Food production became concentrated outside the household. Social stratification manifested itself in the form of classes as well as castes. The upper caste and upper class women came to be confined within the household. The introduction of iron-plough based agriculture and the subsequent development of a defined family structure, private property, patrilineal succession, and the state further sharpened the caste, class and gender divisions. This process of transition became well-marked by the sixth century B.C. (Chakravarty 1993: 581; Jaiswal 1981: 58). R.S. Sharma (1983: 34) observes: 'Later Vedic society marked the beginning of the transition to class society and state formation. . . . But it was really in the post Vedic times, in the age of the Buddha, that the *varṇa* divided and state based society was founded'.

The changing socio-political situation and the increasing differentiations were based on power which was used to maintain a 'hierarchy of privilege'. The authority of the ruler was based upon the major social hierarchies and his vested interest lay in its perpetuation. The decline in the importance of large scale sacrifice (*rājasuya* and *ashvamedha*) giving way to rituals associated with individuals was due to the far-reaching changes such as the emergence of the state, and an increasingly complex socio-economic order. Rituals validated 'the existing and emerging hierarchies based on *varṇa*, gender and patrilineal kinship structure' (Roy 1985: 142). In fact, the period from the mid-first millennium BC witnessed significant and far-reaching changes.[1] Caste purity through a closely guarded system of marriage, legitimate reproduction, strict rules against adultery, and patrilineal succession were prescribed both by the normative and the prescriptive texts.[2] The patriarchal family that became family rooted not only created the institutional edifice of the state's economic, political, military and religious power but was also in turn constantly recreated by the expansion of these overarching institutions of power. As can be easily derived, the major victims of this shift to a class, caste and gender-stratified society were women.

The rise of a patriarchal society thus witnessed the beginning of a process of ideological hegemony through control over upper caste women to maintain caste purity and patriliny. Emphasis was laid on marriage according to the prescribed forms with prescribed partners. The importance of ancestor worship and legitimate motherhood was recommended in order to fit in the patriarchal arrangement. The upper caste women were exhorted to follow the ideology of *strīdharma* as advocated in the Brahmanical literature. Discussing it as the 'master-stroke of Hindu-Aryan genius', Chakravarty (1993: 583) writes that this firmly established patriarchy as an ideology since it was 'naturalized'. *Strīdharma* and *pativratā* were not only accepted but were venerated by women themselves as concepts. The huge mass of Brahmanical literature prescribing laws and customs and social codes bear testimony to trends keeping women within the patriarchal structure. An attempt to legitimize the emerging socio-political order by 'reinforcing the notion of hierarchy at a number of levels, and by inculcating a belief in the "inevitability" and "naturalness" of systems based on superordination and subordination' is evident (Roy 1985: 142).

In this context, linkages between property and marriage are not difficult to co-relate. As in all other patriarchal civilizations, in the

Indian society too, the transfer of property, both movable and/or immovable, to a woman took place on the occasion of her marriage. Yet, as the practice of forbidding daughters from inheriting land became the norm to prevent the transfer of property to husband's family at marriage, women were permitted to take a portion of movable property with them at marriage as dowry (Thapar 1963: 477). It may be thus argued that as the process of delinking women from property rights began, at empts were made to adequately compensate her at the time of marriage which marked her transfer from her own patrilineal descent. To quote Romila Thapar again, 'the purpose of marriage was the furtherance of caste (*jāti*) relations, essentially a social and political concern, and where it existed, marriage was aimed at the consolidation of property'. There were, however, exceptions, but they were generally the result of 'the interplay of patrilineal and matrilineal groups which have been active for many centuries until recent years. . . . Family and social relationships did follow either of the two dominant forms or an intermingling of the two, and this is sometimes suggested even by contemporary family structures. This in part accounts for the regional variations in the status (both implied and actual) of women in various parts of the country' (Thapar 1975: 12). This appears to have cemented the symbiotic relationship between property, marriage and dowry. Women's acquisition of property was almost synonymous with marriage and her control over it depended on the form of marriage she was wedded in indicating thereby her caste and class status. A look at the forms of marriage would be useful at this juncture.

Forms of Marriage and Dowry

The forms of marriage have a direct bearing upon our subject of dowry. While the proprietorial rights of women were dependent on her marital status, the approved marriage forms emphasized the concept of gift-giving in the form of movables and immovable at the time of *kanyādāna*, i.e. the gifting of the daughter to the groom. These approved forms of marriage took precedence over the other forms as the hold of the Brahmanical order and expressions of patriarchal control got strengthened and codified. Yet no simple uniform structure of marriage, kinship or property developed. Complexities and fluidity are discernible despite the detailed norms of conduct laid down for all caste groups. Different marriage forms flourished despite the tight structure of marriage advocated. One is thus more struck by diverse forms of marriage than by a common code. While the Brahmanical tradition under-lined the approved forms, other marriage forms were common and open to probably all those who were outside the Brahmanical tradition.

The oldest known surviving record of marriage is in the tenth book of *Ṛgveda* (*RV* X.85; also see Altekar 1956; Apte 1978). This is apparently devoid of complexities of rites that characterized a marriage ceremony in the later texts. Marriage was solemnized by the grasping of the bride's hand by the groom accompanied by prayers for progeny, long life and well-being by invoking different Gods through sacrifices (*RV* X.85.36 in Shastri 1990: 28). References also reveal that considerable freedom was enjoyed by both men and women in choosing their marriage partners (*RV* X.27.12; *RV* X.85.21 in Bhargava 1988: 3 and Indra 1955: 42-3). It is evident that the bride was to be from outside the family (see Apte 1978: 9). This becomes more apparent in the later texts. Clan exogamy is not mentioned (Apte 1978: 14), thus reflecting a transitional society when social norms and hierarchy have still not rigidified. In the *Ṛgveda* itself, no mention of alternate forms of procuring a wife are to be found. However, as Sastri and others have pointed out, the existence of different marriage forms in their rudimentary stages can be traced to the early texts (see Sastri 1972: 139; Sarkar 1928: 80; Apte 1978: 16). For example, references to self-choice by the maiden, or payment to the guardian of the bride serve as pointers to the specific forms that developed later. References are also available of variations such as the mother of the bride playing an important role in arranging the marriage, or of a brother-sister marriage, etc. (see Apte 1978: 10-12).

By the middle of the first millennium, as Romila Thapar points out, 'tribal egalitarianism had surrendered to the evolution of a system of government that, whether oligarchic or monarchical, was explained as concerning itself with the problems of social disharmony, the need for authority, and the justification for revenue collection' (Thapar 1978: 45). This brought about the development of caste structures out of a variety of interrelationships between groups. 'The purity-pollution dichotomy which, above all, demarcated the Brahman from the untouchable and which was absent in the earlier period, [was] now well established' (Thapar 1978: 47). The dichotomous ethnic, linguistic, and cultural differences gave way to a social order based on the use of Sanskrit and the observation of *varṇa* rules. The maintenance of the purity of castes required not only the ban on commensality among members of different castes but also enforcement of rules of caste endogamy and exogamy. The struggle between the new and the older tribes, the emergence of social stratification and defined family structures on the *varṇa* and caste lines had thus their implications upon the complexities that led to the need for the codification of laws, and the creation of Dharmasūtras.[3] Emerging complex patterns in society also became apparent in marriage forms and rituals that subsequently arose.

While historical accounts of changing preferences in marriage styles and forms are limited and vague, one of the best examples of changes in the ideals of marriage can be seen in the *Mahābhārata* itself. Scholars are now unanimous in assigning a late date to the *Mahābhārata's Anushāsana Parva*, as compared to the *Ādi Parva*.[4] One of the reasons for such assumption is difference in views expressed on marriage in the two Parvas, which suggests not only their composition in different periods but also the changing emphasis on the ideal marriage type. As Talbot aptly demonstrates that 'the epic progresses from extolling purely *kshatriya* forms to recommending *kanyādāna* for brahmins and *kanyādāna* or warrior-like marriages to *kshatriyas* and in the final phase advocates *kanyādāna* for everyone'[5](Talbot 1980: 61). Similarly, D.C. Sircar writes that,

> it is evident from works like the Mahabharata and the Manusmriti that the way of securing a wife and a son in ancient India was rather irregular in comparison with the definite and regular systems of later days. Many of the marital unions of early times can hardly be reconciled with the social ideals of modern India. The *gotrantara* seems to have become a regular feature of marriage only after the popularization of later ideas in the Indian society. It seems that forms of marriage not involving *gotrantara* were quite popular at least down to the fifth century AD[6]. (Sircar 1967: 209)

From the Smriti period onwards, the approved and unapproved forms of marriage developed with growing Brahmanical influence. These were coded in the *Manusmriti* as eight forms of marriage and graded according to contemporary norms providing preference of practice for some and condemnation of others. Thus began an attempt to structuralize the society according to the ideal type 'order' envisioned by the dominant class or classes. Manu described these eight forms of marriage as follows (III.27-42):

The first or the most ideal form is described as the *Brāhma* form of marriage. This characterized the gift of a daughter after decking her (with costly garments) and honouring (her by presents of jewels), to a man learned in the Veda and of good conduct whom (the father) himself invited. Further, the son born of a *Brāhma* form of marriage was believed to purify ten ancestors and ten descendants, thereby of great spiritual value.

The *Daiva* rite of marriage was marked by the gift of a daughter who has been decked with ornaments, to a priest who duly officiates at a sacrifice during the course of its performance. The son of a *Daiva* form purified seven descendants each in the ascending and descending lines.

When (the father) gives away his daughter according to the rule, after receiving from the bridegroom, for (fulfillment of) the sacred law, a cow and a bull or two pairs, that is named the *Arsha* rite. This signified their lesser merit as the son born of this union purified only three ancestors and three descendants.

The gift of a daughter (by her father) after he has addressed (the couple) with the text "may both of you perform together your duties", and has shown honour (to the bridegroom), is called in the Smriti the *Prajāpatya* rite. (This also denoted an act of great religious merit as the son born of this form purified six ancestors and six descendants.)

When (the bridegroom) receives a maiden, after having given as much wealth as he can afford to the kinsmen and to the bride herself, according to his own will, is called the *Asura* rite.

The voluntary union of a maiden and her lover one must know (to be) the *Gandharva* rite, which springs from desire and has sexual intercourse for its purpose.

The forcible abduction of a maiden from her home, while she cries out and weeps, after (her kinsmen) have been slain or wounded and (their houses) broken open is called the *Rākshasa* rite.

When (a man) by stealth seduces a girl who is sleeping, intoxicated, or disordered in intellect, that is the eighth, the most base and sinful rite of the *Pisāchas*.

The eight forms were summed up by Mayne (1883: 123) as gift of the bride, sale of the bride, and self-choice by the man and the woman. In ancient texts, of the above-mentioned marriage forms, the first four were considered *dharmya* or socio-culturally acceptable, and the latter four as *adharmya* or against socio-cultural norms. The most important characteristic of the *dharmya* forms of marriage was greater emphasis on the bride's father who was required to arrange the marriage and bestow the gift of daughter according to prescribed rituals for each form. The father or guardian who gifted the girl in marriage according to *dharmya* forms, as the digests claim, gained merit for himself and for the girl (Sternbach 1965: 347-423). The emergence of *kanyādāna* ideal, as opposed to the gift-receiving as in the bride-purchase of the earlier *Asura* form of marriage, may be indicative of the growth of a patriarchal set-up. It may also be a consequence of the growth of the concept of *dāna* or gift in the later Vedic period. *Dāna*, as a religious non-reciprocal gift-giving, over the time appeared to be more accessible to all caste groups than the elaborate sacrifices prevalent earlier. Exhortations by the Digests for the *dharmya* form of marriage indicate the growing rigidification of patriarchal elements within the society.

Marriage as a sacrifice of great religious and spiritual merit came to be historically binding on all castes and classes. The marriage rituals deified gift of the bride and gift-giving. Even the *Ārsha* form whereby the bride's father received a pair of cattle for sacrificial purposes from the groom's family was strongly condemned. 'It is a sale, it matters little whether one accepts a large sum or a small one . . .' (*Manu* III.53). In fact, in course of time the very word 'take', according to Pandey (1949: 289), on the part of the bride's family was removed from the very auspices of marriage.

The significance of gift-giving as exemplified and eulogized in the ancient scriptures is pertinent to comprehend evolving linkages of dowry with *dharmya* marriages. As a symbol of affection, and also having definite moral and religious merit, gift-giving came to be observed at first among the established classes. It came to signify 'better social and ritual status' even though its intent and content were different in the various stages of cultural and historical development of the society. It also served as a useful vehicle to gain social mobility. 'Making gift was a visible sign of prosperity . . . either for distributing tribal wealth or for gaining prestige and dominant status' (Nath 1990: 85-6). The epics and the Puranas are full of references to large scale gift-giving, the dowry accompanying Sita on her marriage to Rama being a typical example of such luxurious expenditures among the propertied classes.

Besides, the type of marriage and its co-relation with the quality of offsprings produced also influenced the acceptability of the options of *dharmya* marriage forms. Sons born out of such marriages were considered to be endowed with Brahmanic glory and respected by cultured persons. 'Endowed with beauty and the quality of goodness, possessing wealth and fame, with full enjoyment and righteousness they lived for a hundred years' (Sternbach 1965: 374-5). Moreover, since the efficacy of gift-giving and *kanyādāna* increased with the worthiness of the receiver, the notion of hypergamy took shape. Its merit was certain if the donor did so selflessly. The practice of hypergamy thus became an integral part of the *dharmya* or *kanyādāna* forms of marriage. The specific marriage form that was closest to this ideal was accorded general approbation.

Evidently, as almost all the digest writers indicate, the *Brāhma* form was regarded as the highest and the most ideal form of marriage. It was always mentioned first in all the Smritis in the list of the forms of marriage. It is said that 'he who gave a girl in marriage according to the *Brāhma* rite brought her into the world of Brahman (after her death), and entered the world himself'. It was the highest and the best world (Sternbach 1965: 372). References in non-Brahmanical literature also point to *Brāhma* form of marriage as the most approved one among all the marriage forms then in existence. The Jain texts suggest the prominence of three forms—arranged marriage, *svayamvara* and *Gandharva* form. The first had come to be characterized by caste restrictions. It required either a payment to the bride's parent by the groom's family or the accompaniment of money, estate or goods with the bride to her marital family (Jain 1947: 148 and 155-6; also Jain 1967: 50-1). For example, the king of Varanasi gave to his son-in-law 'one thousand villages, one hundred elephants, plenty of treasure, one lac of foot soldiers and ten thousand horses in marriage'. On the other hand, bride-price was practiced by the lower castes (Jain 1947: 148-55).

The socio-culturally disapproved or *adharmya* forms of marriage were characterized by their denial of patriarchal set up. They were remnants of earlier tribal forms of marriage which featured the capture and purchase of, or elopement with a girl by warriors and others on the one hand and self-choice or *svayamvara* through *Gandharva* form by men and women themselves. These forms may have developed in historically successive periods. None of them required either active participation of the father of the daughter or her bestowal with rituals. Opposed to the patriarchal order of Brahmanic society, these marriage forms were disapproved for higher castes and were considered to be appropriate only for the lower castes (Sharma 1983: 53; Thapar 1978: 42-7). Baudhayana, for instance, holds that since the wives of the lower castes were involved in agricultural activities, control over them to abide by *dharmya* forms was difficult. On the other hand, the withdrawal of the upper castes from the production process made women more dependent upon men and the approved forms could be enforced by the latter. Besides, it also behove the upper castes as upholders of the social order or *dharma* to observe the approved marriage forms (*Bau. Dh.S.*, I.11.14-16 in Sharma 1983: 53; Apte 1978: 83).

Such *adharmya* forms of marriage as *Asura* and *Rākshasa*, along with the *Gandharva* form, were earlier considered to be commendable for the *kshatriyas*. The case of Subhadra's abduction by Arjuna in the *Mahābhārata* and its approval by Krishna as the only suitable marriage mode illustrates this. Yet in the thirteenth book of *Mahābhārata* (*Anushāsana Parva*), the *Rākshasa* and the *Gandharva* forms are considered unsuitable for all castes. They became gradually associated with Vaishyas and Shudras. They were widely condemned in an attempt perhaps to extend the lawfulness of the essentially Brahmanical *dharmya* form that characterized the gift of daughter. The practice of the payment by the groom as required in the *Asura* form received criticisms. A wife thus 'bought' could not perform sacrificial rites and the act of such a marriage was supposed to destroy seven families (Baudhayana in Apte 1978: 144). The adaptations in the ritual was effected by the Brahmin who were, or became over the time, the sole repository of the Vedic rituals. It is obvious, however, that their influence was limited to the upper castes primarily because the existence of the *adharmya* forms were not denied. They were accepted as prevalent forms and worthy of note and codification as eight categorized forms of marriage.

The disapproval notwithstanding, *adharmya* forms co-existed with *dharmya* forms of marriage. Once coded and legitimized, these marriage forms were mentioned in most of the texts on Hindu social system from ancient to modern times. They were, however, considered of varying merit suitable for different groups of people. The order in which the forms appear in the texts denote their relative moral value in a particular historical time.[7] Attempts to elaborate and standardize the marriage forms can thus be consistently discerned in the ancient texts. As gift-giving gained in meaning and importance it came to influence the lawfulness and religiosity of the marriage forms. Marriage rituals and rites increased and so did the significance of the gift of a daughter. Each *varṇa* came to be associated with a set of ideals, norms and even marriage forms, but no uniform set of notions or prescribed code of conduct could be enforced. The viability of each option of marriage modes thus cannot be disputed or ignored as disappearing remnants of the previous ages. At best, these *adharmya* forms appear as, what Trautmann and Hara write, 'norms for conduct, culturally determined patterns of behavior, based on underlying symbols of the essential attributes of the four *varṇas*' (cited in Talbot 1980: 2). Basham (1954: 169) thus correctly observes:

> Some authorities have tried to explain away the less reputable form of marriage and to prove that they were non-existent or very rare, but it is hardly likely that the law givers would have admitted these forms, of which they wholeheartedly disapprove, if they had not a solid basis in ineluctable social custom. It would seem that with surprising realism they recognized a wide range of relationships.

Yet, it was the *kanyādāna* form of marriage to which the cultural and religious genesis of dowry and its emergence as an institution can be traced. The most ideal of this form of marriage, i.e. the *Brāhma-vivāha,* is marked by the voluntary giving away of daughter to an honourable man after having decked her with ornaments. The bedecking of the daughter with ornaments has been variously described by the Smriti writers. It is said: 'the maiden be decked with ornaments (endowed, dressed and adorned)'; or 'she had to be decked with ornaments, i.e., with gold, or endowed with wealth'; 'she had also to be honoured with many valuable presents such as jewels and wear new bangles'; 'the dressing (endowment) had to carried out according to the best ability of the person who was obliged to supply these ornaments (endow the girl)' (Sternbach 1965: 369).

This reflects that the dowry in a palpable form was an essential part of the *kanyādāna* form of marriages. The obligation to bestow dowry was on the father or the guardian of the bride. The Smritis justify the bestowal of dowry by explaining that the girl was honoured by the giving of gifts. It is said that 'where women are honoured, there the gods rejoice; where on the other hand they are not honoured, there all rites are fruitless' (*Manusmriti* 3.56 cited in Sternbach 1965: 370). Dowry in terms of goods or estate can thus be considered integral to the *kanyādāna* form of marriage which advocated '*alaṁkritya sutadānaṃ*' or 'decking the girl with ornaments before giving her away' (Apte 1954: 38).

While the Dharmashāstras unanimously recommended gift-giving in the *kanyādāna* form of marriages, they differed on the validity and desirability of the wealth that accompanied other marriage forms. This is especially so in respect to the *Asura* form of marriage, the universality of whose practice in ancient times in many societies of the world has been demonstrated by Westermarck (1926: 166-71). Vashishtha, for instance, calls the *Asura* form as the *mānusa* rite, i.e. the form prescribed for ordinary mortals (Sastri 1972: 160; also in Jolly 1885: 74). Nuptial fee was not condemned if it was provided to the brides. Digest writers, such as Devenabhatta, Nilkantha, etc., supported this view. Gradually, this came to constitute a part of presentation that formed *strīdhana.* Brides thus received dowry either from the groom or through their guardians (Sastri 1972: 265; also Jolly 1885: 232-4).

On the other hand, Baudhayana, Manu and other commentators believed that the amount received as payment for the bride was meant for the bride's parents. They do not speak of the bride's share in the payment (Sastri 1972: 160). *Manusmriti,* in fact, condemned the *shulka* or bride-price and suggested scriptural rules to prevent further expansion of this practice. It held that only 'blamable offspring would be born' of such a marriage. It also mentions that 'nor have we heard even in former creations, of such (a thing as) the covert sale of a daughter for a fixed price, called nuptial fee' (in Verghese 1980: 58; and Altekar 1956: 39). R.S. Sharma holds that condemnation of the *Asura* form in which bride-price was practised was probably due to its association with the lower *varṇas* (Sharma 1966: 32; see also Apte 1954, and 1978:17). References to the bride-price payment occur in the *Grihya Sūtra, Atharvaveda* and other texts too. Apte concludes that rich fathers gave generously to their daughter out of 'love and affection', while suitors who were not qualified enough gave bride-price to be accepted (Apte 1978: 13; see also Altekar 1956: 70).

Evidences of the historical roots of modern dowry thus can be seen in both the *kanyādāna* and *Asura* form of marriages. It was, however, more the culturally and ideologically predominant *kanyādāna* form, requiring the father to bestow the daughter in marriage with gifts, earning maximum spiritual merit to its performers, and with gift-giving, property, hypergamy and caste restrictions inherent in it, that gradually gained currency. This prompted the institutionalization of the dowry system and facilitated its evolution as an all pervading part of the modern marriage system.[8] Yet the fact that dowry did not assume a menacing proportion in pre-modern times can be attributed to two factors. First, the institutionalization of *kanyādāna* form of marriage did not mean an end to, or denial of, other form of marriages which continued to exist till modern times, often in symbolic replica of the older custom in tribal and village societies.[9] This resulted in several options of marriage forms available and greater variation in rites and rituals in spite of the efforts by the Dharmashāstra-writers for standardization. Second, because of the fact that the *kanyādāna* form was prescribed especially for the hierarchically upper castes and elites in the society, the custom of dowry remained limited to a numerically small group. This was also the group that could afford gift-giving because of its status. It was only when its status role began to change or decline that dowry along with other factors also became a burden.

Inheritance Rights, *Strīdhana* and Women

The symbiotic relationship between marriage, property, and dowry becomes more apparent when we examine the nature of women's rights to inheritance, and *strīdhana*, i.e. women's property. Women's rights to property are mentioned in ancient texts in the context of their rights to the *strīdhana*, i.e. wealth given to them at marriage which, at least normatively, was inviolable to a large extent. Besides this, a strong normative injunction to provide for an unmarried fatherless daughter's marriage or for her upkeep was also laid down. A brotherless daughter, however, could inherit on certain conditions.[10] Most schools of thought, however, disapprove inheritance of property by girls. The *Ṛgveda*, for example, rejects it on the grounds that girls migrate to another family (*RV* III.31.9 in Vishnoi 1988:16-18). In another instance, only life-interest is accorded to women in family property without the power to sell or gift it. A woman is regarded incompetent to inherit, so she is gifted away by her father while her brother is not (Yaska III.1 in Indra 1955:159). Several other references also state explicitly that women are incapable of inheriting property.[11]

While it is difficult to conjecture the actual property rights of women, the normative injunctions provide some insights into the working of this complex web of social and material relationships. The Codes of Manu presented the earliest exposition of property rights. It subscribed to the view that the unmarried daughters were to be given a quarter of their brothers' share of patrimony for the purposes of their marriage. 'But to the maiden (sister) the brothers shall severally give (portions) out of their shares, each out of his share one-fourth part, those who refuse to give (it) will become outcasts' (Manu IX.118). Elsewhere too, provisions for the unmarried or the-not-so-well-settled daughter are referred to. Gautama, for instance, provided for property of the deceased father to be inherited by a poorly settled daughter (Gautama XXIX.II in Bhattacharji 1991: 507).

In most texts, provisions were especially made for the daughters in the context of the settlement of marriage. Kautilya, for instance, mentioned that the 'unmarried daughters shall be paid adequate dowry, payable to them on the occasion of their marriage' (*AS* III. V.161). Yajnavalkya too called for one-fourth of the brother's share in patrimony to cover marriage expenses of the daughters (Yaj. II.124 and 125 in Indra 1955: 162; Vishnoi 1988: 88). For those who remained unmarried, maintenance was provided both from patrimony and the maternal estate (*RV* II.17.7). Brihaspati and Katyayana both reiterated the provision for one-fourth. The latter clarified further 'if the fund be small, sons must give a fourth part to daughters, deducting it out of their own respective shares' (in Vishnoi 1988: 88). Medhatithi condemned those who did not regard it necessary to provide the required one-fourth but only the amount which fulfilled the expenses in marriage. He emphasized that the one-fourth portion was to be set aside for the sisters of the same caste as the brother (IX.118 in Vishnoi 1988: 112).

Thus, what may be termed as the inheritance rights were limited and considered exclusively for marriage only. Other texts reveal reluctance on the part of many on sharing the patrimony with women and especially sisters. Both the *Baudhāyana Dharmasūtra* and the earlier *Taittirīya Saṁhitā* of eighth century BC regarded women as incompetent to inherit (Bhattacharji 1991: 507). Vishnu and Narada both insisted that the amount specified in other texts, i.e. one-fourth, was to be used only for the daughter's marriage and the already married sisters were not entitled to a share (Vishnu XVIII: 34-5 and Narada XIII: 13 inVishnoi 1988: 88). The norm prevails even today as the daughter is assured a marriage that will provide security and equal or better level of standard of life as in her natal household. Transfer of wealth still takes place at the time of marriage and often is used to procure a desirable match. Altekar reasons that since marriage had become obligatory, provisions were made for the daughters' wedding expenses even if it entailed spending 'reasonable amounts for their suitable marriages out of their (sons) family estate' (Altekar 1956: 242). In any case, an unmarried daughter enjoyed relatively more rights in the patrimony than her married sister (*Dāyabhāga* XI.2.4; Yaj. II.135 in Vishnoi 1988: 88-9).

In later texts too, the same stand on inheritance is reiterated. Alberuni mentions that the chief rule of the Hindu law of inheritance is that

> the women do not inherit, except the daughter. She gets the fourth part of the share of a son according to a passage in the book of Manu. If she is not married, the money is spent on her till the time of her marriage and her dowry is bought by means of her share. Afterwards, she has no more income from the house of her father. (Sachau 1971: 164)

On the basis of evidence referred to above, many scholars conclude that daughters had a share in parental property[12] which became gradually wider in scope. I would suggest that this 'share' was, however, linked to a woman's marital status. If unmarried, she was to be provided maintenance, otherwise it was expected to provide her a good marriage according to the status of the family concerned. Her rights in parental property began and ended with marriage. This brings up the question of *strīdhana*. How far did it mean inheritance or property rights of women? And, to what extent was it connected with dowry?

The discussion of women's status in ancient India usually equates women's rights to *strīdhana* with the right to property and inheritance. Often, *strīdhana* is depicted to glorify, or to demonstrate, the better position of women in the Indian society. It was provided to the unmarried daughter at the time of her marriage. In fact, *strīdhana* was the earliest recognized form of women's property. The Smritis and the Dharmashāstras have enunciated it in great detail. Some believe that the *strīdhana* originated from the practice of bride-price or *kanyāshulka* given to the bride by the groom's family. The existing mores, however, denounced receiving any gift from the groom's family and probably to avoid such denunciation the girl's parents partly transferred the *shulka* amount to the girl as her dowry (Altekar 1956: 217; *Taittirīya Saṁhitā* VI, 2.1.1. in Vishnoi 1988: 16).

A great diversity of opinion exists in the various doctrines as regards the exact nature and scope of *strīdhana*. The earliest reference to gifts accompanying the bride are mentioned in the wedding hymn of the *Ṛgveda* (*RV* X.85.8). These gifts, primarily ornaments, were earlier known as *parinahya* and later comprised a part of *strīdhana* (*Taittirīya Saṁhitā* VI.5.8.2 in Vishnoi 1988: 16). The scope and ownership rights become explicit, however, only in the later texts. The division of property among sons was well-established in the Vedic Age and the succession was decided accordingly. The daughter's rights in all likelihood, comprised of movables such as gifts and ornaments and these were provided to her at the time of marriage according to one's status. Baudhayana recognized only one kind of *strīdhana*, i.e. ornaments, while Vashishtha mentioned only nuptial presents or *parinahya* as *strīdhana* (Banerjee 1962: 119-20). The epics also refer to such gifts. The *Rāmāyaṇa* mentions it as *kanyādhanaṃ* over which women exercised full ownership. The *Mahābhārata* refers to *vaivāhikaṃ, parichhadaṃ, harnaṃ, jñatideyaṃ* and *yautakaṃ* as the gifts and movables possessed by a woman. These later became known as the *strīdhana* (Vishnoi 1988: 20).

Manu laid down: what was given before the nuptial fire (*adhyāgnika*), what was given on the bridal possession (*adhyavāhanika*), what was given in token of love (*prītidattā*), and what was received from a brother, a mother, or a father, are considered the six-fold separate property of a married woman (Manu IX.194). Manu also included the ornaments that a woman wore in her husband's life-time as her property. The Jain literature also confirm the above constituents of *strīdhana* with the difference that all these were fully under the control of women (*Bhadrabāhu Saṁhitā*, 83-7 in Vishnoi 1988: 25).[13] Narada elaborates further by adding 'the property given to her by her husband through pure affection, she may enjoy at her pleasure after his death, or may give it away, except land or houses' (Colebrook's *Digest Book* V: 476 in Banerjee 1896: 291). Gifts from sons, kin, her fee on supersession by another woman were added to the *strīdhana* by Vishnu (Banerjee 1896: 291; Altekar 1956: 220). Its scope also extended to property obtained by inheritance, purchase, partition, acceptance, finding and what was earned through working—though the earnings of a woman were mostly considered as belonging to the family rather than the woman herself (Banerjee 1896: 298-301).

Katyayana's view of *strīdhana* was acceptable to most digest writers (Bhattacharyya 1988: 68). He defined it as 'all property (whether movable or unmovable) obtained by a woman, either as a maiden, or at marriage, or after-marriage from her parents or from husband and his family (except immovable property given by husband) is included within the scope of *strīdhana*' (quoted in Vishnoi 1988: 75; and Bhattacharyya 1988: 69). Lest one may conclude about the generosity and adequacy of the property endowed to a woman, references are also of limitations prescribed for a *strīdhana*. Both Katyayana and the *Arthashāstra* (3.2.14), for example, place a limit of two thousand *paṇas* and unlimited ornament as *strīdhana* (Basham 1954: 179; Pande 1988: 133).

The succession to *strīdhana* has been dealt in detail and separately from the other property of the family and further indicates the extent of women's rights over it. Most jurists believed that it should devolve upon daughters alone as it consisted of things which she could use. But variations exist in the texts of the various authors. Gautama (in Banerjee 1962: 119) prescribed inheritance of *strīdhana* by unmarried and unsettled daughters and in their absence, the right over it went to their uterine brothers. Vashishtha and Baudhayana also held that all wedding gifts were to be inherited by daughters.[14] Kautilya (*AS* 3.2.31) included sons as well as daughters. Manu (IX.192) too reiterated that but emphasized claims of unmarried daughters over separate property of the mother (IX.131). Yajnavalkya (first-third century A.D.) opined that all of mother's property and *strīdhana* belonged to the daughter, and sons alone were to pay off any debts incurred by their mother (Yaj. II.117).

From the tenth century onwards, the *Dāyabhāga* of Jimutvahana (A.D. 1100-1150) and Vijnanesvara's *Mitākshara* (1080-1100) became the chief source of Hindu law. While the former accorded ownership rights of *strīdhana* to the woman which, if not willed, was to devolve equally upon sons and unmarried daughters, the latter gave priority to the unmarried as well as to the unprovided though married daughters (Bhattacharyya 1988: 69). While the *Mitākshara* included in *strīdhana* any property belonging to a woman, the *Dāyabhāga* school did not include immovable property within its scope. These differences in opinion of the jurists show the absence of any uniform pattern. The scope of *strīdhana* was wide and liberal to some and quite limited according to others (Vishnoi 1988; also Jolly 1928: 48-51). This cleavage in the opinions remained throughout.

On the basis of Manu and the *Mitākshara's* comments on *strīdhana*, Indra maintains that women in ancient India, in keeping with their circumscribed religious, political, and social rights and status, enjoyed only a limited legal status over it (Indra 1955: 182). Manu had enjoined women to consult their husband before using *strīdhana* (Manu IX.199). If borrowed by the husband for purposes of religious matters, illness, or if imprisoned, then he was not under obligation to return it (Yaj. II.147). But if he seized it in any other manner or under other circumstances, he must make it good (Banerjee 1896: 341). Two categories were made to distinguish ownership rights of women over *strīdhana*: *Saudāyika* over which women had complete control, and *Asaudāyika* which may have included immovable property gained through inheritance. The latter could be used by women but could not be alienated. Although some texts (e.g. *Mitākshara*) even included all property, however acquired, as *strīdhana*, one can easily agree with Indra (1955: 176) that

> such enlargement of women's rights has not been accepted by any other legal authority . . . and the term *strīdhana* must be limited to comprise only such property as the woman acquires otherwise than by inheritance and partition and over which she possesses plenary powers of disposal and which on her death devolves upon her own successors.[15]

The devolution of *strīdhana* was also linked to the form of marriage a woman was wedded in. In case of the four approved forms, if there was no successor, a woman's property devolved to her husband, or in his absence to her nearest relative. In all the other forms, however, her property was acquired by her parents or next of kin (*Mitākshara* II.145 in Indra 1955: 177; *AS* 3.2.17-18 and Manu IX.196-7). It is interesting to note that while in the first four approved marriage forms, the husband could enjoy and make use of the property if mutually acceptable, complaints could be lodged against husbands who, if married in the *Gandharva* and *Asura* marriage forms, did so and the amount used along with interest was to be recovered from them. In the *Rakshasa* and *Paisacha* forms, the appropriation of such property by husbands amounted to theft (*AS* 3.2.18).

Broadly, two points are discernible in the provision of *strīdhana*. First, while *strīdhana* may have included the daughter's portion of inheritance, her control over it was far from complete. Second, *strīdhana* cannot be equated with dowry. In dowry, the transaction of gift was from bride's father or guardian to the groom or his guardian and not to the daughter alone. As such, it did not constitute *strīdhana* only but more. Even in modern times, as M.N. Srinivas notes, the dowry is not *strīdhana* because it is transacted at the instance of the groom or his family (Srinivas 1984: 12). Women's limited rights and control respectively over inheritance and *strīdhana*, however, confirm that the transmission of property to the daughter as a gift was the common practice. The occasion for the transfer of property as gifts ideally arose at the time of the daughter's departure from her natal family to marital household; i.e. at the time of marriage. Such practices were sanctioned and legitimized by the patriarchal social order. The origin and evolution of the dowry system can be traced to these practices.

The inextricable linkages of marriage and property are thus apparent. It is, therefore, not surprising that the *Bhāradvāja Grihya Sūtra* names four inducements for marrying a girl as wealth, beauty, intelligence and family (in Bhattacharji 1991: 507). In ancient texts, women are often referred to as objects of property along with such other items as gold, etc.[16] A woman's acquisition of property was almost synonymous with marriage and her control over it also depended on the form of marriage she was wedded in indicating thereby her caste and class status.

The importance of patrilineal succession also necessitated maintenance of caste purity which in turn perpetuated the control over women. Marriage and legitimate motherhood within a distinct family structure came to be regarded as obligatory. Kautilya even mentions giving preferential shares of *strīdhana* to the sons of the wives of superior *varṇas,* (to ensure and emphasize the purity of the upper castes), thereby recommending *anuloma* marriages (*AS* 3.7.17-22; also in Manu IX.149-57; Yaj. I. 95). Vashishtha also emphasized *anuloma* marriages and prohibited a Brahmin's marriage with a low caste woman (Vishnoi 1988: 43). Similarly, 'the sons, born of wives of the castes in the reverse order (*pratiloma*), though entitled to maintenance (*bharanīyāḥ*) are excluded by Vishnu, and their sons are excluded even from the ancestral property' (Banerjee 1962: 118). The predominance of the upper castes and caste purity through marriage were thus sought to be preserved.

Caste System and Marriage

In the earlier section, we have discussed evidences regarding the practice of various forms of marriage with numerous differing rites, rituals and customs elaborated in the normative *shāstric* texts. In the successive historical periods, pressure to standardize the approved marriage forms increased. The Brahmanical control and hegemony was sought to be established through a rigid caste structure, a formalized marriage system with the prescription for age and choice of partners, as well as a tight control over women through pre-puberty marriage, economic dependency, and emphasis on chastity and celibacy. Ceremonial purity among the Brahmins was observed and expected. Xuan Zhang mentions the 'strict observance of ceremonial purity' by the Brahmins [Watters: 168; also Sharma (1) 1966: 41]. The Brahmins at the apex of the social order, enlisted the support of the state and *Kshatriyas* to maintain ceremonial purity. The *Kshatriya* king's greatest service was considered to be the prevention of inter-mixing among caste divisions [Sharma (1) 1966: 45]. Together they attempted to clasp bonds of the caste system through highly compartmentalized marriage rules (Kane 1946 (III): 1-3). These brought about the hierarchical ordering of the society according to caste and gender.

In the practice of growing caste restriction in marriage, the attempt was to put an end to the proliferation of several sub-castes and to maintain the purity of the castes through a tight control over its members. Although the customary law was to pursue the occupation only of the caste lower than their own, occupational diversity even among the Brahmins, however, came about and new sub-divisions emerged within each caste [Sharma (1) 1966: 38-43]. References of the caste of the progeny being dependent upon the caste of the mother also abound (Sachau 1971: LXIX.156). A hundred mixed castes are mentioned in the Smritis.

Besides this, castes also appears to have borne out of *anuloma* and *pratiloma* marriages. Scholars have pointed out that different combinations of *anuloma* and *pratiloma* marriages took place and many new *samskāras* emerged (Sharma 1988: 49). In Medhatithi's commentary on the social life of *circa* eighth century A.D., while marriage of a woman to a lower caste man (*pratiloma*) was not accepted socially, the reverse was tolerated if the difference between the two castes was not substantial (see Singh 1959: 121). Along with this, serious injunctions against free mixing of the sexes find reference in the texts which show that the Brahmanical norms for pre-puberty marriages, etc., were not uniformly conformed to.[17] The assimilation and absorption of new influences, foreign as well as indigenous, also kept liberalizing tendencies alive. For example, the marriage of Hunas with the Brahmins or *Kshatriyas* made them a part of these castes [Sharma (1) 1966: 329].

At the same time, caste restrictions in marriages formalized customs and codes and became an inseparable and integral part of the Brahmanic social order. This led to a growing emphasis on virginity and monogamy. The birth of a son was valued both by kings and commoners alike (Singh 1959: 121; Sharma 1958: 169).

Daughters began to be considered as an expensive luxury in some sections of the population, particularly the Rajputs, largely because of the huge costs incurred for their weddings. Infanticide became common among some of these sections (Dass 1866: 153; also in Gupta 1987: 21).

In the *Harshacarita*, Prabhakarvardhana refers to three major concerns a father confronts due to the birth and marriage of a daughter. He says that although a daughter is entitled to the same treatment as a son, yet people are dismayed at her birth; the girl's marriage is the greatest anxiety for the parents of the daughter, as it was their concern; and the bridegroom is almost always an outsider, often unconnected by blood [Chap. IV: 140-1 in Sharma (1) 1966: 10-11]. The *Ratnāvalī* of Harsha (seventh century), *Upamitibhāvaprapañcakathā* of Siddharsisuri (tenth century), and the *Bṛhatkāthakosha* of Harisena (tenth century) mention about the first concern, while the second is recorded in the accounts of Xuan Zhang and Alberuni. The latter records that it was forbidden to marry female relations both of the direct descending line or the direct ascending line (Watters: 162; Sachau 1971: LXIX.155). The Smriti writers of this period also disallowed marriage with a *sapinḍa* and *sagotra* girl [Sharma (1) 1966: 11]. At the same time references to cross-cousin marriages are found in both south and western India [*Upamitibhāvaprapañchakathā* as quoted in Sharma (1) 1966: 11].

The formalization of caste divisions in marriage systems emphasized stricter observation of caste endogamy and clan exogamy.[18] These caste restrictions or caste marriage, as later accounts of foreign travellers, Persian chronicles as well as contemporary literary sources indicate, became important factors for the growth and prevalence of the dowry system at first among the rich and well-to-do families and gradually among the commoners (Ojha 1956: 263).

In fact, rituals accompanying marriage increased in their complexity in each successive historical period so much so that only the 'rich and great persons like kings' could observe them (Murti 1988: 8-32). Complexities entered in the system of marriage with injunctions such as no marriage with the native population, between brother and sister, father and daughter, observations of monogamy and exogamy. This obviously implies prior existence of such practices and efforts to control them.

For a more effective control on women, pre-puberty marriage was advocated strongly by Samvarta, Parasara, Vyasa, Samkha and other

Smriti writers, especially for the upper castes. References of the desirability of early marriage alongwith the proper age, time and features of the groom and the bride are found in most post-Vedic texts (Indra 1955: 43-52; Sheth 1979: 92-3; Apte 1978: 151). If a Brahmin did not marry his daughter to a suitable groom within her pre-puberty years he was considered unfit for 'conversation and dining in the company of the other members of his caste' [*Parāsara Smriti* VII.7 as quoted in Sharma (1) 1966: 15]. Alberuni, in his discussion of the medieval Indian society observed that the Hindu marry at a very young age and were not allowed to marry a girl above twelve years of age (Sachau 1971: LXIII.131). It was not uncommon among the Brahmins to have a marked age difference between husband and wife (Gupta 1987: 38-42). Manucci (1907: 54-9) observes that 'often their daughters are married even before they have learnt to talk'. Ikram (1964: 230) mentions six to eight years as the ideal age of marriage for girls among the Hindus as well as Muslims during the Mughal period.

Despite these injunctions to conform to the norms, different marriage forms flourished. For example, even in the later Vedic and the Sutra periods, prescriptions of the pre-puberty marriage were flouted. Both *Kāmasūtra* and *Kathāsaritsāgara*, point to child marriages existing along with self-arranged marriages performed at a mature age (*Kāmasūtra* III.2-4; *Kathāsaritsāgara* 24.124 in Vishnoi 1988: 3). Basham too holds that 'it is very doubtful that the child marriage of girls was at all common until the late medieval period. The heroines of poetry and fiction are apparently full grown when they marry, and the numerous inscriptions which throw much light on the customs of the time give little or no indication of child marriage' (Basham 1954: 167).

Moreover, Jain canonical literature indicates that both matrilocal and patrilocal marriages were existent. The prevalence of *svayaṁvara* and *Gandharva* forms imply that the marriage age varied and was not low in all cases, and that among commoners different patterns of marriage existed as against the elite and upper caste population. The literary texts such as *Kādambarī* and *Priyadarshikā* refer to the legality of *Gandharva* marriage while the *Upamitibhāvprapañcakathā* mentions self-arranged marriages recognized by the girls' parents [see Sharma (1) 1966:13].

At the same time it was also said to be the parents' duty to arrange a daughter's marriage. The mothers are, says Rajyashri's mother in

Harshacharita, 'nothing more than nurses. In bestowing them the father is the final authority' [Sharma (1) 1966: 14]. In fact, the significant role of father in a marriage had, as indicated earlier, begun with the introduction and institutionalization of the *kanyādāna* form of marriage. For example, in the *Mahābhārata*, one finds that when Dushyanta urges Sakuntala to become his wife, the latter immediately responds, 'my father has gone out of the hermitage to gather fruits, O King. Wait a while. He himself will give me away to you.' Or, in an another instance, Tapati, refusing to acquiesce to a *Gandharva* union with King Samvarna, says: 'I am not my own mistress, Sir, for I am a girl with a father. If you have pleasure in me, ask my father for me' (cited in Talbot 1980: 14 and 64). The role of father in gifting away the daughter, as we shall see in the next chapter, continued to be a major consideration in contentious issues regarding the legality of marriage in the Anglo-Indian Court during the colonial period.

Such substantial variations based on marriage forms, property rights, and caste reflect the existence of numerous patterns of arranging a marriage. Accordingly, a whole range of social practices coexisted along with dowry and bride-price.

By the medieval period, one starts getting explicit references of dowry as part of the marriage rituals and ceremonies. Instances of dowry marriages appear to be gradually increasing and becoming socially legitimized. Dowry as an integral part of the *kanyādāna* marriage is mentioned in many of the works in contemporary literature. Various explicit terms for dowry in different regions are now commonly discerned. In Bengal and Orissa, marriage presents were known as *jautaka*, while in Bihar, parts of modern U.P., and Rajasthan they were termed *dahej* or *daeej*. Mukundaram and Dvija Madhava termed it as *pan* (Ojha 1956: 266-7). In popular literature, it was predominantly the word *daeeja*, or its Arabic *jaheja* and Persian *daheja* instead of original *dāna* and *dakshiṇā*; i.e. gifts, to denote the marriage payments. Tulsidasa in his *Rāmacharitmānasa* refers to the un-speakable amount of *daeej* received by Rama (see Bālakāṇda, *doha* 100, 101 and 325 in Tulsidasa: 47 and 140). The word *daeeja*, if its etymology is linked with the Sanskrit root words *da* or *daya*, we get the meaning of nuptial gifts or portion of inheritance. The shift in meaning of gifts in marriage or dowry from *dāna* to *daeej* suggest different connotation that dowry acquired over the time and referred to probably nuptial gifts or portion of inheritance. Such explicit reference of dowry is not present in the Dharmashāstras' prescription of the bestowal of daughter in marriage after having decked her with ornaments.

Dowry along with the *kanyādāna* form of marriage, during the medieval period, had begun to expand. Different forms of marriage are only scantily mentioned in the chronicles by Muslim writers. Abul Fazl refers to eight forms of marriage recognized by the Smritis but he finds the *Brāhma* form most prevalent in the contemporary society (Chopra 1963: 27). Marriage ceremonies described in these writings correspond to the *Brāhma* form though *Asura* and *Gandharva* forms are also mentioned as practised by lower castes and even *Kshatriyas*[19] (Singh 1981: 83). Such evidences demonstrate shrinking marriage options as well as the institutionalization of the *Brāhma* marriage as the most popular form. The expansion of this form of *kanyādāna* marriage along with gifts or dowry entailed huge expenditures especially among upper castes. This turned the daughter's marriage into a social burden so much so that Ibn Batutah notes that efforts were made to combat the menace by providing financial relief to the parents for the marriage of their daughters. During the reign of Sultan Balban, Fakhruddin Kotwal made arrangement to provide dowry for poor girls (Nand 1989: 201-2). Firuz Shah Tughluk is said to have established the '*Diwani-Khairat*' under the supervision of Sayyid Amiri Miran, for providing relief to the financially handicapped parents. After investigating each case, grants were given to them of 50, or 30, or 20 *tankas* (Islam 1950: 41). In the south, King Deva Raya II of Vijayanagar (1422-49) enacted a law to prevent payment for the bride which had become common among the south Indian Brahmins of the fifteenth century Padaividu kingdom. He made all money transactions connected with marriage as legal offences for both the giver and receiver (Verghese 1980: 57). An inscription of this period also points to the prohibition of the sale of land to outsiders or even its gift as dowry (Nanaiah 1992: 135). In the north, Manucci refers to the prevalence of the practice of purchasing brides in Bihar, U.P. and Bengal up to mid-eighteenth century (Storia III: 61). Polygamy is referred to often among the upper caste Hindus (Gupta 1987: 79).

In Rajputana region, dowry was prevalent among the aristocracy in the thirteenth and fourteenth century A.D. and gradually 'grew in rigidity' among the propertied classes (See Hooja 1968: 415, Pandey 1949: 286). According to R.B. Pandey, such a change in conception of marriage was due to its status of a sacrifice which raised the importance of rituals such as *dakshiṇā* (Pandey 1949: 374). Pomp and show marked the pre-marriage as well as actual marriage ceremony. Dowry began to be linked with such pre-marriage ceremonies as *tilak* or *pān* given prior to, or at, marriage. Among the wealthy, dowry consisted of 'costly jewels and metals, ornamented furniture, landed property, elephants, chariot horses, servants and maids beside other items of luxuries and necessaries of life' (Ojha 1956: 268; also in Gupta 1987: 71-5).

Abul Fazl and Badaoni too refer to large dowries during Akbar's reign both among Hindus as well as rich Muslims. Badaoni records that Raja Bhagwan Das gave his daughter at the time of her marriage to Prince Salim 'several strings of horses, one hundred elephants, boys and girls of Abyssinia, India and Circassia, and all sorts of golden vessels set with jewels, and jewels and utensils of gold, and vessels of silver, and all sorts of stuffs, the quality of which is beyond all computations' (cited in Chopra 1963: 35). For the poorer subjects Akbar appointed *Tui-begs* to keep check on those who demanded exorbitant dowries. Empress Nurjehan apportioned funds to about 500 girls in the seventeenth century to meet marriage expenses [Lanepool 1951 (II):218; also Verghese 1980: 85]. Muslims emulated the Hindu marriage pattern and supported the dowry system because of their reliance on higher castes for ruling purposes. At the same time, references provide evidence of Hindu-Muslim marriages, *svayaṁvara* or self-chosen marriages, and marriages among mature couples taking place 'particularly among the higher sections of the society' (see Gupta 1987: 43-5).

Marriage since ancient times was also used as a means for political alliance by the ruling elite. We have earlier examples of such alliances in the Gupta period and in all successive periods. According to R.C. Majumdar, the Guptas established the policy of forming political alliances through marriage with powerful and important royal families. The consideration of such marriages, however, were above the caste or other restrictions that were being increasingly formalized. The considerations were only to augment political rule or to gain social respectability[20] (Majumdar 1954: 21). Such practices gradually expanded and became increasingly prevalent in medieval period among kings and chieftains. Aurangzeb is said to have demanded the fortress of Ramgiri when his son Prince Sultan Mohammad was to wed a princess from

Golkunda to establish a gainful marriage alliance. Dowry appears to have thus existed more among the rich and the powerful than commoners (Mishra 1967: 131).

Concluding this, marriage and its linkages with society and polity of the time, though sometimes conflicting in form and nature, reflect a variety of options as well as differences in opinion. Regional, cultural and temporal patterns and variations existed which lent diversity and dynamics to the prevalent social pattern. The ancient texts while being prescriptive in their content also recognized and reflected the changes in the practice and customs of the people, as evident from the diversity of opinions expressed in them. Dowry co-existed with bride-price. The four higher marriage forms that were approved were characterized by the dominant role of the father, elaborate rituals and gift-giving. The latter four were considered inappropriate for the higher castes. The *Kshatriyas*, however, could marry by the latter four forms, even give bride-price. These marriage forms did not require dowry. No single tradition thus existed in spite of continuous efforts to homogenize various marriage forms by emphasizing higher spiritual merit of the *Brāhma* form. Yet, the right to property and marriage for women appears to be inextricably enmeshed. The patrilineal system of devolution of property was effected for women through *strīdhana*. It was normatively under the control of women and consisted of usually a portion of movable property offered at the time of marriage. In the context of the fluidity of the pre-modern marriage forms with dowry usually being limited to upper castes or elites, the question thus naturally arises: what made dowry such a pervasive and integral part of marriage in modern times affecting the majority of population in Indian society?

NOTES

1. Both Sharma (1966 and 1983) and Thapar (1978 and 1984) have aptly demonstrated the social, political, and economic consequences of the large-scale changes in Indian society during the first millennium B.C. Throughout this study reference to Sharma (1) implies B.N. Sharma's publication *Social Life in Nothern India (AD 600-1000)*, New Delhi, 1966.
2. References of such developments, for example as Chakravarty (1993: 581) notes, can be found in *Āpastamba Dharmasūtra* II.6.13.7 and Buddhist texts such as *Dīgha Nikāya* III.80ff.

3. Romila Thapar (1978: 47) writes that 'the complexity of the new society is clearly reflected in the need for codifying the laws of the various social groups, which is what is aimed at in the Brahmanical *Dharmasūtras.* The purpose of the laws is to differentiate between the various social groups generally identified as those of *jana, jāti,* and *varṇa.* These, however, are made part of a cohesive view of society. There is an implicit belief that the demarcation of differences would lead to a resolution of tensions, an attitude that could only have been feasible in the absence of a situation of conflict. Also implicit in the *Dharmasūtras* is the Brahmins' claim to being the arbiters of the law. There was no overt challenge to this claim since the codification did not aim at a uniformity of laws, but, on the contrary, to the recognition of their diversity'.
4. For a fuller discussion of these issues see Talbot 1980.
5. For example, one finds that 'the *Gandharva* form is singled out for special praise by Dushyanta, a *Kshatriya,* while the *Rakshasa* is also commended. Brahmins meanwhile are urged to marry by one of the first four marriage of the eightfold list. Bhisma cites the *Svayaṁvara* and *Rakshasa* as the warriorlike marriages.' The Anushasana passage stands apart from others in its rejection of abduction and its advocacy of daughter-giving for all (Talbot 1980: 26).
6. After marriage, the change of a woman's *gotra* or clan name, referred often as *gotrantara,* is an essential feature of the Hindu marriage system which has continued till the modern times. That signifies that she breaks her connection with her father's *gotra* and is adopted by her husband's family. The change of the bride's *gotra,* according to digest writers, takes place either with the *sapta-padi-gamana* (seven ceremonial steps walked by the bride and bridegroom after marriage) or *caturthī-karman* (consummation of marriage by sexual intercourse performed in the fourth night of marriage ceremony). Moreover, such changes in the bride's *gotra* took place only if the marriage was performed according to the *Brāhma, Daiva, Ārsha* or *Prajapatya* forms which required *sampradāna* (ceremonial offering of the bride by her father) or *kanyādāna.* See D.C. Sircar (1967: 204-9).
7. Sastri (1972) provides a detailed description of varying order accorded to the forms of marriage in the different texts.
8. The modern linkages of the *kanyādāna* form with the system of dowry has been explored in detail in the third chapter. It also attempts to explain how and why did the system of dowry pervade large sections of the north Indian society.
9. For example, the system of marriage through elopement has been found to still exist in a small tribal locality in Rajasthan (See *India Today,* 15 May 1994). While many of such forms of marriage started

rapidly disappearing during colonial period, a massive anthropological report on the Indian people find the custom of bride-price still practised although in a handful number of communities. Before the entrenchment of the colonial rule, such so-called *adharmya* form of marriages were however very common among low as well as several specialized occupational castes. See Census Reports.

10. The earliest reference to *putrika* is found in *Ṛgveda* but the first exposition of it is in the *Dharmasūtra* literature (see Vishnoi 1988:18).
11. For a detailed description see Vishnoi (1988: 16 and 53); Bhattacharyya (1988: 66); Indra (1955: 158), etc.
12. See, for example, Upadhyaya (1941: 48).
13. *Strīdhana* has been extensively dealt with in Derrett (1957), L. Sternbach (1965), Banerjee (1896), Mayne (1883), Pal (1938), Kane (1941 and 1946, Vol. II and Vol. III), etc.
14. See *Gautam Dharmasūtra,* also *VDS* XVII.46 and *Bau.Dh.S* II.43 referred in Banerjee 1962: 119 and Vishnoi 1988: 51 for detailed description.
15. Patriarchal joint families did not encourage alienation of landed property by any member of the household least of all by women. Because of the attitude of a typical patriarchal society based on private property, R.S. Sharma (1983: 43) notes that the Brahmanical law did not allow any proprietary rights to women. Women's rights in actuality remained restricted to jewels, ornaments and presents made to her. Bhattacharyya (1988: 71) states that apart from *strīdhana,* no 'natural right' over father's property was enjoyed by women. He also asserts that even the one-fourth of brother's was 'more an expression of moral obligation than of a legal compulsion'. Why gender-based different methods of devolution and accumulation of *strīdhana* and patrimony evolved has hardly been addressed by most scholars.
16. In an illuminating discussion on co-references to woman and property in the Epics and Puranas, R.S. Sharma (1983: 43) points to two obvious conclusions. 'First, the institution of private property and family centering round the wife were not only held to be the chief reasons of the origin of the state but also looked upon as the main motives for social action. Secondly, since woman and property are bracketed together in several references, there is no doubt that woman herself was regarded as a sort of property. She was considered incapable of exercising her independent will, and could be given away or loaned as any item of property. This was like the attitude of a typical patriarchal society based on private property.'
17. The contradictory and conflicting nature of evidence were the result of the constant changes in the social mores and organization. 'An attempt to reconcile the Aryan tradition and the usages of the non-Aryan tribes' was made, yet as source material they appear 'varied

and complex' (Goyal in Vishnoi 1988: xi). 'Placed as they were between the eternal law as represented by the rules of *Dharma* and the innumerable customs and usages of this vast sub-continent that constitute the living positive law, the commentators were able to suggest a number of different, sometimes contradictory interpretations all based upon the same authority of the Dharmashāstras. Thus, certain practices, often different from each other could be legitimized and recognized. Their method had the advantage of conferring to the interpretation a pliancy which could never have been obtained had the Dharmashāstra been dealt with as temporal legislation. The complexity of the Indian world could hardly accommodate a more uniform type of law' (ibid: xii-xiii).

18. By the medieval period, such restrictions had further solidified. About the caste marriage of Hindus, Abul Fazl mentions: 'In the present *Kali Yuga*, no one chooses a wife out of his own caste, nay, each of these four being sub-divided into various branches, each subdivision asks in marriage only the daughter of their own equal' (*Ain.* III in Mukherjee: 1972: 21).
19. Ashraf (1969: 180-1) provides a detailed and graphic description of a typical marriage ceremony of the *kanyādāna* form which includes among other customs and ritual dowry as an integral part. Such Hindu practices of the upper castes, according to him, also influenced the Muslim nobility.
20. Mishra (1967) mentions that through such marriage alliances women were thus being used to play a secondary role in political life.

CHAPTER THREE

Institutionalization and Expansion of Dowry in Colonial Period

For any study of modern Indian society, a comprehension of the role of 'culture', 'caste', and 'religion' alone is not adequate. In fact, till the beginning of the colonial rule in India, both caste and Hinduism have remained vibrant and fluid entity.

> Neither caste nor Hinduism, nor Islam had yet been fixed and codified for use by colonial authorities. These 'traditional' institutions were undergoing profound changes from the impact of the same basic social forces that were giving rise to the modern classes of the sub-continent; caste, sect and class, as these are known now, were being formed simultaneously and interactively'. (Stein 1991: PE-9)

Stein further remarks:

> Not even the most obdurately nationalist student of early modern India (and many of later times) would dispute the ideological importance of caste and Hinduism or dismiss them as some sort of trivial false consciousness. However, that does not mean conceding to these peculiarly Indian institutions the centricity which caste, religion and other cultural forms continue to enjoy among modern social scientists. . . . Situating caste and Hinduism within a class context means to provide them with a useful ideological content in place of what is most often an undefined and unconditioned global explanatory privilege. (Ibid: PE-17)

This analytic approach highlights the simultaneous and interactive relationship between the traditional socio-cultural institutions, like caste and Hinduism, and the contemporary socio-economic forces like classes and the state. As such, it provides a better comprehension of the world of cultural difference and heterogeneity and its concomitant social customs and rituals, which is often misleadingly assumed to be only a representation of traditional or human past. More importantly, it helps us to view the persistence of various 'traditional' or 'historical' social and cultural forms in the present not merely as legacies of the past but also as the product of modern social, political and cultural processes. In this context, the present chapter attempts to situate the social custom of dowry not only within the 'traditional' but also reinterpreted and rearticulated caste system and Hinduism arising out of the colonial state's codification of the social order and the imperatives of the contemporary socio-economic process.[1]

The linkages between the colonial state's restructuring of the socio-economic order within a reconstituted tradition and the monstrosity of dowry system in modern India has been noted by M.N. Srinivas. He writes that,

> modern dowry is entirely the product of the forces let loose by British rule. . . . The attempt to equate the huge sums of cash, jewellery, clothing, furniture and gadgetry demanded of the bride's kin by the groom's, to dakshina is only an attempt to legitimize a modern monstrosity by linking it up with an ancient and respected custom, a common enough and hoary Indian device. (Srinivas 1984: 13)

How has the charade been so successful? What was the rationale behind modern dowry? How was the dowry linked with the modern attempts to reconstitute and reinforce Brahmanic tradition and caste system?[2]

The British Reinvention of Tradition and Law

The customary fluidity and diversity in the institution of marriage of the ancient and medieval Indian society was most affected by socio-political and economic changes which accompanied the establishment of the British rule in India. New interpretations of Indian, and especially Hindu tradition, rituals, and customs within a broad and rigid framework—created to facilitate the colonial state's subjugation of India, accelerated the process of the institutionalization of a single form of marriage system. This displaced, several other customary forms of marriage as, if not totally illegal, deviant patterns of the newly established and recognized form. The 'invented tradition'[3] and its codification suppressed the dynamism of the earlier system. The diversity and complexity of forms of marriage as it historically evolved within the framework of socio-economic contexts lost its *raison d'être*.

Most significantly, the recognition of a form of marriage as the standard progressively declined the social legitimation and options for other forms. It ultimately led to a characteristic development which was marked by, first, the institutionalization of a form of marriage which was intricately linked with dowry and, second, the universalization of this form leading to its emulation by, and prevalence among, almost all of social groups and castes, albeit through the progressive restructuring of their respective tradition and rituals. What it brought about was not the simplification of the diverse forms of marriage systems but the move from one complex system to another with dowry as its integral part. The development of the dowry system, as it exists in the contemporary Indian society, can be traced to these significant changes beginning with the British rule in India.

The precise nature of the socio-economic impact of the British rule in India is a matter of polemical debates among scholars.[4] So are the questions of British imperative for the 'reinvention of the tradition' and its extent. Yet the significance of the colonial state's impact on the socio-economic order as well as of its large project of documentation and codification of tradition cannot be denied. We shall focus on the second aspect of the colonial state not only because of its more direct linkages with the problem of dowry but also due to the fact that the state project, to a large extent, was formed in simultaneous interaction with contemporary socio-economic imperatives. In fact, it was essentially a project for cultural legitimacy leading ultimately to the political legitimacy of the colonial state.[5] It sought to select from plural traditions, at the expense of other powerful, historically evolved, and conflicting interpretations, those strains which served their interests best and to unify it within a singular overwhelming framework. What it led to was not more fluidity but a newer rigidity.

The major instrument of the application of this project of codification and unification of the tradition was law exercised through the Anglo-Indian Courts. As the preface of the first English work of this project, *A Code of Gentoo Laws*, states that 'the importance of the commerce of India and the advantages of a territorial establishment in Bengal' could be maintained only by 'an adoption of such original institutes of the country as do not intimately clash with the laws or interests of the conquerors'[6] (in Sharma 1983: 4). Expressing the contemporary popular perception, a commentator later wrote that the High Courts are now doing the same task which the *mahātmās* did in interpreting the Dharmashāstras. As the *mahātmās*' comments differed in ancient period so did those of the High Courts in the contemporary period [*Stree Darpan* 1915 (13:1): 86].

One thus marks the emergence of law and the courts as the colonial state's most important weapon to appropriate and redefine the social order.

The development of a colonial legal system provided for the occasion for undertaking the project for codification of local customs into a Hindu Family Law. Such customs which varied from region to region and were subject to different interpretations according to the natural evolution of local socio-cultural environment were now put into a compact and serviceable body of law. The project began late in the eighteenth century with the establishment of High Courts and the promulgation of the Civil Courts Act. The purpose was the regulation of the jurisdiction of other earlier courts in each province in respect to succession, inheritance, marriage, caste or religious institutions in view of contrary practices based on local law and customs. 'The history of the British administration of Hindu Law', as Lucy Carroll notes, 'is largely the story of the erosion of customary law in the face of a judicial preference for law that could be found in the (judicially recognized) texts . . . it illustrates the role of the judicial branch of the British raj in the process of propagating values of orthodox Hinduism and 'Hinduizing' castes and tribes on the fringes of Hinduism'(Carroll 1989: 2; see also Carroll 1978: 233-50). The need to bring some semblance of uniformity within a larger framework of the Hindu Family Law required recourse to the study and comprehension of ancient written documents in Sanskrit. The British courts looked to these documents for the sources of current social customs and practices.

Earliest sources of law, as discussed in the last chapter, were found to be in the Code of Manu and the texts of Yajnavalkya, Narada and Brihaspati. These texts were followed some five hundred years after Narada by the *Mitākshara* (A.D. 1000-1100) commentary on Yajnavalkya applicable for most part of India. Two other commentaries, especially the *Dāyabhāga* (A.D. 1200-1400) and the *Vyavahāra Mayūkha* (*c.* A.D. 1600) were found to be specific respectively to Bengal and Gujarat and Bombay regions. These were the latest interpretation of the Family Law which combined together with earlier Brahmanical Sanskrit texts became the basis of almost all the judgement and law administered by the British courts. The Hindu Family or Civil Law was thus seen to be solely of Brahmanical origin.

The search for sources of local customs and practices and its gradual transformation into a unified treatise of the Hindu Family Law had two characteristic patterns. First, a concerted effort was made to comprehend ancient discourses on law and its application in modern legal cases. For this purpose, the British undertook the project of the translation of the earlier texts. The initiatives taken by Warren Hastings and Sir William Jones are noteworthy in this respect. The earliest work which attracted European attention was the Institute or Code of Manu. It was considered to be something which came into force on a particular day, like the Indian Penal Code, and which derived all its authority from being promulgated by him. It was not realized that the Code of Manu never had any legislative authority in the modern sense. It actually described what its author believed to be, or wished to be, the law. It was addressed primarily to Brahmins. But it admitted that conflicting customs and practices in the locality and the family existed and that ought to be respected (see Banerjee 1896: 1-2). Sir Jones translated the Code of Manu in 1794.

Similarly, commentaries of Vijnanesvara's *Mitākshara* and Jimutvahana's *Dāyabhāga* were rendered into English by Colebrook in 1810, and of Nilakantha's *Vyavahāra Mayūkha* by H. Borradaille in 1827. Hastings was also responsible for commissioning the preparation of a digest of Hindu law, better known as Halhed's *Gentoo Code.* This digest was compiled by Halhed in 1776 at Calcutta with the help of eleven Sanskrit pundits from a Persian translation of *Vivādārṇava Setu.* Another digest, known as *Colebrook's or Jagannatha's Digest,* appeared later with translation of excerpts from original Sanskrit texts. It was actually the *Vivāda Bhangārṇava* compiled by Jagannatha Tarkapunchanana at the instance of Sir William Jones. Edited by the famous Sanskrit scholar and lawyer, H.T. Colebrook, it became an important legal guide for courts. Translation and compilation of ancient and predominantly Brahmanical legal treatises provided an anachronistic reference point to judge contemporary local practices and customs which often lacked any written texts to prove their traditional usages.[7]

Moreover, the colonial discourse on the Hindu family laws often did not take into account the precise relationship which the Brahmanic law defined between individual and joint families. The new interpretations ignored the joint family context of these laws. As Kapadia writes:

The whole history of the Hindu family unfolds one significant fact, viz. that even when the trends towards individualism were recognized and attempts were being made to harmonize them with the interest of the joint family, the family constitution was unequivocally declared to be, and maintained as, joint and agnatic. . . . The destruction of the joint family by legislation is therefore rightly considered to be non-Hindu. (Kapadia 1966: 244)

Second, Sanskrit pundits were attached to the courts to consult the judges on cases where doubts existed. Brahmins by caste and trained in ancient scriptures, these pundits naturally tended to discourage any departure from conventional orthodox views. They usually clung to their views even when altered social conditions and established local customs demanded departure from the ancient interpretations. As Mayne succinctly puts,

The pundit, however bigoted he might be, was at all events a Hindu, living amongst Hindus, and advising upon a law which actually governed the everyday lives of himself and his family and his friends. He would torture a sacred text into an authority for his opinion; but his opinion would probably be right, though unsustained by or even opposed to, his text. (Mayne 1883: 37)

These pundits often magnified the authority of their own texts to the extent of even corrupting the original meaning. Moreover, their decisions were often influenced by schools of authority or seats of learning such as the Banaras School, and the Bengal School to which they belonged. As Sir William Jones notes that 'even if there was no suspicion of corruption on their part, the science they professed was in such a state of confusion that no reliance could be placed on their answers' (quoted in Dodwell 1932: 390). Difficulties in administering legal cases on the basis of the pundits' partisan Brahmanical views and the variance between *futwahs,* customs, and texts even brought in caste heads to the courts for opinions. It was essentially the result of law outgrowing the ancient authorities.

Moreover, it was the colonial official who had the privilege of the final authoritative decision in civil matters. Thus despite the pundits' involvement, the right to interpret their *vyavasthās* was appropriated by colonial officials. It was because, as Mani writes,

the *Nizamat Adalat* judges, the Governor General and his Council who determined which *vyavasthās* were 'essential' and which 'peripheral'. The authority of the pundits was problematic. The fact of being native simultaneously privileged and devalued them as reliable sources. The pundits were essential to 'unlocking' the scriptures for officials. But they were also believed by officials to be the 'devious minority' against which it was the mission of colonization to protect the 'simple majority'. (Mani 1989: 102)

But prevailing confusion and more importantly the British growing confidence in administering the Hindu civil laws as compiled by them finally led to the abolition of the practice of attaching pundits to the courts by the Act XI of 1864.

What the colonial project for the unification and codification of tradition led to was the search for ancient solutions to modern problems. It also brought about a somewhat uniform Brahmanical application of texts in disregard to the growth of particular family and local conditions.

The belief that Brahmanism was the law of India was so much fostered by the pundits and judges, that it came to be admitted conventionally, even by those who knew better. The revenue authorities, who were in daily intercourse with the people, were aware that many rules which were held sacred in the court, had never been heard of in the cottage. But their local knowledge appears rarely to have been made accessible to, or valued by, the Judicial Department. (Mayne 1883: 41)

Moreover, civil rules of conduct as practised in the society were not distinguished from religious ordinances. They were in fact legitimized not by the Court but by the religious practices evolving over the time. The rules or laws relating to marriage were thus contained, not in the chapter on *Vyavahāra*, or jurisprudence, but in the part treating of *Achara*, or the ritual. These were administered by private tribunals and were highly elastic in nature. They thus kept evolving by the assimilation of new usages and interpretation and reinterpretation of ancient texts in accordance with altered social situations. During the medieval period, only negligible interference in the Hindu civil law was made by the state which was more interested in tax-collection. The spontaneous growth of the Hindu civil law was thus 'suddenly arrested by the administration of the country passing to the hands of the English, and a degree of rigidity was given to it which it never before possessed' (Banerjee 1896: 7). The law thus evolved in the colonial period failed to establish either the anachronistic Brāhmanical tradition or a modern system of rules and regulation which the growth of a more complex civilization required. 'The consequence was,' as

Mayne (1883: 38) writes, 'a state of arrested progress, in which no voices were heard unless they came from the tomb. It was as if a German were to administer English laws from the resources of a library furnished with Fleta, Granville and Bracton, and terminating with Lord Coke.'

The nature and extent of the British reinterpretation of tradition, as mentioned earlier, is a matter of polemical debate among scholars. The crux of the debate, however, centres more around whether new interpretation of tradition emerged from conflicting traditions or the British colonial outlook. It is true that it was not the British who first reinvented the tradition. The powerful tradition, as Bayly notes, was constantly reinvented throughout history. It is also true that the pre-colonial social structure and practices were not devoid of rules and regulations or of set patterns of conducts and rituals. In the last centuries before colonial rule, he notes that

> the growing power of Brahmins and scribal people and the desire of new dynasties to legitimate themselves in terms of orthodoxy ensured that this was a powerful tradition in the process of constant reinvention. And it was from the adepts of this tradition at Nadia in particular that H.T. Colebrook derived the material and ideology which was to form the basis of his Hindu law code prepared for the use of Warren Hastings's neo-traditional administration in Bengal. (Bayly 1988: 156)

According to Bayly, it is therefore untenable to argue that 'traditional India was not a rigid society. It was British rule which made it so codifying many localized and pragmatic customs into a unified and Brahmanized "Hindoo Law" and classing people into immutable castes through the operations of the courts and ethnographical surveys' (ibid).

He, instead, insists that new interpretations of the society in India was only indirectly stimulated by the British. The latter codified and legitimized a system of civil customs and practices which had begun to emerge in the last centuries before the colonial rule. He thus concludes that the attempt of early British officials to rank and grade the Indian social order was more to understand and control it.

> So James Tod's neo-Gothic extravaganza, *The Annals and Antiquities of Rajasthan* 1829-32 itself became a reference book for the princes of that region in histcry and marriage customs. In the same way British law began to dispense to all castes and communities the high Brahminical and

scholarly traditions derived from the seminaries of Nadia or Tanjore. Yet the colonialists did not create this interpretation of India; rather they speeded up and transformed social and ideological changes which were already in train. (Bayly 1988: 158)

For our present purposes, it is a moot question whether the colonial state was directly or indirectly involved in the reconstitution of tradition or whether it was a fresh or continuous process. What is more important is that the colonial state undertook a cultural project to define the tradition and in doing so preferred to project one interpretation as culturally authentic. The locus of this authenticity, as Lata Mani, in an illuminating essay on 'Contentious Tradition,' writes, was found to be in Brahmanic scriptures. It generated a colonial discourse on Indian tradition and society, which

> did not emerge from nowhere, nor was it entirely discontinuous with pre-colonial discourses in India. Rather, it was produced through interaction with select natives; though . . . officials clearly had power over the natives in question. . . . This greater power had several consequences. It meant that officials could insist, for instance, that Brahmanic and Islamic scriptures were prescriptive texts containing rules of social behavior, even when the evidence for this assertion was problematic. (Mani 1989: 90-1)

Instead of taking into account varied and remote local systems of customary law, it was easier to prove or disprove a case in reference to written ancient legal treatises which both the British and Indian judges (who themselves were usually Brahmins) studied. As Bayly himself concedes that

> in the early nineteenth century . . . the spirit of hierarchy and ritual distinction became more pervasive. The British peace speeded the rise of high Hindu kingship, Brahminism and the advance of principles of purity and pollution in the countryside. . . . [H]ierarchy and the Brahmin interpretation of Hindu society which was theoretical rather than actual over much of India as late as 1750 was firmly ensconced a century later. (Bayly 1988: 157-8)

It thus transformed Brahmin or high caste Hindu family norms into statutory Hindu Law. Customs and norms approved by the traditional Brahmanic codes of conduct became the yardstick to validate or invalidate socio-cultural practices prevalent among other sections of differentiated Hindu society. Brahmanism thus emerged as one of the key factors in the colonial appropriation of the whole of Hindu society.

The British legitimacy to the priority of Brahmanical rules and laws of social order over customary local practices of various rural groups affected the law of marriage, succession, and adoption. It provided juridical sanction to certain patriarchal practices to the disadvantage of all Hindu women whether rural or urban. It influenced the way in which the custom of marriage and succession to the property was enjoyed by the majority of population. How did the growing Brahmanization of the social order affect the marriage forms and how did it lead to the entrenchment of the practice of dowry?

Brahmanization and its Impact on Marriage and Dowry

In the late eighteenth century, the trend toward moulding the customary social order within the framework of Brahmanization began the process of rigidification of forms in the marriage patterns, caste system and rules of succession. All these combined together ritualized, promoted and universalized the practice of dowry giving as a necessary ingredient of the Hindu marriage. Examining the implication of Brahmanization in the marriage patterns, Van der Veen (1972: 25) notes that 'Brahmanic ideals led to a preference for the dowry marriage'.

Of the eight forms of marriages enumerated in the laws of Manu, as discussed in the last chapter, only four, i.e. *Brāhma, Daiva, Ārsha* and *Prajāpatya* rites, were considered acceptable to the superior ideals of Brahmins. These four forms in some way or another were 'variations of dowry marriage'. The other four forms, based on bride-price and different types of abduction, were considered inferior and permissible only for the lower castes. Unlike the first four forms which result in the birth of *shishṭa* (civilized) sons, the last four forms of marriage cause, as Manu writes, the birth of sons 'who are cruel and speakers of untruth, who hate the Veda and the sacred law' (Manu III. 39.41 quoted in Van der Veen 1972: 26). One of the important aspects of the trend toward the Brahmanization was the establishment of the legality of the *Brāhma* form of marriage.

In the late nineteenth and early twentieth centuries, British ethnographic surveys and census reports indicated the obsolescence of all other forms of marriage mentioned in the ancient texts except for the *Brāhma* and *Asura* forms. Mayne (1883: 84) notes that 'it is stated generally, that the *Brāhma* is the only legal form at present, and probably this may be so among the higher classes. . . . But there is no doubt that the *Asura* is still practised . . . among the Sudras, it is a very common, if not the prevailing form' (see also Banerjee 1896: 87). Blunt's Census Report of 1911 too notes the prevalence of two forms of marriage: one requiring the payment of dowry or the dowry marriage practised among the high castes, and the other was the bride-price marriage common in the low castes (Blunt 1912: 221). The dowry marriage referred to the *Brāhma* form and the bride-price marriage to the *Asura* form.

(a) *Institutionalization of the Brāhma Form of Marriage*

In colonial India, Banerjee notes that legally the *prima facie* assumption was to consider all the marriages in the *Brāhma* form. This is witnessed in court decisions in cases relating to Uthikesavulu *v.* Ramanujam, *ILR*, 32 Mad. 512; and Chuni *v.* Suraj, *ILR*, 33 Bom. 433. In the case of Chuni *v.* Suraj (5 April 1909), the court noted that 'unless rebutted by evidence', 'the *prima facie* presumption no doubt is that every marriage under the Hindu Law is according to the *Brāhma* form' [*ILR* 1909 (XXXIII): 437]. Yet, the court did not consider the solemnization of a marriage in *Brāhma* form if no transaction of gifts from the bride's side to the other took place along with the *kanyādāna.* In the above-mentioned case, it rejected the consideration of an *Asura* marriage to be of the *Brāhma* form in spite of the fact that it was solemnized according to the rites prescribed for the latter form.

> Where the person who gives a girl in marriage receives consideration for it, the substance of transaction makes it, according to Hindu Law, not a gift but a sale of the girl. The money received is what is called bride-price; and that is essential element of the *Asura* form. The fact that the rites prescribed for the *Brāhma* form are gone through cannot take it out of that category. (Ibid)

Thus, the court considered all Hindu marriages to be of the *Brāhma* form only on the ground that no gift or payment was received by the bride's side in consideration of marriage. There was however tacit approval of the one way transaction of gift or dowry from the bride-side along with the gift of daughter. The colonial state thus not only legitimated dowry as an integral part of the *Brāhma* marriage but by promoting this form also supported the expansion of dowry practice. This was in contrast to the Muslim rulers who made at least some active efforts to curb such practices (see chapter two).

Turner in his 1931 Census Report of the United Province remarks that 'by far the most prevalent custom is that of the bride's family providing the dowry' (Turner 1933: 313). 'At the present day', Blunt similarly notes, 'one of the most common of all forms of marriage amongst Hindus, even the highest, is the "dowry" marriage, where the bride's father pays a bridegroom price in the shape of a dowry with his daughter. That payment is necessary: without it the marriage would not take place at all. It would presumably be classed as a *Brāhma* marriage' (Blunt 1931: 318-19). The court in almost all the cases linked dowry to the *Brāhma* form of marriage, which characterized gifting away of daughter (*kanyādāna*) by the father, and legitimized such gift-giving. For instance, where father had died, the court upheld the validity of gift-giving to the daughter at the time of her marriage and interpreted the unmarried daughter's entitlement as consisting of dowry. In an 1826 case, Justice Lord Gifford opined that even within the *Mitākshara* law, a Hindu widow had, 'for certain purposes a clear authority to dispose of her husband's property, and might do it for religious purposes, including dowry to a daughter' (*Clarke's Rules and Orders* 1826: 91). Another judge in a different case remarked that 'whichever view be accepted, it is clear from *Mitākshara* that the maiden daughter is entitled to a share, which represents her dowry and marriage expenses, and such share is one fourth of what she would have been entitled to receive, if instead of being a daughter she had been a son'[8] [*ILR* 1909 (XXXVII): 6]. In the *Brāhma* form of marriage, the judge observed that 'the gift could be defended on the ground that, apart from the circumstance that it was a provision for the married couple, it was believed to enhance the merit of the primary act, namely the giving of a virgin in marriage, which from a religious point of view is supposed to be productive of considerable benefits to the parents' (ibid: 8).

In fact, as marriage was linked with property and inheritance, the legal validity of marriage was to be sanctioned for claiming one's share or entitlement. With women's right to property not considered in earnest until the Hindu Law of Inheritance (Amendment Act) of 1929 and the more elaborate Hindu Woman's Right to Property Act of 1937, the most accepted *Brāhma* form of *kanyādāna* marriage with gifts or dowry to the bride appeared the only way to legalize one's property interests under the rule of inheritance on the one hand and to provide for the daughter within a customarily accepted form on the other. Most of the legal cases involving marriages therefore not surprisingly pertain to property or its succession disputes. Considerations of property and the colonial state's interpretation of the traditional rights to succession naturally favoured the promotion of the *Brāhma* form of marriage.[9]

Recent studies by Madan (1975) and Miller (1980) find that dowry has been an integral or the predominant form of marriage payment in the *kanyādāna* form of marriage particularly among propertied groups in north India. Nirmala Banerjee (n.d.), who explores both the economic and cultural factors as crucial determinants for the position of women links the prevalence of *kanyādāna* form of marriage and dowry to the diminishing role of women in the process of production and the acculturation of other castes through Brahmanic influence.

The growing incidence of dowry marriages during the colonial period was, in fact, also the result of admissibility of the *Brāhma* form of marriage even for the people of low castes, who numerically constituted the majority of population. All persons, as Banerjee (1896: 87) notes, 'are at the present-day' held competent to marry in that form.

> *Prima facie* one would imagine that a *Brāhma* marriage, from its very definition was inadmissible for a Sudra; and Manu certainly seems to contemplate only the last four as applicable to the case of the lower three classes. But there is no doubt that the *Brāhma* marriage has long since ceased to be the property of any class; and the Madras Sudder Court have held that, in the case of Sudras, the mere fact that the bride is given without bestowal of any gift by the bridegroom, constitutes the marriage one of the Brahma form. (Mayne 1883: 83-4)

Its prevalence among the high castes and its subsequent legality during the British period thus also made it as the most valid and perfect form of marriage to be practised by all those groups connected with the process of Brahmanization. In the 1911 Census of the United Province, Blunt found that besides most Brahmin and Rajput castes and clans, the custom of bridegroom price or dowry was practised among the Aheria, Udhiya, Baiswar, Basor, Bhat, Bhatiya, Bind, Dangi, Golapurab, Gujar, Jat, Kachhi, Kayastha, Khangar, Kingaria, Kurmi, Lodha, Pasi, Sadh, Sejwari and Sonar (Blunt 1912: 221).

Finally, the *Brāhma* form of marriage, as discussed in chapter two, required the gift of the daughter (*kanyādāna*) with costly garments, ornaments, and other precious items to a well-versed person invited by the father. As such, Blunt correctly questions the assumption of dowry in its contemporary forms as a gift to the bride or a mere token of affection not essential to the *Brāhma* marriage ceremony (Blunt 1931: 319). The fact that there is one way transaction of gifts demonstrates gradual historical shift from the traditional definition of the *Brāhma* form of marriage to the treatment of marriages without any payment from the groom to the bride as the *Brāhma* marriage. As elaborating the practice of dowry among Rajputs and Kunbees of Gujarat, Forbes' *Ras Mala: Hindu Annals of Western India* (1878: 615) informs:

On the conclusion of a match between the parents a sum of money is sent to the father of the youth by the father of the girl. The sum is not large, probably about the tenth of the amount of 'Juheez', or dower. This is a sort of earnest money, and when the ceremony of 'Tilluk' is completed the father of the youth cannot recede from the engagement.

After this comes the 'Luggun', when half of the dower agreed upon is paid, and the date for the nuptial procession, called the 'burat', is settled. The Burat, or chief marriage ceremony, to which all the relations and friends are invited, is the occasion of the most profuse expenditure in feasting them; the greater the multitude fed, the better satisfied is the pride and vanity of the father of the girl, who, at the same time, pays the remainder of the dower. This sum varies according to the rank of the parties, but is generally enough to throw the father into debt and difficulties. Unless a handsome sum be offered, a husband of the good caste is not to be procured; and, unless the feasting be profuse, and the invitation to the marriage feast general, then the girl's parents are held up to public scorn, as stingy or poverty stricken.

The requirement of bride bringing money and property with her and no counter presentation from the bridegroom in exchange for the bride made the *Brāhma* marriage coterminous with the dowry marriage. The growing prevalence of the *kanyādāna* form of marriage also witnessed the simultaneous rise of the practice of the gift of daughter bedecked with costly clothing and ornaments as its integral component. Trautmann notes that the ideal *kanyādāna* and the 'traditional' dowry are intricately connected with hypergamy, non-reciprocity between wife-givers and wife-takers, and the unidirectional flow of gifts. Because a bride is severed from her father's house and has no claim on him or his property, she is given a dowry of clothing, ornaments and other goods (Trautmann 1981: 292).

Moreover, as the *kanyādāna* or *Brāhma* form of marriage also required the invitation to the bridegroom for marriage, the extent of dowry also worked as a necessary incentive to establish the marriage alliance. The dowry thus also functioned as the bridegroom-price legitimized with reference to the *kanyādāna* or *Brāhma* form of marriage.

> It is nowhere laid down explicitly that Brahmins should give dowries; and renunciation of bride-price asking, is sufficient condition for Brahmanization. Nevertheless, as social affirmation of economic capacity and high ritual status, the dowry stands as a symbol of Brahmanization. . . . The introduction of the dowry marriage, like the refusal to do agricultural work, is only part of the total process of Brahmanization. (Van der Veen 1972: 27)

Dowry in its contemporary form was thus culturally expressed and couched in potent terms like *dāna* and *dakshiṇā*, sanctified by the predominant Brahmanic religion, associated with hypergamy, and integrally linked with the highest form of marriage, i.e. the *Brāhma* form, and its historically evolved socio-cultural practice represented much more than, in spite of being originally rooted in, what is referred to as a part of the 'pre-mortem inheritance' by Goody and Tambiah (1973).

(b) *The Status of Asura Form of Marriage*

Opposite to the *Brāhma* marriage was the *Asura* form of marriage. It required presentation of gifts or payment from the bridegroom or his kinsmen in exchange for the bride. This form of marriage, as noted by Manu, is the one in which 'the bridegroom having given as much wealth as he can afford to the father and paternal kinsmen and to the damsel herself, takes her voluntarily as his bride' (Manu III, 31). Linked with so-called non-Aryan form of marriage by scholars, its practice was throughout condemned by the Sanskrit texts. Manu strongly denounces all those fathers who receive even a small amount as gratuity for gifting daughter in marriage. It is, therefore, not surprising that the *Asura* form was prevalent most among so-called low castes—the ones which remained outside the Brahmanic social order.

During the early colonial period, Blunt found the practice of bride-price prevalent among many of the hierarchically lower castes. He lists such castes and notes the average amount of bride-price transacted in their marriages: Musahar (Rs. 1-1/4); Ahir, Chamar, Dhangar, Habura (each Rs. 2); Bhar (Rs. 2-1/2); Patari (Rs. 3); Byar (Rs. 4); Bansphor (Rs. 4-1/2); Bhuiya, Chero, Dom, Dusadh, Kharwar, Kol, Korwa, Majhwar, Panka, Parahiya (each Rs. 5); Khatik (Rs. 7); Bhuiyar, Dharkar, Sahariya (each Rs. 8); Tharu (Rs. 9); Agariya (Rs. 10); Ghasiya (Rs. 12); Bhajgi (Rs. 40 to 50); Bhil (Rs. 30 to 60); Nat (Rs. 25); Khapariya (Rs. 100); Sansiya (Rs. 500); with Soiri, Raji, Kingariya, Kalwar, Jat and Gond (Blunt 1912: 71). Turner in the 1931 Census Report, however, finds the fast declining control of tribal customs or caste panchayats over the amount of bride-price. He, however, notes that its amount was now getting settled more and more in the nature of business transaction and not by traditional customs (Turner 1933: 312). The Court thus determined a marriage to be in *Asura* form if there was some pecuniary benefits to the giver of the bride even if same ceremonies as of *Brāhma* form were performed.

Wedding ceremonies of these hierarchically lower ranked castes, however, differed greatly from those of the upper ones. Composed mainly of pre-Aryan and non-Brahmanical elements, their distinct patterns have been noted by such early anthropologists as Crooke (1896), Risley (1915), and others, in mid-nineteenth centuries.[10] For example, Chamars, unlike the upper castes, paid bride-price and not dowry. When the marriage was settled, fathers of the bride and the groom jointly sacrificed a pig to the local goddess and had a feast. Their wedding ceremony was very simplified and lasted for not more than one day as compared to usual three days among the upper castes. The groom presented the father of the bride-to-be with ten seers of flour, one saree, and five rupees. There was no direct participation of Brahmin priests (see Cohn 1955: 58). This reflects a distinctive marriage pattern characterized by the bride-price and simpler wedding ceremonies prevalent among the lower castes.

Yet it appears that the *Asura* or the bride-price form of marriage was prevalent not only among the lower castes or Shudras but also some Brahmins and Rajputs occasionally practiced it. It arose mainly out of economic compulsions and transcended caste rules and barriers. The 1931 Census Report finds that

> owing to the stress of economic conditions . . . marriages by purchase are

undoubtedly on the increase, although they are looked down upon by those in better circumstances. The increase is most marked among poor Brahmins and Rajputs. Again if the bridegroom is old or suffers from some defect or other he has to pay a bride-price. In some parts Sonars take a bride-price either through poverty, or because of the relatively fewer women in their community. (Turner 1933: 313)

Another factor for the bride-price marriages, according to the 1931 Census Report, was hypergamy. Lower ranked Brahmins and Rajputs, probably with better financial conditions and unable to secure brides for their sons in their own branch, brought brides from somewhat higher branches of their community by paying them between Rs. 100 and 500. Vaishyas also often paid a large sum as bride-price, the amount of which was fixed by either private intermediaries or the Panchayats (Turner 1933: 313).

Blunt views these practices to be originating from the traditionally approved Arsha form of marriage. For him, the Arsha form differs from the Asura only in degree, in the former a nominal amount was paid and in the latter a large amount or as much wealth as the bridegroom could afford was paid to the bride's family. On this basis, he classifies majority of the castes mentioned earlier as practising the *Ārsha* form of marriage and the rest the *Asura* form (Blunt 1931: 316-18). Distortions might have come in these two forms due to the overlapping of marriage patterns and its adoption as caste customs over the time. But the bride-price marriage was not traditionally considered approved or desirable among the upper castes. The 1931 Report indicates that when the brideprice is paid openly the marriage is celebrated at the bride-groom's house and is known as *dola kadhana.* This was, however, considered very derogatory especially for upper castes which usually paid the bride-price discreetly and held the marriage at the bride's house only.

(c) *Shift from Asura to Brāhma Form of Marriage*

The impact of Brahmanization on the *Asura* marriage practice was evident in two trends. First, there was a progressive decline of the *Asura* form of marriage in preference of the *Brāhma* form. Second, ceremonies usually associated with *Brāhma* form were increasingly adopted by those still practising *Asura* form. It was the result of Anglo-Indian Courts' establishment of the *Brāhma* marriage as the most standard and legal in terms of Hindu, customary, and British laws. The *Asura* marriage was considered legal only on the basis of regional customary practice.

The Brahmanizing, Hinduizing or Sanskritizing castes of the British period gradually began to shift from bride-price to dowry marriages to demonstrate their upgradation on the social ladder in response to the state's attempt to sharpen social cleavages on the basis of caste hierarchy. It was most notable in castes like Ahir, Chamar, Teli, etc.—which were noted to be practising bride-price marriages by Crooke (1896) and Blunt (1912 and 1931) in the mid-nineteenth century. In his study of the Chamar society in post-Independent north India, Cohn found their domestic ceremonies increasingly fashioned according to those of Thakurs and Brahmins. Where there was once bride-price, 'the practice of giving dowry has been introduced, although the boy's father still gives a token payment to the girl's father: here the transition between bride-price and dowry can be seen in progress' (Cohn in Marriot 1955: 75; see also Beteille 1969).

There was also a greater emphasis in observing or modelling marriage ceremonies in terms of rites and ritual associated with the *Brāhma* form. The courts' insistence on proving the legality of traditionally disapproved *Asura* form of marriage predominantly by such evidences as the proper celebration of ceremonies provided a fillip to their adoption. For example, Cohn notes the lengthening of Chamar weddings from one day to three days to resemble Brahmin weddings, prevalence of child marriages in preference to the earlier marriage age of between twelve to sixteen, and employment of Brahmin priest for every ceremony except the final rite. He thus remarks that 'recent changes have moved Chamar religion directly toward the main stream of the great tradition of orthodox Hinduism' (Cohn 1955: 75). Such changes started becoming visible in many lower castes during the colonial period and established as norms during the post-Independent era. 'Sanskritization, which was the principal idiom of social mobility in the past', Beteille (1969: 119) remarks, 'appears to have special significance today for castes in the middle and the lower middle regions of the hierarchy'. Such shifts reflect the pervasiveness of the *Brāhma* form of marriage along with dowry and related rituals in the larger section of society. Lower and lower middle castes, which were also turning into significant socio-economic classes in the wake of industrialization, increasingly opted for more universally accepted *Brāhma* form in place of the *Asura*.

Moreover, the examination of the validity of a particular marriage in the Court required the extent to which ceremonies were appropriately observed. Detailed descriptions and standardization by the Court of an appropriate marriage ceremony meant reinforcement of a particular set of customs and freezing of all others. It was prepared and approved in the perspective of Hindu law, customary law, and the statutory law. Hindu laws as administered by the Anglo-Indian courts, Carroll notes, 'was a mixture of *Shastric* laws, custom, and case-law, with a hardy dose of English legal concepts and notions, simplified and standardized for ease of application and administrative convenience. Not surprisingly, the end result contained several anomalies' (Carroll 1989: 7). The case of Anjana Dossee *v.* Proladh Chunder Ghose, for example, dealt with the question of validity of a Hindu marriage even without involving the questions of right to property. The officiating Chief Justice Norman observed: 'We think that the court must have jurisdiction in such suit to declare the marriage void, if procured by fraud or force, and celebrated without the consent of necessary parties or without the formalities necessary to render it a binding marriage according to Hindu law' (Banerjee 1896: 107). The case involved Proladh Chunder Ghose's abduction of Anjana Dosee's daughter Kuppoora and performance of marriage ceremony with her at the house of a third party. Only marriages actually and properly celebrated were considered to be legally binding (Mayne 1883: 97). In some cases, courts took this view that 'when the fact of the celebration of marriage is established, it will be presumed, in the absence of evidence to the contrary, that all the necessary ceremonies have been complied with' even if these celebrations were in violation of a previous agreement to marry another person; or it has been performed without the consent of the person whose consent ought to have been obtained (ibid: 97).

While the courts took into consideration the customary ceremonies of the family, i.e. *kulāchāra*, in making judgement on the legality of marriages, it was limited to the family of elites or high castes or kings. All other practices were treated as deviant liable to make a marriage void. The legality of marriage ceremonies of the Adi Brahmo Society of Bengal was a matter of debate for quite sometime. The court considered them Hindus on the basis of their birth in the community. The opinion of the English Advocate General, Mr. Cowie was against the grant of the validity of their marriage ceremonies which was different from those prescribed and approved by the court in the case of the Hindus (Banerjee 1896: 105). Similarly, the *Gandharva* marriage was held valid for Kshatriyas in one very old case of Hujmee Mull *v.* Ranee Bhadoorun of 1817 by the Bengal Sudder Court. In later years it was refused legal recognition as being contrary to morality (Blunt 1931: 318).[11]

Moreover, the judgement of the legality of a custom was often an arbitrary process especially in cases of families and castes not prominent on the social ladder. For example, the Chief Justice in Calcutta, Sir Charles Gray, observed that 'Although in this country we cannot go back to that period which constitutes legal memory in England, viz., the reign of Richard I, yet still there must be some limitation, without which a custom ought not to be held good' (in Banerjee 1896: 12-13). A custom to be held valid, in case of Calcutta, must have existed from before the year 1773, when the Act of Parliament established the Supreme Court, and in case of Mofussil, from before the year 1793, when the practice of the maintenance of registry of regulation began. Since these dates the power of making laws had become vested in the British legislature, therefore, no change could be effected in the Hindu Law by any other agency. The custom to be held valid thus required proof that it was 'uniform', of 'ancient origin', 'continuous', 'definite', 'unopposed to morality or public policy', upheld by courts, panchayats, or such experienced persons as pundits. Blunt thus observes that 'even in the most favorable circumstances it would be difficult (and expensive) task to prove the validity of an overriding custom' (Blunt 1931: 315).

The attempt to standardize the ceremonies associated with the *Brāhma* form of marriage affected the society in two ways. First, there was move by the new Brahmanizing castes to adopt the *Brāhma* or *kanyādāna* form of marriage, and second and not less importantly, attempts were made to follow the essential rituals, such as dowry, linked with this form. Such developments, as we shall see later, provided for the *kanyādāna* or the gift of daughter with costly garments and jewelleries and in addition of, or in lieu of, the latter with gold and cash within a modern set-up influenced by the growth of industrial economy and consequent monetization. The groom-price or the 'modern dowry', as referred to by Srinivas, thus grew out of the traditional dowry coextensive with the *Brāhma* form of marriage. The primacy which Brahmanization accorded to the *Brāhma* form of marriage over the other traditionally approved forms arrested the growth of such customs and practices which were naturally evolving over the time and different from the existing pattern.

The Colonial Restructuring of Socio-Economic Order: Caste and Class in Marriage and Dowry

(a) *Social Mobility during the Colonial Period*

During the early colonial period, the reinforcement and expansion of the 'traditional' *Brāhma* form of marriage with dowry as an integral part took place in a situation when the local socio-economic order itself was getting restructured. Pressures from the colonial state's own brand of capitalism reshaped avenues of social mobility through its redistribution of existing and creation of new resources. Land settlements reallocated ownership more on the basis of contract than status. This displaced *rajas, zamindars,* tax-collectors and other remnants of Mughal nobility in some places and reempowered them in the other—but all within the context of private property and 'free market'. The colonial rule thus without so much actually destroying the caste hierarchy, patterns of local power and socio-religious institutions changed the context within which these traditionally functioned. The process of cultural reinforcement proceeded side by side with the restructuring of economic order unleashing newer social forces. What speeded up this restructuring were changes like the commercialization of agriculture, emergence of new market centres along the newly introduced railway routes, creation of a service sector for the colonial administration, displacement of rural indigenous handicraft industries by urban industries, and incorporation of regional economies into a single unified economy linked with the world capitalist economy.

So much so that in the early nineteenth century the basis of Indian social and economic order had become substantially different from that of hundred years back. 'India,' Bayly (1988: 144) writes, 'as it is commonly conceived, a land of settled arable farming, of caste Hindus, and of specialist agricultural produce, was very much a creation of this period. The stranger, older India of forest and nomads where the agricultural frontier was as often in retreat as on the advance began to disappear. The more homogeneous society of peasants and petty moneylenders which emerged in the later nineteenth century was a more appropriate basis for a semi-European colonial state.' Settled agriculture and peasant petty commodity production arose out of the colonial state's compulsion to extract surplus, expand revenue collections, and control in effective manner the wider area of society through creation of new classes and production of legitimizing ideologies. This provided fillip to the emergence of a dominant unified socio-economic system within the colonial world of market economy.

Plural cultural traditions characterizing regions with their exclusive socio-economic set up began to melt away. Tribals, and nomads, such as Gujars, Bhattis, Rangar Rajputs, Mewatis, and the traditional trade carriers, Banjaras, were gravitated towards settled agriculture. Their mobility was restricted by the introduction of the revenue assessment of waste land and rigid property rights which spread cultivation to the old grazing land.

> The partnership between the company and the moneylender-trader which had facilitated the subjugation of India now proceeded in the conquest of India's internal frontiers. Monied settlers from the plains trickled into the central Indian tribal zone secured by the types of landlordism and forms of debt recovery alien to the domestic economy of the tribal people. Colonial administrators, solicitous for the stability of revenue, conferred on them proprietary rights and legitimized their bonds through the colonial courts. (Bayly 1988: 141-2)

Lower castes were permitted to hold land after the abolition of interdicts against such practices after 1812. The colonialists abolished by 1850 those practices which smacked of the extreme form of slavery. Domestic and field serfdom for the untouchable declined. This coupled with the spread of cash crops and money economy eroded the traditional patronal ties and turned many groups of the low castes to agriculture for subsistence. In central India, Chamars soon emerged as small landholders; in Bihar, low caste farmers began to take tribals as bonded labour; and in artisan towns, displaced specialist weavers and spinners turned to intensive cultivation as either poor peasants, tenants or agricultural labourers. The overall growth and homogeneity of the landholding peasants and the agricultural labour class characterized the early nineteenth century rural society.

This was followed by the simultaneous breaking off of the old warrior peasant communities. Some of their most eminent lineages either vanished in the war or became domesticated aristocracy. Others found the basis of their power and authority increasingly eroded under the colonial land settlements. 'Even if there was some physical continuity of the families of the village magnates of 1800 through to the small group of "rich peasants" of the second half of the nineteenth century, the nature and context of their power had changed' (Bayly 1988: 148). The village-controlling brotherhood communities of Rajputs and Brahmins under the *pattidārī* or *bhaichārā* system of the landholding too tended to decline. Many of them persisted as a part of the wider peasant body. Unable to meet the settled revenue demands they were forced to auction off their rights to new landlords. Others precariously maintained rights in their domain by physical or legal battles against the outside encroacher.

The above trends are evident in Cohn's (1968 and 1969) seminal study of structural change in rural society in districts of Banaras, Ghazipur-Ballia, Jaunpur, and Mirzapur between 1795-1850. It points to the nature and direction of change in general in north India. His study found that in all the above districts 54 per cent of the sellers of land were Rajputs, followed by 14 per cent of Muslims and 10 per cent of Brahmins. During the same period, the largest percentage of buyers of land at auction were Baniyas and Bhumihars who constituted 52 per cent of the total. The occupation of the maximum number of buyers of land was commerce and money-lending, followed by the *zamindari*. The Raja of Banaras was the single most largest buyer.

More importantly, Cohn's list of the social origins of landholders in 1885 reveals that the largest category belonged to 'new men' who paid 31 per cent of the total revenue. They were followed by the eighteenth century aristocrats (mainly the Raja of Banaras), traditional aristocrats, commercial families, religious institutions, and those of unknown origin paying respectively 25, 21, 13, 1 and 9 per cent of revenues. Most of these new men earned their wealth from activities associated with the British rule in the Banaras region and held such administrative positions as tahsildar, sarrishtadars (head clerks), deputy collectors, and amins and sadar amins (lower court judges). Out of them only three were Rajputs. Cohn (1969: 80) writes that 'this is another indication that until the end of the nineteenth century, new opportunities of gaining wealth were not taken by the Rajputs, whose position was based on landholding in the pre-British era and whose economic position . . . was most likely to be declining in relation to other groups'.[12] Similarly, Metcalf's (1969: 123-41) study of Awadh demonstrates that while the shift of the *talukdars* from *rajas* to landlords forced them to maintain their dominance over the rural society by radically altering the basis of their power to ties of rent and revenue, it created a situation in which there was a progressive decline of the village *zamindars* and permanent tenants (*khud-kasht Asāmis*) and their replacement by a new cultivating class or tenants-at-will.

Such developments indicate a major trend characterized by the increasing importance of wealth and landholding as opposed to status and caste categories in the social mobility and formation of classes. Wealth provided the traditionally non-cultivating classes to purchase land and enter into the ranks of peasants or to purchase the rights to collect revenues to become *zamindars* and attain a status at the local level. Money and money payments had also begun to erode the systems of dependence traditionally marked by the ritualized patron-client relationship by the eighteenth century. 'The economic changes introduced alongside the colonial rule in the early nineteenth century', Bayly (1988: 141) notes, further expanded and cemented 'the labour-for-money element in the relationship and tied it to the creation of surplus for export markets'. Jan Breman's study of Dubla debt-serfs of Anavil Brahmins in Surat highlights newer exploitation bereft of the traditional patronage and based more on labour agreement arising out of the condition of usury and debt during the colonial period and after (see Breman 1972). The colonial modernization thus created such a situation in which the primacy to wealth and wealth generation began to undermine the social order providing opportunities for the rise of new elites and the social mobility of many caste groups.

Outside the rural world, growth of industry, education, and service sectors promoted wealth generation in newer activities at the expense of traditional sources. Searching for new sources for wealth generation and social dignity, new families of middle or lesser status (as opposed to *mahajans* of the highest status connected with the *rajas* and *nawabs*), found in the colonial trade an avenue for social mobility. In Banaras region, the hinterland Agrawal families from Chunar and Jaunpur were thus first to raise their status through cotton trading and passing of Company *hundis* to the west and south (Bayly 1992: 241). While there was continuity in the sense that the traditional merchant castes were not displaced, these newer developments reflect some of the subcastes emerging as more powerful and successful in acquisition of wealth and status during the colonial period.

The establishment of European military stations, and expansion of towns like Allahabad, Agra, Meerut and Kanpur along the railway routes witnessed rise of service villages. This provided opportunities to Chamar leather workers, Teli oilmen, Kahar carriers, and Kalwar liquor distributors to engage in work with Europeans as cooks, stableboys, bearers and domestic servants. These positions were probably difficult to be obtained within a traditional set up governed by Hindu rulers (Bayly 1992: 215). In Bengal, Sanyal (1975: 88) notes that

> opportunities created by these developments attracted many of the artisans and traders belonging to the Teli, Gandhabanik, Maira and Tanti castes who had earned some fortune through their transactions with the East India Company. Among these the Tillis were the most important. They extensively availed themselves of the opportunities and became landholders in different parts of Bengal.[15]

In fact, social mobility of these artisan and inferior merchant groups, which rapidly acquired wealth and status by the mid-eighteenth century, is evident in most of the cities of north India. In Banaras, men of Barhai castes, which cultivated betel-nut, and Teli, which pressed oil, became successful city entrepreneurs after 1750. In Agra, Chamars were accepted as creditworthy merchants. In Mirzapur, Kassera (brass-workers) and Kalwars (liquor distillers) similarly rose to positions of locally prominent entrepreneurs. Explaining the features of social mobility in nineteenth century India, Bayly (1992: 340-1) writes:

> At any time from the mid-eighteenth century onwards, one can point to examples of lower caste families rising to wealth and honour within the community. Lists of works of 'public utility' maintained by magistrates in Agra and Benaras mention distillers, tailors, oil-men and water carriers establishing wells, tanks, temples, and public wharves. But the logic of

status system and the form of commercialization both required that this should be a flexible, but not an 'open' society. Those who had passed through the gate had a strong interest in closing it behind them. Yet by the same token, we cannot speak of unchanging, traditional institutions. For both the state and the market had played a part in modifying relationships which superficially seemed to be played out in the same ideology of shares and redistribution.

Thus, the colonial period witnessed increasing social mobility which the expansion of state and monetization of economy provided. English education and new professions both in private and public sectors provided opportunities to go up in the social ladder and emerged as alternative status symbols. Yet, its feature was marked by the fact that those social groups which climbed up on the social ladder of mobility established themselves as separate sub-castes and often severed their relationship with those members of their own or *byahut* sub-castes which were left behind. Adopting Brahmanized customs, especially in marriages, they perpetuated their distinct entity.

It must also be pointed out that the process of social mobility exacerbated by the colonial structure was gendered. One of the most important features of the colonial period was the diminishing role of women in the production activities. Census Reports of 1911 and 1931 both highlight this fact. Table 3.1 [Banerjee (n.d.): 10] is illustrative of this trend.

The fall in the percentage of women workers were primarily due to the replacement of the household industry by the factory industry which affected women the most. In the decade preceding the 1931 Census, it was pointed out that whereas the 'increase in male adult industrial workers amounts to 38.2 per cent . . . female industrial workers have increased by only 15.9 per cent, and have not increased at all in the last five years' (Turner 1933: 53). It was

TABLE 3.1: WORKFORCE PARTICIPATION RATE OF WOMEN IN SELECTED AREAS

States	1911	1931	1961
Bihar	34.71	26.09	27.13
Uttar Pradesh	33.33	29.08	18.10
Bengal	18.79	13.19	9.44

also reported that the 'female earners and working dependents are actually and proportionally lower now than they have been at the last two censuses' (ibid: 410). The fall in number of female worker was significant in industries like cotton ginning, cleaning, pressing, spinning, weaving, rice pounding and husking. The growing economic dependency to which women were forced into contributed to a large extent in, what some scholars have referred to as, the negative net worth of women. This augmented the structural factor for the expansion of dowry among the larger section of the populace. Moreover, social mobility of some classes might have also led to their restrictions on women to work. An article in *Stree Darpan* [1915 (Dec.: VI): 418-24] perceptively notes the link between women's economic decline and the rise of dowry system. It says that the new rich classes that have emerged demand ten times more dowry than they did before because women, even of respectable families, have lost their traditional occupations due to the rise of mill industry and also because women's work for living has now bad connotations for the status maintenance. The rise of 'modern' dowry thus needs to be seen in the perspective of social changes noted earlier.

(b) *Emerging Social Order—Caste/Class in Marriage and Dowry*

During the colonial period, the characteristic rigidity and openness in the restructuring of the caste system had its impact on the marriage practices and dowry. The *Brāhma* form of marriage with its integral component dowry was further reinforced by newly emerging caste rigidities. The impact of the process of Brahmanization or Sanskritization on the development of such trends have been ably discussed by many scholars.[14] It is generally agreed that there was a constant process of several lower and lower-middle castes to model themselves in the fashion of upper castes due to increased opportunities of social mobility. Yet this modelling, unlike the pre-colonial period, did not change their caste affixation or labels. What it did change or strove to change was usually their status within the caste-based local hierarchical social ladder through the process of Sanskritization.

In the pre-colonial era, the fluidity of the political system at the lower level and availability of large tract of land for agriculture, as Srinivas notes, provided opportunities for mobility to different castes. A caste taking over the local power often proclaimed for itself a higher status. Or, families of a caste opening up land in barren areas and shifting to agriculture established new regional societies and were often accorded a new status by the king. For example, such dominant peasants castes in south India as Marathas, Reddis, Vellalas, Nayars, and Coorgs, Patidars in Gujarat claimed Kshatriya status when they became powerful in eighteenth century. There were 'Shudra' dynasties like Pals in medieval Bengal. The Kshatriya were historically recruited from a wide variety of diverse castes which periodically became politically influential. In fact, K.M. Panikkar notes that every known royal family ever since Mahapadma Nanda in the fifth century BC has come from a non-Kshatriya caste (Panikkar 1955: 8 quoted in Srinivas 1968: 190). Or in case of Brahmins, A. Baines writes, 'There is . . . no section of Brahmanic hierarchy into which recruitment from the outside has been more extensive or to which the claims to membership have been more numerous' (Baines 1912: 30 quoted in Srinivas 1968: 190).

Moreover, Hindu kings, by virtue of their position as the head of the social order, had power and authority to not only settle caste disputes but also to raise and lower the ranks of castes as rewards and punishments.[15] Muslim kings and even the early British exercised power to settle caste disputes. It was only during the beginning of the twentieth century that the extension of the British juridical authority gradually eroded Hindu kings' jurisdiction in caste matters (see Srinivas 1968: 189-91).

The growing entrenchment of the colonial state in India during the late nineteenth and early twentieth centuries, however, began to restrict the nature of social mobility. Opportunities to throw off caste labels or create new caste categories were no longer available to the emerging upwardly mobile social groups which claimed their higher status by adopting customs and rituals of upper castes and made their own subcastes distinct from their *byāhut* ones. This, to a great extent, was the result of the grand colonial project of defining the castes and rank them in accordance to social precedence which was carried out during various census operations, most notably the one of 1901. Avenues for social mobility which were often reached through the process of Sanskritization and new economic opportunities now did not mean a shift from one to other caste categories and kept the mobilization limited within the castes. Thus Srinivas notes: 'The establishment of the British rule resulted, on the one hand, in closing the traditional avenues to mobility and, on the other, in opening several new ones. More important, it set forces in motion which altered fundamentally the overall character of society' (Srinivas 1968: 191). 'In short, the attempt to use the census to freeze the rank of castes had the opposite effect of stimulating mobility, and also increased intercaste rivalry' (Srinivas 1966: 100).

During the colonial period, the social mobility thus remained within the caste structure. The codification of castes as carried out by the British census and other officials precluded any shift from a caste label or formation of new caste categories. It merely made some of the castes more acceptable/high in the hierarchical social order. As Rowe (1969) notes that 'although the recording of caste claims by census officials and the attempt in 1901 to rank castes in the Census gave an opening to the socially mobile, many if not most groups failed to be accorded the right to claim membership in a higher *varṇa*.' Table 3.2 illustrates such claims and the judgements.

As is evident from Table 3.2, most of the castes petitioned for changes in their caste affixation or labels in preference for new names aligning them with the upper castes. In the United Provinces alone, the Superintendent of Census received 175 claims from different sub-castes for assigning higher caste categories or new Sanskritized names (Srinivas 1966: 98-9). For example, K.C.S. Verma, a contemporary commentator on caste matters, wrote with regard to such claims that:

> The Khattri who would fain rank himself with the Sesodias of Mywar, with the Jadus of Karauli, or with the Bhatis of Jaiselmere, still remains a Panjabi Bania; and no species of argument will ever transform the quill-driving caste of Kayasthas into a Rajput clan. It is rather late in the day for these would-be Kshatriyas to claim a higher status than that which for centuries past they have been entitled to, and have accepted without question. [Verma 1904, quoted in Rowe 1969: 204; for studies on Kayastha's claim see, Rowe (1969); Carroll (1978), etc.]

Decentralized procedure to judge claims of castes resulted in the approval of such claims in one area and disapproval in other. The general tendency was to proclaim the 'approved' regional sub-caste superior and deny its relationship with 'disapproved' and 'backward' section and thus rejecting claims for the general

TABLE 3.2: CASTES CLAIMING HIGHER STATUS

Castes	Names Claimed		Remarks
	1911	1921	
Ahir	—	Ahir Kshatriya Jadubansi Rajput Nandbansi Rajput Yadava	—
Barhai	—	Maithil, Ojha, Panchal, or Vishwakarma Brahman	Some 75 families in Aligarh
Barhai Dhiman	—	-do-	—
Belwar	Belwar Brahman Sanadh	Belwar Brahman Sanadh	Recognized in 1911
Bhat	Brahmbhatt	Brahmbhatt	—
Bhuinhar	Brahman	Bhuinhar Brahman	Recognized in 1911
Chamar	—	Jatav Rajput, Jatav	
Dhobi		Chhatri	Benaras
Gadariya	Kshatriya	Pali Rajput	—
Halwai	Madhesia Vaisya	Yogya Saini Vaisya	—
Kachhi	—	Kachhwaha Rajput	—
Kahar		Kashyap Rajput	Lahore
Kahar, Rawani	—	Chandrabansi Kshatriya	—
Kalwar	Batham Vaisya	Batham Vaisya Haihaiya or Shoundik Kshatriya	Bengal, Bihar and Orissa
Kandu	Madhesia Vaisya	—	—
Karnwal	Kshatriya	—	—
Kayastha	Chitraguptabansi Kshatriya	—	—
Khangar	—	Khangar Rajput	—
Khattri	Kshatriya	Kshatriya	Partly admitted in 1901
Vaishya	Kshatriya	—	Benaras, and Bara Banki
Koeri	—	Kushwaha Kshatriya	—
Kori	—	Kush Kuleen Rajput Tantuvai Vaishya Jaiswar	— —

Kumhar	—	Rajput Vaishya Jaiswar	—
Kurmi	Kurmi Kshatriya	Kurmi Kshatriya	—
Lodha	—	Lodhi Rajput	—
Lohar	Visvakarmabansi Brahman	Dhiman Brahman	—
Nai	—	Kuleen or Pande Brahman Rajput	
Sonar, Mair	Mair Kshatriya	Mair Rajput	—
Sonar, Tank	Tank Kshatriya	—	—
Sonar, other	—	Mathur Rajput Kanya Kubja Vaishya	—
Tamboli	—	Nagbansi Kshatriya	—
Taga	Brahman	Kokas Panchal Brahman	Old claim
Teli	—	Vaishya	—

Source: Blunt 1931: 227-8; and Turner 1933: 529-32.

mobility of the whole caste. Such developments reflect on the one hand a great deal of movement within sub-castes of a caste. 'Approved' sub-castes intermarried and established various relationships among themselves. On the other hand, these created the basis for the growth of caste and sub-caste rigidities due to the state's restrictions to normally accord a higher status or name to a caste.

An expression of these rigidities were caste *sabhas* or associations which played an important role in perpetuating the caste interest and in guiding the caste to achieve a higher status through the process of Sanskritization. As Srinivas notes:

> The coming into existence of caste sabha or association was an important factor in the spread as well as the acceleration of mobility. Initially their aims were to reform caste customs in the direction of Sanskritization, to lay claim to high rank, to undertake such welfare activities for caste fellows as building hostels, houses on a cooperative basis, and even colleges and hospitals in some areas, and to found journals and endow scholarships. With the gradual transfer of power from the British to Indians, caste associations tended to become political pressure groups. . . . (Srinivas 1968: 195-96)[16]

One of the most crucial impact or expression of the characteristic social mobility of castes and sub-castes is discerned in the marriage customs. The 'superior' sub-castes, through the process of Sanskritization distanced themselves not only from 'backward' sub-castes but also from customs and rites of their own caste-marriage rituals. Adopting *Brāhma* form of marriage, they became dowry givers and takers and interacted with those who followed the same practices in the context of the custom of hypergamy in marriage. Blunt (1931: 51) notes that till recently a change of occupation, social or religious customs, as well as changes involving pollution, increased prosperity, and caste quarrels were enough to produce fission in sub-castes and the formation of new endogamous groups. In general, 'the system of marriage sections in most castes is perfectly simple. The caste is divided into endogamous groups; these are occasionally further subdivided into smaller groups of the same nature; finally the endogamous subcaste or sub-subcastes is broken up into exogamous sections' (ibid: 49). However, 'nowadays, instances of fission due to a change in social practices are uncommon; a subcaste as it rises in the social scale, will separate itself from its humble relatives, and give up certain customs which are not consonant with its newly acquired dignity: but the change of custom is the result of the fission and not its cause' (ibid: 53). The sub-caste endogamy was thus not as rigid or immutable as the caste endogamy. It could be set aside due to above mentioned changes by the Brahmins, new powerful sub-caste elders, or family and caste associations either through purification ceremony or fines till these became accepted as local norms. Permanent excommunication was rare.

Bayly notes the changes from the 'rather flexible society of the eighteenth century' to a more or less rigid social structure in the nineteenth century. In 'traditional India' of the eighteenth century, short supply of men and skills made marriage outside caste groups common.

> Great peasant caste-clusters such as the Kunbis of western India and the Jats of the north allowed their males to take concubines from related or lower caste groups. The sons of these liaisons were considered Jats or Kunbis in the next generation. Even some Rajput subcastes which were rigidly endogamous in the colonial period married outside caste in the eighteenth century. Caste status in the countryside was in fact a rather fluid matter. (Bayly 1988: 29)

Yet by the mid-nineteenth century, these great agriculturalist castes became 'less permeable and more internally divided themselves'. They began to forbid taking of concubines, seclude their women and adopt complex rules for marriage. 'Rural Rajput clans who had been exogamous or even in some cases had married with lower-caste military people (such as the Pasis in Awadh) to enhance their power had become endogamous by the mid-nineteenth century' (Bayly 1988: 158). Noting the practice of Rajputs in Gorakhpur District, Martin [1838 (II): 464] too informs:

> The men of high birth make money by marrying the daughters of rich chiefs of inferior rank; but they are in great trouble how to dispose of their daughters, because they will not in any account give them to persons of lower rank, and most of the higher rank wishing to marry low girls with large fortunes, there is the utmost difficulty in procuring husbands for their daughters.

Customs of keeping concubines which were prevalent among some castes in earlier periods were gradually losing current and were being replaced by those customs practised by Brahmanized castes. In the nineteenth century, one finds that, among the upper caste Hindus, keeping concubines was considered to be the most extreme act of impurity causing the excommunication of person from his caste. Martin [1838 (III): 744] informs:

> No pure Hindu in Bengal can lawfully keep a concubine of any sort, whether he is married or single. But some of the impure tribes allow men to form a kind of left-hand marriage, called *Nikā*, with widows of their own tribe. The contract is accompanied by religious ceremonies, and the same fidelity, both in the man and woman, is expected as in proper marriage (*Vivāho*); but in general neither the *Nikā* nor her children are so much respected as the virgin spouse, especially if the caste approaches in any degree to purity; for in some very low castes there is little difference shown.

One of the important signs of a Sanskritizing or Brahmanizing caste was therefore not surprisingly the eschewing of the custom of widow marriage, known variously as '*sagāī*' or '*nikāh*' marriages. Some of these castes, as Risley (1915: 186) writes, 'have got so far as to throw off sub-castes distinguished by their abstention from widow marriage'. For example, in several castes like Kalwar, Lohar, Nai, and Teli, a '*byāhut*' sub-caste emerged as the result of the abandonment of widow marriage. The Sainthwar sub-caste of Kurmis in Padrauna, Gorakhpur, which became prosperous, similarly gave up widow marriage and despised Baiswar and Jaiswar Kurmis of Sitapur who practised it. On the same ground, Purbi and Paschimi Sonars of Banaras too did not intermarry and interact.

Census Reports, and colonial surveys of caste customs especially by Crooke, Risley and Blunt are replete with such examples of the growing rigidity among the sub-castes on the one hand and their 'openness' in the direction of Sanskritization on the other. While this promoted and reinforced endogamy, some of the sub-castes became exogamous too and practised the custom of hypergamy if their subcastes lacked social mobility on the whole or if their change of occupation and wealth made them closer to the other sub-caste groups in the area.[17] In Azamgarh, Bhars became divided into two exogamous sections, the Patait and Khuntait of which one reared pig and the other did not; they did not inter-marry. The Jadubansi and Nandbansi Ahirs who were formerly endogamous were found to be on the way to amalgamation and inter-marriage. Hardoi Belwars who left the cattle trade and indulged in other fruitful occupations began inter-marriage with the Sanadh Brahmins, to which they earlier claimed their origins. Saraswat Brahmins took brides from Gaur, Gaurs and Kanaujias from Sanadhs, and Kanaujias also from Jhijhotiyas. Karen Leonard's (1978) historical study of the Kayasthas of Hyderabad too aptly demonstrates such changes within a caste group. She finds that from 1880s onward and especially after 1930s, cross-sub-caste marriages along class lines were steadily becoming prevalent among the Kayasthas. Asthanas, Bhatnagars, Srivastava, Saxena, and Gaur families formed a pool for such marriages. Thus while Asthanas intermarried with Saxenas, they only took girls from the Mathurs; at the same time gave girls to Srivastava families of wealth and status in north India but avoided alliances with Hyderabad Srivastava families.

Thus, the characteristic pattern of marriages witnessed prevalence of sub-castes' move in both endogamous and exogamous directions along class lines but within a rigidified endogamous caste system. This exacerbated social mobility within endogamous sections of a caste with such 'openness' being the result of newer socio-economic opportunities and the consequent rise of social classes. Yet, the caste rigidities were not only maintained but greatly reinforced through the Courts. This is most evident in the reassertion of restrictions on the intercaste marriages, *anuloma* and *pratiloma* marriages. These kinds of marriage were already getting obsolete during the pre-British era but there was now greater prohibition emerging out of the Court's disapproval of its legality under the Hindu law. 'Upon the authority of certain texts of the Puranas,' Banerjee (1896: 71) notes, 'intermarriage between different castes is now absolutely prohibited.' Mayne (1883: 89) too notes that 'the prohibition against marriages between persons of different castes is comparatively modern. Originally, marriages between men of one class and women of a lower, even of the Shudra class, were recognized, and must have tended strongly to produce that amalgamation of the customs of the Aryas and the aborginies'. Manu as well as Sutra writers admitted that offsprings resulting from mixed marriages might in seven generation rise to highest class. As late as the time of *Mitākshara* there is recognition of mixed marriages. It may be also due to the right of kings, as mentioned earlier, to grant upward or downward movement to a caste. The court, however, initially went to the extreme extent that 'marriages between persons in different sub-divisions of the same caste, e.g. of Brahmin or Sudra, are . . . invalid unless sanctioned by local custom' (Mayne 1883: 90). The legality of inter-caste marriages remained often denied. In a 1906 case, Padam *v.* Suraj, the Allahabad Court refused to grant legality to a marriage between a Brahmin and a Chhatri [*ILR* (28: II): 458]. It categorically announced that 'whatever may have been the case in ancient times, and whatever may be the law in other parts of India, at the present day a marriage between a Brahmin and Chhatri is not a lawful marriage in these Provinces and the issue of such a marriage is not legitimate'. Similarly, in the case of Melaram *v.* Thanooram during 1867-8, the Court attempted to impose Brahmanic laws on castes which customarily had flexibility in marriage. The plaintiff was a Dome Brahmin and the girl he married was a Haree. The Court declared that the two belonging to distinct castes could not have a 'good' and 'binding' marriage sanctioned by the general Hindu law. The only recourse for them, which after an appeal was provided by the High Court, was to prove that it was a local custom.

The primary question in such cases was what constituted caste and where that caste stood in the hierarchy—as is evident from numerous cases for upgradation of caste categories and in the activities of various caste associations in early twentieth century. While the Court normatively considered local customs it, however, made the judgement according to its own interpretation. The customary role of caste panchayats was declared to be not binding. In 1876, the Bombay High Court ruled that the Courts of Law will not recognize the authority of caste in pronouncing a marriage void, or allowing a woman to remarry (in Kannan 1963: 38). With the role of caste panchayats to practice and affect changes according to local customs and changing scenario denied, the Court's interpretation and judgement according to frozen and antiquated customs rigidified the caste system and marriage practices.

The 'openness' evident in sub-caste/class within a rigid caste structure promoted the *Brāhma* form of marriage or the practice of *kanyādāna* as a result of Sanskritizing tendencies. This also encouraged and reinforced hypergamy and consequently the practice of dowry. Blunt (1931: 70) notes that

> the bridegroom price takes the form of a dowry with the bride and is usual among the better classes. It is, partly, at all events, the result of hypergamy. The bride's family are necessarily of inferior social position, and have to pay for marrying her to a man above her in rank, whilst they also desire to make a show of wealth as a set off to the bridegroom's social advantages. If the bride is herself of high rank, it is often difficult to find her a husband of still higher rank, and her family have to pay accordingly.

This meant the narrowing down of the field of selection for a marriage partner, which in turn impelled the father of a girl to avail himself of the earliest opportunity of finding any boy for his daughter, if he did not want to run the risk of an unsuitable match. The colonial state's insistence on the reinvented Brahmanical tradition along with the promotion of the *Brāhma* form of marriage thus played an important role in the institutionalization and expansion of the dowry system especially among the large number of sub-caste/classes emerging out of the social, political and economic consequences of the colonial rule. Moreover, what made the *Brāhma* form of marriage along with the dowry so pervasive especially among the emerging socially mobile sub-castes and classes was that it was accepted as legally the most approved form which the Court took into consideration while deciding on issues of inheritance and division of the property. Numerous court cases and reinterpretation of marriage forms to determine the legal heir or partition of the property attest to this. Once institutionalized and expanded, the specific nature of modern dowry—like huge demands for cash and other expensive items, evolved within the framework of increased monetization, significance of modern education in job opportunities, better communication and transport networks, and spatial mobility. The origin of modern dowry thus can be traced to the negative impact of the socio-political and economic forces unleashed by the colonial state.

The colonial state, as we shall see in chapter five, had no interest in bringing about any fundamental reform as far as women's right to property and inheritance was concerned. With the state's reassertion of the antiquated Brahmanic tradition and its own reinterpretation of the *Mitākshara* and *Dāyabhāga* texts in granting women's right to property and inheritance, structural conditions for obsolescence of the practice of dowry never emerged. Instead, the characteristic pattern of the emerging socio-economic order as detailed above facilitated its institutionalization and expansion in the north Indian society. How did women respond to the growing menace of dowry is the subject of the next chapter.

NOTES

1. This chapter is a considerably expanded version of my ideas originally put forth in an article in the *Economic and Political Weekly*. See Sheel (1997).
2. More broadly, was not this similar to the recent phenomena of the reemergence and escalations of dowry in post-Mao China which, as Helen Siu demonstrates, was due to a sudden prosperity combined with a largely untouched tradition? (Siu 1990: 6).
3. Our discussion of the concept of the 'Reinvention of Tradition' is influenced by Hobsbawm and Ranger's work on the various dimensions of traditions and its socio-historical impact (Hobsbawm and Ranger 1983).
4. The classic debate focuses on the beneficial or harmful impact of the colonial rule on Indian society. In its various dimensions, this debate continues to stir scholars labelled by such categories as nationalist, Marxist, liberal, conservative, imperialist, etc. What is most important is to note that none disagrees with the fact of profound socio-economic changes wrought by the colonial rule.
5. As Cohn and Dirks (1988: 225) write: 'The legitimizing of the nation state proceeds not only in the public enactment of its self-defined traditions, but by constant reiteration of its power through what have become accepted as natural (rational and normal) state functions, of certifying, counting, reporting, registering, classifying and identifying. The documentation and certification projects of the state have become naturalized as the fundamental activities and legitimate provenance of the modern state. . . . The legitimation

project is both constituted and represented by the forms of knowledge the state creates, accumulates, and organizes to mark and measure the health, wealth and welfare of its citizens.' Its instrumentalities range from 'the expansion of state power to officialize domestic acts, to mark and define marriages, to establish an official definition of home, to control the location and nature of work,' to other spheres (ibid: 225).

6. For a critical analysis of the British work on ancient Indian social order see R.S. Sharma (1983: 3-22). The fact is that such 're-invention' of tradition often distorted historical reality. As R.G. Bhandarkar commenting on tendencies to quote ancient scripture in support of modern reforms, writes: 'In ancient times girls were married after they had attained maturity, now they must be married before, widow marriage was then in practice, now it has entirely gone out. . . . Interdining among the castes was not prohibited, now the numberless castes cannot have intercommunications of that nature' (cited in ibid: 10).
7. 'This approach on the part of the British judiciary', Kapadia (1966: 277-8) writes, 'had very significant drawbacks. First, for the nineteenth century conditions they were accepting the law as it was expounded in the eleventh and twelfth centuries, ignoring thereby the momentous development of the law in the writings of Nanda Pandit, Nilkantha and Balambhatta. And second, by accepting Vijnanesvara and Jimutvahana as the expounders of the personal law of Hindus, the natural evolution of Hindu law over centuries was ignored; for instead of recognizing its essentially dynamic character they accepted it as a stereotyped system based on a particular principle.'
8. The other view refers to the text of Vishnu that was quoted by the lawyers to state 'that the marriage ceremony of the unmarried daughter should be performed according to the father's wealth', and that the word 'quarter' is here used, not in its plain sense, but simply to enjoin the allowance of as much as will suffice for the marriage of the sisters.
9. Lucy Carroll's (1991: 791-809) 'Daughter's Right of Inheritance in India: A Perspective on the Problem of Dowry' attempts to link dowry with the daughter's property rights in her own family. It may be argued that a marriage in an illegal form had the danger of depriving the daughter with whatever limited rights she had under the customary rules in her own family.
10. W. Crooke's *The Tribe and Castes of the North Western Province and Oudh* (1896: Vols. 1-4) provides probably the most exhaustive description of the socio-cultural customs including the marriage practices of numerous castes and tribes of north India.

11. In Bahoni *vs.* Maharaj Singh (*ILR* 311, 738), it was observed that no ceremonies were necessary in the *Gandharva* form which was little better than concubinage. But a different view has been taken in Brinda *vs.* Radha (*ILR* 12 Mad 72) in which it has been held that ceremonies are necessary in *Gandharva* marriage (Banerjee 1896: 86).
12. K.K. Trivedi (1975: 47-67) in his study of 'Changes in Caste-Composition of the Zamindar Class in Western Uttar Pradesh' notes substantial changes in caste-compositions of zamindars. He finds that 'everywhere the money-lending castes, notably Banias, not even once recorded as Zamindars in the *A'in* [*-i-Akbari*] in western Uttar Pradesh, appeared with sizeable holdings by *circa* 1900'. Between *circa* 1870 and *circa* 1900, the percentage of the total areas under Rajput *zamindaris* reduced from 47.64 to 42.36. In the same period, the Brahmins, Banias, Khatris and Kalwars increased their *zamindaris* mainly at the cost of the Rajputs, Kurmis, and Kayasthas (ibid: 56).
13. See also Rajat K. Ray's (1975: 97-104) 'Differential Modernization in a Colonial Society: Bengal Under the Lieutenant-Governors' for dimensions of social mobility.
14. For example, Srinivas (1966 and 1968); Beteille (1969); Cohn (1968 and 1969), etc.
15. Crooke [1896 (II): 145] notes such grants of Brahmin status by local kings and chieftains. He writes: 'In Partabgarh there is a current legend that the celebrated Oudh chieftain, Manik Chand, created Brahmans wholesale out of various Kurmis, Ahirs, and Bhars. A similar case occurred in Fatehpur. In Unnao, again, a story is told of Raja Tilok Chand . . . [who] asked a Lodha . . . to fetch him some water. . . . The Raja after drinking the water discovered that the owner of the vessel was a low caste man, so he asked him to call himself a Brahman under the title of Pathak of Amtara, as he was watching the mango (*am*) tree. This title still remains with his descendants, who are acknowledged as Brahmins.' See also Stein (1991) for such fluidity within the pre-colonial social structure.
16. Noting caste *sabhas* move toward Sanskritization, Srinivas (1966: 98-100) further writes: 'This often involved the giving up of the forbidden meat and liquor . . . , and the donning of the sacred thread; and in Uttar Pradesh and Bihar, the shortening of the mourning period to correspond with that of the twice born castes. . . . [T]he formation of caste *sabhas* [also] resulted in increasing the "horizontal stretch" of castes. A classic example of horizontal stretch is provided by the Ahirs, who founded the Gop Jatiya Sabha in 1912, and which included, in a few years' time, cowherding *jatis* from all over North India from the Punjab to Bengal'.

17. The custom of hypergamy modified the marriage rules within many castes in the sense that it classified exogamous groups according to their social position and fixed a norm of a higher group taking brides from but not giving brides to lower ranked groups. Besides Rajputs, Blunt (1931: 46) found this practice most prevalent among the Bhat, Byar, Dharkar, Gujar, Jat, Kanaujia and Jijhotiya Brahmins, Kharwar, Khattri, and Patwa. See also Risley (1915: 156-65) for different aspects of hypergamy.

CHAPTER FOUR

Dowry and Women's Movement in India during Nineteenth and Twentieth Centuries

Beginning with the colonial period, the institutionalization and expansion of dowry witnessed its unprecedented reach over the modern Indian society. In congruence with the emerging patterns of socio-cultural, political, and economic order, it assumed manifold dimensions and reflected a major social malady affecting the dignity and status of women. The growing phenomena of dowry naturally provoked intense responses from women and their organizations. In fact, dowry was one of the most crucial issues which consolidated contemporary women's movement in India in the late 1970s and 1980s and was considered synonymous with the women's movement. Yet, during late nineteenth and early twentieth centuries when the first organized stirring of women began at the national level, dowry was not the major issue of agitation. It was a concern mostly voiced and debated at the regional level. To understand differing perceptions on dowry at both the levels, it is necessary to look at the nature of the historical development of women's movement.

What led to a focus on women's issues and the rise of women's movement at the time of the nationalist struggle against the colonial rule? Scholars point to both indigenous and external stimuli for its origin. Externally, the onslaught of Western ideas and the colonial impact on the socio-economic structure, and internally, efforts to preserve or alter the tradition to confront new challenges provided necessary backgrounds for its growth. The variety of ideas and differences in perception and approach to the question of contemporary women's problems amply manifest divergent strains of thought on women's question in the late nineteenth century. Subsequently, one finds the growth of diverse campaigns, strategies, and organizations for reforming women's conditions. In the beginning, the initiative was taken largely by men but by the early twentieth century 'women's activism' had come on its own.

A 'new' phase of the women's movement crystallized in the late 1970s and early 1980s in post-Independent India. It is often referred to as the second phase which was marked by the emergence of several fresh women's organizations and the revitalization of the old ones. It was different from the earlier phase as far as issues, practices and strategies were concerned. The dowry issue became the major focus and facilitated emergence of a large scale independent women's movement. Intense anti-dowry campaigns and local and national debates unmasked manifold dimensions of dowry and converged society and the state's focus on this major problem in contemporary Indian society.

In the earlier context, this chapter focuses on the nature of women's movement's response—both in its conceptual as well as in the organizational aspects, to the issue of dowry. It traces the emergence of women's movement and its development beginning with the social reform movement of the early nineteenth century and examines its divergent streams of ideological thought, activism and strategies in the light of its protests against dowry. Divided into three parts, the chapter first provides a brief background to women's issues in reformists' and revivalists' intellectual currents prevalent in the social reform movement of the late nineteenth and early twentieth centuries. It discusses the impact of the two pronged nature of the social reform ideology on women's movement. Secondly, it deals with lacunae present in the 'male-dominated' social reform activities and women's own perception of such reformers and their actions with particular reference to dowry as discussed in contemporary prominent women's journals in the north Indian Hindi belt. Finally, it analyses the linkages between dowry and contemporary women's movement in India.

Women and the Social Reform Movement of Late nineteenth and Early twentieth Centuries

(a) *Ideological Origins*

The ideological background to the social reform movement divulges the basis of the predominant concern of colonial officials and the indigenous elite for the status of women. The concern did not encompass dowry but originated from distinct and diverse sources. While the Orientalists brought into focus India's past glory and lamented her present decline in their learned writings,[1] the Anglicans, especially the Christian Missionaries, primarily pointed at the innate degradation and immorality of the natives including women within the fabric and texture of Indian society. Mill, for example, wrote that the Hindu women were in a 'state of dependence more strict and humiliating than that which is ordained for the weaker sex. . . . They are held in extreme degradation, excluded from the sacred books, deprived of education and (of a share) in the paternal property' (Mill 1840: 312-13). Even more severe were the criticisms of Hindus and Hinduism by Alexander Grant in *India and India Missions*, and by Duff who called for an increased effort on the part of missionaries and Christianity to dispel the areas of darkness and ignorance (Kumar 1993: 20). The attempt to civilize the native population provided the ideological legitimacy for the protective and interventionist role of the colonial state.

Within the British frame of reference, the position of Indian women was unsatisfactory. This frame of reference was also subsequently adopted by the Indian elite when they included women in their social reform agenda. Belonging to either reformist or revivalist groups, their consciousness on the subject of women was overwhelmed by their notion based respectively on the Western liberal doctrines or images of past glory. They responded by developing the ideology of an ideal Hindu womanhood as embedded in the ancient texts and traditions in sharp contrast to the Westernized woman.[2] At the same time, they also made efforts to abolish those practices which inhibited the progressive portrayal of women.

In fact, both the revivalists as well as the reformists converged in their efforts towards the location and search for a 'glorious, precolonial, caste-based "tradition" in which the "corrupting" Muslim rule had brought about undesirable changes' (Mukhopadhay 1990: 9-28). The whole debate on women, in the absence of objective historical study of women's question, too became synonymous with 'scriptural interpretations' (Mani 1989: 90). For example, Rammohun Roy and Lord Bentinck both used *shāstric* texts to show that the *satī* was not an obligatory or a religiously sanctioned practice. Ishwar Chandra Vidyasagar too began his campaign for widow remarriage in the early 1850s on the premise that widow remarriage was acceptable to the Dharmashāstras and even debated the issue with the pundits in Sanskrit. The attempt was to determine the 'authentic' cultural tradition based on primarily Brahmanical scriptures. Many organizations were engaged in the task of highlighting the ancient scriptures. Some even translated the texts from Sanskrit to the local language for more effective impact. The Tattva Bodhini Sabha founded by Rabindranath Tagore in 1839, for example, was pledged to spread knowledge of the Vedas and the Upanishads and to portray ancient India as a 'great centre of learning and theological study' and where there was parity between men and women (Mukhopadhay op. cit.).

Consequently, the Vedas and Upanishads, above all the other texts and practised traditions, were declared as the only 'natural basis of Indian History'. The Vedic women, represented by the examples of Gargi and Maitreyi, were presented to epitomize the 'high' status of Hindu women in ancient India and to provide models for women's upliftment (Bader 1925; Dutt 1888). Swami Dayanand Saraswati, a champion for the cause of revival of Vedas, exhorted for a return to the original spirituality in order to meet the crisis posed by the foreign rule. Spirituality was emphasized as an essential feature for all women. For 'the regeneration of the nation', women were to follow the high ideals of motherhood in service of others. Rammohun Roy also used the argument of women being 'infinitely more self-sacrificing than men' and possessing 'virtuous knowledge'. The focus however, was on the upper caste women who had enjoyed a relatively privileged position in the past. Gandhi too stressed the complementary sex roles and viewed women as 'embdiment of sacrifice, silent suffering, humility, faith and knowledge' (Everett 1981: 76).

Similar emphasis on the Aryan society with its ideal of 'womanhood' and women as *sahdharmiṇī* without whom a man could not perform any religious function was reiterated by Vivekananda [1958 (II): 504-5]. Virtues of Indian womanhood and motherhood were extolled and chastity was emphasized. It was also believed that 'a race that produced Sita, even if it only dreamt of her, has a reverence for women that is unmatched on earth' [ibid (V): 231]. The female aspects of Hinduism—Shakti-Shiva, and a religious tradition of male and female equality in ancient Vedic times were highlighted. According to Everett, the Hindu revivalist movement represented by the Arya Samaj, Ramakrishna Mission and the Theosophical Society placed women in a position of honour, expressed concern over the status of contemporary women, and enlarged the definition of religious activities to include social service and reform activities (Everett 1981: 39-55).[3] Their subsequent promotion of women's education rested on the basis provided by the Vedic practices and religious ideals.

Later, the bygone Hindu glory also reflective of racial solidarity and an 'Aryan theory of race' was adopted to evoke Hindu nationalism. The question of womanhood accordingly became synonymous with national identity. Different images of womanhood came to be celebrated by the women leaders themselves, many of whom internalized and evoked such glorification. While Annie Besant extolled the 'self-sacrificing' Hindu woman', the image of 'self-sacrificing Indian mother' was projected by Sarojini Naidu. Margaret Cousins talked of women as the representatives of 'the great Hindu race' and 'the strong Muslim people'; and Kamaladevi with her socialist influence, glorified the 'self-sacrificing' peasant woman (Kumar 1993: 79).

Thus, for varying compulsions, a particular kind of past and its womanhood was constructed and also legitimized by exigencies of the colonial period. Such portrayals of women helped early nationalists not only to project the superiority of unpolluted traditional patriarchal order but also to rebuke the colonial hegemony on grounds of its all polluting effect on women. The Westernized elites, on the other hand, sought to create images of womanhood on the basis of prescriptions presented by the contemprary Western liberal or religious doctrines. These varying tendencies resulted in ambivalent construction of womanhood and consequently affected the nature of the reform put forward and effected.

In such a situation, dowry was often treated as a particular social issue not extricably linked with the women's question or the construction of 'ideal' womanhood.

(b) *Nature of the Social Reform Movement*

The reform movement for women was at first initiated largely by men who for different reasons and with diverse ideologies confronted the problem of women's question in Indian society. It consisted of several strands characterized by regional diversities and variations in terms of the nature of campaigns and issues raised. Aparna Basu divides growing efforts at women's emancipation, which the social reform movement came to symbolize, into three stages. The first stage was during the early nineteenth century when the religious basis of practices such as *satī*, ban on widow remarriage, and child marriage was questioned. The second stage began in the mid-nineteenth century when women's education received the uppermost attention. This was followed by the third stage marked by women's entry into political struggle which removed many restrictions and familial taboos and allowed women to undertake political activities (Basu 1976: 39-40).

Throughout the period of the three stages, the susceptibility to two simultaneous contemporary trends of revivalism and reformism determined the nature of the project for reform. Concerns of the first for women's existing situation, and the second for reform of women's position on the basis of equal individual rights presented ambivalent solutions for the contemporary problems of women (Thapar 1963: 481). Ranade thus recommended and approved three distinct strategies for reforms. The first comprised of an attempt to reinterpret old texts to make it compatible with the present needs (e.g. Bhandarkar, Dayanand and others); a focus on morals and emotions to appeal to the conscience of the people to judge right and wrong as well as good and bad (e.g. Vidyasagar and Malabari); and finally, an emphasis on legal restraints to be imposed upon the failure of the first two strategies. Ranade disapproved and discouraged any drastic break from the traditions in the course of reform. In fact, his view that 'change is sought not as an innovation but as a return and restoration to the days of our past history' can be held to be representative of almost the entire thrust towards social reform in the colonial period (cited in Mazumdar 1976a: 43-4).[4]

In the early nineteenth century, the issues raised by the reformers included social practices such as *satī*, widow remarriage, polygamy, child marriage, education and property rights of women. They questioned their religious basis and applied 'rationalist' approach. They however took each issue separately and emphasized ultimate solution through legislative measures. Legislation became an index to the success of each struggle (Jayawardena 1986: 80). Accordingly, *satī* was labelled as an offence in 1829. The remarriage of Hindu widows was legally permitted in 1856. The 1872 Native Marriage Act raised the age of marriage of girls to 14 years, and for boys to 18 years. It also made marriage monogamous and allowed for divorce though it was applicable only for non-Hindus. The 1874 Right to Property Act provided the married woman with a life interest in husband's share of property and proclaimed that a widow's share in property, although limited, was to be equal to that of a son. The Age of Consent (1891) raised the legal age of consent for sexual intercourse from 10 years to 12 for girls.[5] In 1925, the age of consent was further raised to 13 years in the case of marital and 14 years for non-marital sexual intercourse. In 1928, recommendations were made for more increases in these ages. Apart from these, legislative measures were adopted against female infanticide in 1795, 1804, and 1870, and child marriage in 1929. Changes in women's property rights were again effected in 1929 and 1937 (Everett 1981: 144-6; Thapar 1963: 482 and 487; Asthana 1974: 21-2).

The British attitude towards reform was rather ambivalent. While driven by a 'civilizing mission', the British were reluctant to oppose the Brahmanical orthodox groups in their imposition of new legislative measures. An example is the case of legislation against *satī*. At the first instance it took over a decade for the prohibition against *satī* to be extended to the whole of British India.[6] The campaign against polygamy was withdrawn in the 1870s due to the criticism of the unwarranted British interference in the traditional family matters of the Hindus. In their reform measures, the British were sensitive to the opposition of the orthodox groups which might lead to 'social instability' by prompting mass reactions (Liddle and Joshi 1989: 27-30). Perceiving threats to its own existence by new reforms, the British also fostered an 'alliance with the conservative forces of Indian society, the landed aristocracy, the wealthy and the communal elements' throughout the last decade of the nineteenth and first two decades of the twentieth centuries (Mazumdar 1976a: 55).

The half-hearted and 'selective' approach of the British to initiate reforms is illustrated in the case of Rukhmabai in the 1880s. In 1884, Dadaji Bhikaji was prevented by the District Court for restitution of conjugal rights with his wife Rukhmabai. His wife was married to him in childhood. She had subsequently educated herself and refused to live with him. The orthodox groups rallied against the decision of the District Court and accused the British court of interfering with Hindu customs. Tilak wrote that education for women was proving 'an attack on our ancient religion under the cover of Rukhmabai with the intention of castrating our eternal religion'. Bhikaji finally won the case, but Rukhmabai refused to obey the court order (Omvedt 1976: 1016). The orthodox Hindu reactions, according to Radha Kumar, were sharper in Bombay than in Bengal probably because the Brahmin power-structures were relatively far stronger in Maharashtra than in Bengal (Kumar 1993: 15). For the British, political expediency guided their rather selective policy of non-interference in the religious practices of Hindus. Suggestions to interfere in the marriage rituals were considered as 'red herrings' in the path of reform (*Pioneer Mail and Indian Weekly News* (19 Feb. 1891): 230 in Sinha 1986: 374). Similarly, confronted by the backlash from the religions orthodoxy, the Age of Consent Bill was defended on humanitarian grounds rather than as change in religious customs (Sinha 1986: 365). After years of deliberations, the age was raised by only two years and no effort was made to comprehensively tackle the issue.

The reform movement was thus guided by a limited perception for change and did not challenge the patriarchal family structure.[7] Women's roles as wives and mothers were idealized. Social reform and female education, it was believed, would 'revitalize and preserve the patriarchal family structure, produce more companionable wives and better mothers, and therefore have a stabilizing effect on society' (Jayawardena 1986: 79). Even the concern for widow remarriage grew partly out of the need to stabilize the family structure for an increasing number of young widows who, being ill-treated in the family, were compelled to take to prostitution. This threatened the status and stability of the family. Reforms were thus only to make conditions for women less deplorable through the realignment of the existing power structure. Accordingly, property rights were limited to widows only and without a provision for alienation of property. Besides no provision was made for daughters. Some of these proved counter productive too, as is evident in the case of making 'voluntary' acts of *satī* legal. It is not surprising that between 1812-16 out of the 400 cases reported, only 10 'illegal' cases were prevented (Vaid and Sangari 1989: 15).

Similarly, the Widow Remarriage Act of 1856 deprived even those women who traditionally had customary rights to remarriage from maintenance or inheritance from their husband's property and custody over children. Under the new rules promulgated, they could remarry only after receiving express permission from their husbands, caste or community. Rights of the children were vested with the dead husband's relatives (ibid: 6).

During this period, only some measures of social reform were addressed to the linkages between caste hierarchy and the structure of Hindu society. Reformers such as Jyoti Rao Phule (1827-90) of Maharashtra founded the Satyashodhak Samaj (1873) at first in Poona and then in Bombay. An anti-Brahmin movement, this aimed at abolishing caste disabilities which were forced upon the low castes by the Brahmin priesthood and their 'oppoitunistic scriptures'. Women's issues remained in the forefront. Its reform measures supported widow remarriage and inter-caste marriage and the marriage ceremonies were performed by non-Brahmin priests. Women's education also received much attention from Phule and other reformers, such as Gopal Hari Deshmukh Lokahitawadi (1823-92) and Darsondas Mulji (1832-71).

The Brahmo Samaj (1828), the Prarthana Samaj (1867) and the Arya Samaj (1875) too questioned the caste rigidities and other structural inequalities. They challenged many forms of obscurantism and rituals oppressing womanhood but at the same time singularly venerated motherhood. They provided the rationale for education and other reforms for women but only in order that the latter could serve their families and communities better. The revival and purification of Hinduism and its golden past was especially stressed upon by the Arya Samaj whose sway extended to much of north and west India (Everett 1981: 39-59). One also finds the proliferation of caste associations and attempts at the simplification of the marriage and caste stratifications during this time. All in all, an ambivalent and sectoral approach to the women's issues characterized the reform efforts of the late nineteenth and early twentieth centuries.

(c) *Rise of Organized Women and the Social Reform Movement*

Efforts of the social reformers established the necessary prerequisites such as education for women and support to associational activities of women by men for the rise of a women's movement (Everett 1981: 45). Consequently, in the late nineteenth and early twentieth century, women themselves entered the public life, organized their own associations either independently or within the larger parent organization, and agitated for further reforms. For the early pioneers of social and religious reform, women were at first objects of their emancipatory efforts, but in the course of the late nineteenth and early twentieth centuries they became more and more subjects in the political and social spheres (Mies 1980: 117). Individual efforts by women like Pandita Ramabai (1858-82), Anandibai Joshi (1865-87), Ramabai Ranade (1862-1924) and Tarabai Shinde (1850-1910) were most notable. These women transcended the familial and cultural boundaries and restrictions in terms of their own marriage and their education abroad. They sought to bring about changes in education, and strongly opposed caste and ritual rigidities, child marriage and enforced widowhood.

The movement for education, employment, and complementary roles of men and women occupied major attention of the newly emerging women's organization[8] which also included several Mahila Samaj, Ladies Associations, and Women's Clubs.[9] The forum for interaction and information for these smaller groups was provided by the Indian National Social Conference founded by Ranade in 1887. The forum organized a separate section called the Indian Women's Conference (Bharat Mahila Parishad), which held annual conferences and organized special educational programmes for women (Liddle and Joshi 1989: 22). Gradually, as activities of the Indian Women's Conference expanded, the focus overwhelmingly shifted to addressing the complex nature of women's issues as well as their regional variations. It, as Mazumdar points out, disagreed with Ranade's belief that social reforms could proceed (beyond a superficial level) without shaking the basic principles and foundations of the Indian social structure, the hierarchic nature of the caste system, and the inequalities inherent in the identification of occupations with stations in life (Mazumdar 1976a: 45). This indeed is a critique which could be extended for most of the reform efforts in the colonial period.

In the second decade of the twentieth century, the National Council of Women in India (Bombay 1925), All India Women's Conference (1927), and also the Women's Indian Association (1917) entered the national scene. Smaller existing women's societies became represented by these larger organizations which claimed a total membership of over 10,000 women (Forbes 1979: 6).[10]

The beginning of the women's movement in India can be traced to the activities of such large-scale women's organization and their supporters who fought for both social reform and political freedom. Forbes (1979: 150), therefore, dates the period of the first women's movement from the 1880s to the 1940s, while Liddle and Joshi (1989: 21) expand it to cover the period from the start of autonomous women's organization in the first decade of the twentieth century to the culmination of the campaign giving women legal and political rights in the mid-50s. Everett (1981: 44) attributes the emergence of women's movement in India to the years 1880s to 1930s when several local, regional and national level women's associations were founded.

The women's movement in its first phase primarily discussed issues of *satī*, female infanticide, child marriage, widow remarriage and advocated changes. It also sought to ameliorate women's educational and employment status. *Ātmashakti* (self-reliance) for women and swadeshi were linked together by organizations such as Sakhi Samiti (Chakravarty 1989: 62). Male-dominated professions such as law, medicine, architecture were encouraged to be taken up by women (Basu and Ray 1990: 10).[11] Attempts were made to bring about changes in women's inheritance laws. The All India Women's Conference (AIWC) urged for comprehensive rather than piecemeal legislation regarding monogamy, divorce and inheritance as all were interlinked (ibid: 49). Revocation of the British-promulgated Prostitution Regulation law was also demanded. The issue of rape of Indian women by the British soldiers was also highlighted. Interestingly, the Nationalists viewed these instances of rape as a violation of community honour rather than as acts of violence against women (Kumar 1993: 37).

Moving initially within the framework laid down by the earlier reform movement, women's organizations in the 1930s and 1940s, particularly the AIWC, demanded the complete reform of the Hindu Personal Law that included inheritance rights, divorce, monogamy, inter-caste and inter-faith marriages with self-choice, and equal rights of guardianship over children.[12] The basis for such demands had already been laid in the fundamental rights adopted at Karachi in 1931 by the Indian National Congress which declared that no discrimination on the grounds of sex be permitted in free India (Chattopadhyaya 1975: 34). Despite this, the debates that ensued over the Hindu Code Bill in the forties still continued to project two distinct images of the ideal Hindu woman—one worshipped as a goddess but needing protection all through life (as per *Manusmriti*), and the other as competent for interacting with others on the basis of equal rights and individual freedom (Everett 1981: 166).

From the 1920s onwards, the major emphasis of the women's movement however shifted to the demand for political emancipation. The AIWC stressed the primacy of the realization of the political goal of self-government in order to fulfil women's aspirations (Kaur 1968: 145). The leaders of the movement also aimed at securing voting rights for women, reform of personal laws and guarantees of sexual equality in the Constitution (Liddle and Joshi 1985: WS-75).

As political questions supplanted the issues concerning social reform, women partook in large numbers in agitations, boycotts, picketing of liquor shops and the *satyāgraha.* They held protest meetings, composed songs, edited journals, distributed leaflets, opened indigenous goods shops, broke salt laws, and participated in increasing number in militant and revolutionary activities. It is not surprising that of the 80,000 persons arrested during the famous salt *satyāgraha,* 17,000 were women (Basu 1976: 18-30; Kumar 1993: 49). In 1926, Dr S. Muthulakshmi Reddi was elected as the first woman legislative councillor in Madras. Although women leaders have been criticized for subordinating the goals of their own liberation to the national cause, the raising of women's questions on the political platform lent a wider recognition to their specific issues.[13] Basu (1976: 40) thus comments that 'it is doubtful if a century of preaching and social work would have brought about the same change in the position of Indian women as was achieved in the wake of the two decades of political struggle in India'.

The women's movement in its first phase thus constructed its demands around women's position and political oppression, and organized autonomously for women's emancipation without simply remaining a part of the freedom movement. Women's issues were continuously kept alive and not subsumed within the national political movement. Mazumdar (1976a: 62-3) attributes this political linkage to the broad perspective that the movement acquired despite its caste and class elitism. The women's movement regarded the two issues of gender subordination and political domination as interlinked. Most women leaders viewed the debilitating social practices deriving from invasions and imperialism as responsible for women's subordination. It was felt that the removal of such practices would allow women to play a more constructive role in national development. Education was seen as the means through which women could play their societal roles meaningfully. Legislation was also considered to be a means to this end. At a later stage, equal rights in terms of legal and social equality were emphasized. Everett (1981: 83) distinguishes two different conceptions of ameliorating women's position. The first was women's upliftment by eradicating evil social practices (e.g. Annie Besant and Sarojini Naidu as its prominent spokespersons), and the second focused on equal rights for men and women in the political, economic and familial spheres.[14] There were other strains too. Some attributed the contemporary problem of women to male-domination alone. Vilasinidevi Shenai in the 1940s emphasized, 'today our men are clamouring for political rights at the hands of an alien government. Have they conceded their wives, their own sisters, their daughters . . . social equality and economic justice' (Forbes 1982: 532). Yet another strain was represented by Kamaladevi Chattopadhyaya who presented a socialist analyses. She argued that rights of franchise were meaningless in a capitalist society (Chattopadhyaya 1939: 1-7).

To sum up, the national social reform movement and the women's movement in the late nineteenth and early twentieth centuries provided the backdrop for the stirring for the upliftment of women through laws against social evils and the empowerment of women through education. This encouraged the entrance of women in public spheres and the rise of women professionals and women's organizations all over India. The shift in the emphasis on women's equality with men in the legal and social spheres was, however, not accompanied by recognition of gender-based differences. A critique of the male-dominated, hierarchical and power-based structure of the family and the society was seldom voiced. 'On the contrary, women's roles within the family as wives, daughters, and mothers were reemphasized and extended, to be in tune with the requirements of the family in a changing situation' (Mazumdar 1976a: 63). It undoubtedly 'made the unprecedented departure from a fatalist, negative position on women's lives and status' by propagating that 'it was not the destiny of women to remain ignorant, illiterate, and oppressed' (Gandhi and Shah 1992: 17-21). The structure on which the inequalities were based, however, remained largely unchallenged. The failure of the movement to address the linkages between the hierarchical and patriarchal societal structure and women's subordination resulted in its concerns primarily revolving around the legislative removal of some social practices under the aegies of resolving the 'women's question'. Dowry and other manifestations of women's subordination, which were growing out of the complex developments as discussed in chapter three, were institutionalized and further expanded as both the social reform and the women's movement did not question them. Thus, despite Constitutional equality and improved legal rights and education, the hierarchical relationship of men and women became more and more institutionalized exacerbating society's discrimination against and devaluation of women. Only in the late 1970s, women's groups at the national level sought to understand 'oppression' along with its bearing on the women's position in the family and society. The unprecedented upsurge of women against evils like dowry and rape in the late 1970s and 1980s was a response to the earlier inadequate attention to women's issues in the society.

Women and the Regional Perception and Critique of Dowry System

As already discussed, the problem of dowry was seldom raised on the national agenda of reform in the late nineteenth or early twentieth centuries. One finds only passing reference to it in the contemporary national organizations for women.[15] However, a survey of women's literature of the first three decades of the twentieth century in the Hindi belt in north India demonstrates serious contemporary concerns with dowry not only as a problem in itself but as the cause of all other evils affecting the society. This concern was accompanied by a critical and impatient attack against the male reformers for their failure to address and tackle the 'monstrous' practice of dowry.

Ambiguities between the national and regional platforms were the natural result of women's organization and articulation of their own concerns at the local level beginning with the late nineteenth century. This was because, as Talwar writes 'women's movement in the Hindu provinces' in the early twentieth century was different from the nineteenth century reform movement. Two distinguishing premises characterize this. First, the former was 'led by women, and in that it raised questions from the standpoint of women rather than that of men'; and, second, with the growth of their own organizations, women 'wrote sharp criticisms of the self-centred egotistic behaviour of men, their privileged position in society, their disparaging attitude towards women and their predilection to exploit and rule over women' (Talwar 1989: 204-6). In addition to the gender inequalities, women's contemporary writings reflect an attack on the structural inequalities inherent in the caste system, marriage customs, class and other values which were duly imposed by an exploitative Brahmanical priesthood.

These writings are the best reflection of the 'stirring' of the high-caste and literate women against dowry. The late nineteenth and early twentieth-centuries' women's magazines vigorously espoused their cause. One finds these replete with articles, stories and editorials taking up dowry as a primary issue afflicting womankind. A cursory look at these issues provides us with glimpses of the social reality of dowry as perceived by these writers. Reflecting in strong tones their utmost concern for dowry, they offer vehement criticisms of the absence of dowry issue in the women's movement at the national level.

Dowry in Early Twentieth-Century Women's Writings in Hindi

Dowry as a phenomenon appears to have been widely prevalent among the high castes and the middle classes that these magazines represented. In *Mahila Darpan* [March-April 1921 (3-4): 104] an article entitled the 'Evil Practice of Dowry,' alleges that the qualities of a girl were of no importance unless accompanied by an offer of wealth. Even the highest caste would be willing to accept a girl who came from a rich family, regardless of the lack of other features. In fact, the attack on the higher castes as perpetuators of dowry occurs frequently in a number of articles. The *Griha Lakshmi* [1916 (7: II): 97-100] criticizes the practice of bargaining by higher castes and classes before the settlement of marriage negotiations. 'Such respectable persons,' according to the writer, Jagat Pyari, 'reveal a greed for money and do not consider it a blot on their respectability when they place a price on their sons' (ibid: 99). Similar sentiments are expressed in articles in issues of other women's journals including the *Stree Darpan* [September 1928 (3): 58-66]. For example, an article in this journal blames the new rich classes for aggravating the dowry problem by demanding and bargaining for ten times more dowry than earlier times [December 1915 (6: 13): 418-4].

The editorial of the *Mahila Darpan* [March-April 1921 (II: 3-4): 155-6] states that the form and nature of dowry was different in ancient times. Dowry or '*Dayaja*' was offered voluntarily to the girl as a gift with no condition attached for cash or its monetary value. Instead, the amount of gift depended upon the bride's father's status and his affection for his daughter. But it is now extracted forcefully. Accordingly, the status of the girl has also undergone a change. Whereas she was earlier welcomed and received with care in her marital household, nowadays even the most accomplished and beautiful girl is rejected. The editorial then refers to the fear of social censure especially among the poor people for failure to comply with the groom's demand for dowry. It emphasizes the usefulness of the earlier practice where dowry depended upon the status and affordability of the family concerned.

In another similar discussion in the *Griha Lakshmi* [1916 (7: II): 99], it is stated that marriage in the ancient times was based on traditions and customs but it was now totally dependent upon wealth. This is surprising since wealth alone cannot make a marriage run. However, it laments the fact of wealth being responsible for easy arrangement of the marriage of a wealthy girl as compared to the poor one.[16]

In contrast, many references include criticism of traditional values and norms as being responsible for women's dependent status and for evils such as dowry. It is noted that whether the family concerned is able to afford or not, the marriage rituals along with the related expenditures have to be observed to save the family 'honour' [*Mahila Darpan* March-April 1921 (3-4)]. They point to inflationary tendencies adding to the misery of the people. In one instance, it was mentioned that in the Khilji period during the fourteenth century, Rs. 10 to Rs. 20 were enough for meeting marriage expenses. Now, despite rise in inflation, the 'tradition bound' people tend to celebrate marriage in the same 'traditional' way and the evil custom of dowry has increased the financial burden (ibid: 106). So much so that even well-to-do people have to resort to loans in order to meet the marriage expenditure. However, they are still unwilling to forego these traditional practices but take care to fulfill all societal expectations regarding marriage. The Brahmanical priesthood has designed and enforced such rituals for its own survival [*Griha Lakshmi* 1913 (4: III): 166].

Women, these writings indicate, themselves suffer from the existence of such burdensome practices as dowry because of the internalization of traditional norms. Traditionally, according to an article in the *Stree Darpan* [1916 (15:1): 57-9], Hindu women were considered 'unfit' for independent existence. Manu's famous adage about a girl being under the guardianship of her father before marriage, under her husband after marriage, and under her son in later years does not accord her the right to earn a living and provides her only a limited access to property and over parts of her *Strīdhana.* Parents absolve themselves of their responsibility towards their daughter at the time of her marriage. They blatantly tell her that: 'This house is not yours now, it is the property of your brothers only' [*Stree Darpan* June 1926 (12): 8-9]. In another instance, it is stated that dowry is given as a 'bribe' to compensate for the 'weakness' symbolized by a girl [*Griha Lakshmi* 1915 (5:1): 49-59]. With norms set by the ancient texts such as the Vedas and Shastras, the plight of a woman from a 'respectable' family is indeed enormous [*Stree Darpan* December 1915 (6: 13)]. Among the lower classes, such as the dhobi, sweeper, gardener and labourer, daughters and wives work hard with men for survival. But the upper class women must abandon their pride when in need and accept help from their relatives and be satisfied with the bare minimum (ibid).

In fact, such strong criticism of patriarchal anti-women societal norms and the low status of women arising out of their propertylessness and economic dependence are a significant part of the women's movement even today. The *Mahila Darpan* [March 1921 (3:3)] laments that deprived of education, power, and articulation women's lives have remained miserable and lowly throughout history. It says that now as soon as a girl approaches 10-11 years of age, parents begin to worry about her marriage. They take loans to prepare themselves for impending expenses. The consideration of marriage as a socio-religious sacrament makes its performance at all costs essential to preserve family honour [*Stree Darpan* September 1928 (3)]. Moreover, dowry, marriage expenses, and anxieties about preserving her chastity make a girl an unwanted person in the family from birth itself. Quoting the Census of India report on the deplorable conditions of women, the article mentions that in the present the 'regret at the birth of female children and our social customs which demand a costly marriage besides a rich dowry have naturally a tendency to create a sort of indifference, if not passive neglect to female infant life. Marriage has become a commercial venture among many communities like the Marwaris, Marathis, etc.' (ibid). The groom's family invariably stipulates a certain amount to be met by the bride's family before a marriage can take place. The value of a boy with a B.A. degree is now worth five to six thousands as compared to five hundred to one thousand quoted earlier [*Griha Lakshmi* 1916 (7: II): 99]. This destructive and monstrous practice has caused many young girls to commit suicide in order to alleviate their parent's misery.

Vindhyavashini Devi in her article 'Tilak-Dahej' in *Stree Darpan* [February 1920 (22:2): 90-1] further elaborates upon the spread of dowry. She states that the practice of dowry has spread its tentacles resulting in the impoverishment of thousand and thousands of households. Girls have become a burden on their brothers. Dowry, according to her, is the primary cause of the utter unhappiness expressed at the time of birth of a daughter. Dwelling upon the reason for the spread of dowry she attributes it primarily to the emulation of the rich by the poor classes. In a satirical fashion, she states, 'if a rich man takes Rs. 5000 as tilak-dahej, then the poor man will question his own self-worth with the remark— If that particular Rai Sahib took Rs. 5000, aren't we worth even Rs. 2000? My son is a student of F.A. Once he reaches the graduate level (B.A.), he will fetch Rs. 4000. So why should I be satisfied with only Rs. 500 to Rs. 1000 as dowry. Is my status any less than that of Rai Sahib's or is my son's education of less worth than his son's'? Education, the reformers had believed, would bring an end to practices like dowry. It, however, became an added status symbol to the family and prompted increased dowry within the hypergamous social set up. The Sadler Commission, as noted in G.S. Ghurye (1969 cited in Mazumdar 1976a: 53), recorded that English education and university degree in particular had acquired a high value in the marriage market.[17]

Vivid descriptions of marriage bargains are found in numerous writings. Jagat Pyari in *Griha Lakshmi* (op. cit.) likens marriage negotiations with the sale of a son. A businessman sells his goods for a price, and similarly, parents of a groom also 'auction' him with the difference that they do not forfeit their rights over the product (i.e. their son) they have sold to another party. Similar criticisms are evident in another issue of *Griha Lakshmi* [1913 (4: VI): 330-1]. It states that 'while in business a broker does the middle man's job, in marriage bargains it is done by two persons: the barber and the priest! Also, while in business a tax is levied there is no tax in the business of marriage!'.

In these writings, dowry thus emerged as a symbol and cause of women's afflictions. The fear of heavy dowry demands made anxious parents in north central India to deny education to their daughters and marry them off at quite a young age (Mazumdar 1976: 52). Tara Devi of Gorakhpur in an article in *Stree Darpan* [May 1925 (5: 33): 210-12] states that dowry is the reason for the misery expressed at the birth of a girl. As a result, the girl's own self-worth gets belittled and she is deprived of education. Dowry was also linked with the practice of polygamy. An editorial in *Mahila Darpan* [March-April 1921 (3-4: II): 155] categorically mentions that the monstrous custom of dowry is the 'primary' cause for the rapid increase in polygamy, marriage of young girls to old men, and widowhood. The custom has so reduced women's status that many innocent girls are put to death at birth, and among those who grow up, many are married to old men married several times before and having numerous wives. The editor conjectures thereby that if the custom of dowry were abolished then a considerable improvement would follow in other social ills besetting the society.

For these women writers, dowry was linked with other oppressive social practices. It appeared as an obstacle to women's education, respectability and dignity. Whereas the social reformers of the nineteenth century attempted to tackle each issue in isolation, dowry in these writings was seen in connection with other problems and identified as responsible for a larger vicious pattern characterized by the oppression of women in the society. For example, Jagat Pyari [*Griha Lakshmi* 1916 (7: II)] writes that 'it is not only women who suffer the consequence of this evil practice, the entire society is beset by problems, yet no attention is paid to the problem'.

Anti-male sentiments were also frequently expressed in the analysis of dowry in these writings [*Stree Darpan* May 1925 (5: 33): 210-12]. An earlier issue of *Stree Darpan* [1916 (15: 1)] even denounces any 'natural or God-made' differences between men and women. It states that such differences are social constructs designed by men as no male-female inequality can be observed among the animals. Hypergamous marriages were also regarded as aggravating dowry. However rich or poor a person was, he usually tried to arrange a marriage of his daughter with someone of his own status if not higher. The marriage expenditures and dowry rates increased in proportion to the status sought. The effect on girls of poor families, however, was of inverse nature, as most girls were forced to marry into families lesser in wealth and status than their own [e.g. *Mahila Darpan* March-April 1921(2): 103-12].

Such realistic portrayal of dowry in its usual occurrence and practice in the society is reflective of the intensity of women's concern. A great outcry against suicide of Snehlata of Bengal also found place in these journals.[18] Snehlata's letter to her father written just before her death was publicized and printed in several issues of many of these journals. Extremely sensitive about her family's anxiety regarding her marriage, she wrote to her father, 'I am unmarried even though I am fifteen years of age' and 'am taking my own life because people criticize and ridicule you for this in spite of your making several attempts to resolve this issue' [Quoted in *Mahila Darpan* March-April 1921(2): 109].

In fact, Snehlata's suicide provoked strong response among women and evoked women writers to investigate the rate of suicide among female as compared to males. They found higher rates of suicide among women [e.g. *Mahila Darpan* March-April 1921 (2): 103-12]. They highlighted the state-wise figures as cited in an official report published in *Jain Hitaishi.*

State	Population	Suicide by	
		men	women
M.P. and Berar	1,39,16,308	441	523
Bihar and Orissa	3,44,90,034	605	1105
Agra and Ayodhya	4,68,20,556	614	1193
Bengal	5,53,29,221	1452	2018

Such figures were provided to draw attention of the society's 'peers' to the increase in suicide rate among females as compared to men. A tremendous pressure to arrange a girl's marriage, the inability of her parents to cope with dowry demands resulted in many cases of suicide by young girls especially from poor families.[19]

Also included in letters to the journal are references to social reformers' neglect of women's issues. For example, one remarks

> ... Many kind-hearted and educated people, both men and women have donated generously to help the orphans left in the aftermath of the Burdwan floods. Many men have discarded foreign items (in favour of swadeshi). Young persons have even begged to collect money to help the South African community. May God bless such kind and generous men. But why don't they focus on the ills besetting their own society? (ibid: 109)

Such bitter attack on social reformers, especially males, epitomised the anger and helplessness at the 'inadequate' attention being paid to the real issues of women. In *Stree Darpan*, the article by Tara Devi [May 1925 (5: 33)] expresses women's dissatisfaction with men engaged in the battle for freedom. She writes 'I pray to those brothers who are lovers of freedom and are fighting for their freedom and rights, and the welfare of their country. These men should first provide freedom to women from social evils . . . without the emancipation of women, the country cannot progress.' Referring to Snehlata's suicide, Jagat Pyari [*Griha Lakshmi* 1916 (7: II): 97-100] alleges that although there is talk of reform everywhere, and some reforms are being affected, evils such as dowry are not being tackled although its terrible consequences were before the people. Similar plea was made in another issue of *Griha Lakshmi* [(4: 6): 330-1] in which the caste reformers are asked to 'destroy the evil of dowry from its roots to arrest the spread of this robbery. . . . Girls will bless such reformers for such efforts from the "innermost core of their hearts".'

Shrimati Bhagwan Devi in her story 'Madan Malti' [*Griha Lakshmi* 1916 (7: 12)] criticizes a male social reformer of paying only lip service to the abolition of dowry and making dowry demands at the time of his son's marriage. Similar allegations are made by Jagat Pyari too (op. cit.) who writes, 'These men who are nation's social reformers do not see the misery of their brethren because they themselves practice it'.

In other writings, women were asked to fight against social evils such as dowry while the men were busy fighting political struggle to free the country from foreign rule [*Mahila Darpan* (2): 112]. Writers like Vindhyavasini Devi (op. cit.) called upon all men to put an end to the practice of dowry. According to her, the first attempt should be made by 'our rich brothers' to give up dowry-taking as practices of the rich and upper classes are emulated by the majority of the population. She, however, praises those reformers who made some attempts to abolish the practice.

The concern against dowry evident in the regional literature possibly led to many contemporary active caste *sabhās* to condemn its prevalent practice. It is however difficult to establish whether the move to condemn dowry came from the reform efforts at the national level or grew out of such regional concerns. In fact, both played a part. But the consequences of the regional literature's vehement criticism of dowry in the initiation of such local stirring cannot be underestimated. In the Census Report, Turner notes that

> the objects to which the various sabhas have so far chiefly directed their attentions are the uplift of the particular community concerned in the social scale . . . , proselytizing and re-conversion, the spread of education, abolition of purdah, encouragement of widow re-marriage, *reduction of expenditure on social and religious ceremonies and at festivals, reduction of dowries,* and the abolition of nautches [dancing] (emphasis mine). [Turner 1933 (1): 552]

As mentioned in the last chapter, the caste *sabhās* and *mahā-sabhās* were essentially a product of the colonial rule and their roles usually limited to frame caste rules and pass resolutions applicable to their caste (Turner 1933: 333). Their injunctions were thus only 'persuasive' and not 'coercive'.[20] They thus had only limited impact over the eradication of the dowry system.

Another impact of these women's writings can be seen in the emergence of such active organizations like the Mahila Mandal of the Kayastha community in Prayag. It suggested several measures to reduce unnecessary expenditures in marriage [*Saheli* April 1933 (1: 4)]. This included (a) checks on asymmetrical marriages in terms of age, status and wealth, and on marriage bargaining, dance by nautch-girls, *bhang* and drinks, and (b) disapproval of the payment of more than Rs. 51 in *Varakshā* and *Tilak* ceremonies. It was specifically stated that no girl was to marry a man above forty years of age. The Mathur Kayastha community which did not demand or give dowry was presented as a model for emulation

[*Griha Lakshmi* 1916 (7: II): 100].[21] The use of moral pressure, and not legal redress, on families with boys to refrain from putting pressure on the girl's family to conform to norms of giving enough jewellery, etc., was advocated (ibid).

Such criticisms were not limited to the Hindi belt. Bengali periodicals published in the early twentieth century also exhorted the youth of Bengal to rise against dowry and other evils in order to bring about healthy changes in the society. Such local periodicals as *Gambhira* (Malda), *Shobhana* (Midnapur), and *Gourprabha* (Howrah) made frantic appeals to take a vow against dowry.[22] *Satsanga* (Murshidabad 1893), *Prachi* (Dhaka 1930), *Samachar Darpan* (1818) were other periodicals which wrote forcefully against dowry (Bhaumik 1986: 393-5). Moreover, societies such as the Satyashodhak Samaj (1873) and Hindu Missionary Society[23] (1830s) attacked marriage customs and advocated simplified and shortened marriage ceremonies to be performed by trained non-Brahmin priests (cited in Kumar 1993: 15). A contemporary work by Jogesachandra Ghosha (1928: 88) mentioned the 'praiseworthy desire . . . amongst some of the educated young men of the day [is] to make a principle to marry without dowries, but it will be long before the fathers of girls, with insufficient means, would derive practical benefit from such noble resolve on the part of a few of our young men.' Many leagues were started in northern India, where pledges against dowry were taken in early twentieth century (Singh 1968: 237).

Such developments may not be of significance in isolation but when viewed as a whole, they can be seen as questioning caste rigidities, patriarchal control and removal of rituals and long ceremonies of marriage as important prerequisite for tackling the problems of dowry and women's subordinate status. Why were these voices of women writers and associations at the regional level not reflected in the mainstream women's organizations? Why were these unable to locate the issue of dowry—which they considered crucial, in the mainstream perspective of the national struggle for women's 'upliftment' and equality? The mainstream women's organizations existed as a part of the nationalist movement. With greater emphasis on political issues, no separate and comprehensive struggle for women's socio-economic problems at that time appeared feasible. The women's movement of the first phase at best remained largely reformative in approach with a firm commitment to the efficacy of legal enactments.

The Contemporary Women's Movement and Dowry

The anti-dowry movement is regarded as one of the 'high marks' of the contemporary women's movement. As already mentioned above, during the colonial period, protests against dowry featured in the women's movement primarily at the regional level. However, in the contemporary women's movement, struggle against dowry occupied the centre stage.

The late 1970s witnessed the rise of several autonomous women's groups which rejected political party affiliation and concentrated on diverse issues affecting women.[24] The obvious forms of violence that dowry and rape correlated, brought the groups together which launched the contemporary women's movement. Three factors appear to have made dowry the one specific issue to which women's groups focused upon and remained committed to. First, a large number of murders or suicides of young married women were noticed and identified as murders for dowry or abetment to suicide for bringing inadequate dowry. Second, a brutal and an extreme expression of violence against women within the so-called 'safe' portals of family life was observed. Lastly, the larger struggle against patriarchy to tackle an obvious manifestation of women's subordination manifested itself in the protest against dowry. So much so that dowry could no longer be regarded as mere gift-giving.

As in the earlier protests before Independence, the middle and the upper middle classes were readily able to identify with the agitation against dowry as it touched them personally. To be sure, dowry had originated among the propertied and upper classes and was still prevalent among them but, as already discussed in the last chapter, it rapidly percolated among the lower classes. Recent studies like those of Epstein (1973), Miller (1980), and Srinivas (1966), confirm this phenomenon. The anti-dowry agitation thus once initiated had the mass appeal.

In 1961, less than two decades following Independence, the Dowry (Prohibition) Act was promulgated by the Parliament. It was however soon realized that the Act, instead of containing dowry, failed to prevent its spread in a drastically altered form to most castes and classes. While dowry demands ranged from consumables to cash for business, education, foreign trip or marriage of a daughter, what caught the attention of women's groups was a large number of 'accidental' deaths of young married women. These deaths, on investigation by a women's group called the Mahila Dakshata Samiti (New Delhi 1977) were discovered to be murders for dowry or abetment to suicide by incessant harassment (Gandhi and Shah 1992: 54).

Women's groups, thereafter, launched a sustained campaign against these 'dowry deaths'. They began an analysis of the root and nature of the problem, gathered data and information, processed it for legislative redressals, voiced most visibly the feminist dictum 'the personal is political', and demonstrated against cases of harassment inflicted on women in the privacy of the home. In fact, the term dowry came to be closely identified with dowry murders and violence against women. This new dimension in the meaning of dowry in the eighties could be seen as the culmination of dowry viewed as 'extortion' in the fifties and the sixties, as nuptial presents or gifts in medieval period, and gifts linked with inheritance in ancient times.

The initial investigations in 1978 by the Anti-Dowry Committee of the Mahila Dakshata Samiti revealed that more than 350 women were burnt to death for dowry in Delhi alone. As Pramila Dandavate, the Secretary of the Samiti observed, 'These were cases of girls pushed on to the burning stoves or driven to suicide for not bringing adequate dowry. Education too has not helped or acted as a deterrent in the increasing incidence of dowry for even lecturers and other professional women have been harassed for dowry' [*Manushi* January 1979 (1)]. The then Prime Minister, Charan Singh, assured the Mahila Dakshata Samiti members that measures to stop the maltreatment of women for dowry would be introduced in the next parliamentary session.

Yet, the widely reported grim statistics tell a different story. According to figures available, in Delhi (1983) on an average, two women died of burns everyday. In a municipal hospital in Bombay, within six months between September and February 1987, 157 burn cases were admitted. In Karnataka, nine cases were reported in 1982 as against 31 and 48 in 1983 and 1984 respectively. Similar increase was evident in other states too. In Uttar Pradesh, for example, in 1984 the figure was 182 and doubled to 323 in 1985; in Madhya Pradesh, 42 cases were reported between June and October 1985; in Maharashtra 129 cases of dowry deaths in 1984 more than doubled in the following year. In addition, there were 411 cases of suicides by young married women in 1983, 652 in 1985 and 662 in the first ten months of 1986 [*Flavia* March 1987 (2: 3)]. The Ministry of Home Affairs observed 1285 cases in 1986. The Compendium of Policy Statements in the Parliament (Budget Session, 1988) reported, on the basis of the data from early seventies to mid-eighties of the Bureau of Public Research and Development, that crimes against women had almost doubled. The Home Ministry's National Crime Record Bureau clocked a 'dowry death' at every 102 minutes and informed that between 1987 and 1991, dowry deaths have increased by 170 per cent.[25] It was reported in *The Hindu* (17 April 1994) under the caption 'The Darkness Has Not Lifted for Women' by Visa Ravindran.

The Phase of Activism: Protests and Demonstration

The spate of the dowry murders and suicides, and dowry as the brutal reality of the symbol of inequality laid the basis for a renewed women's movement. Women's groups, informed first by the widely reported dowry cases in the national and regional newspapers in the late seventies, focused on this problem as one of the most pressing social issue. Gradually with the help of the media as well as legal and social support, attempts were made to disentangle murders for dowry from suicides and accidents, as they had been usually treated earlier. Quick and drastic measures were urged to curb the practice of dowry. The most immediate reaction to the report of dowry deaths was issue-based rallies, protests and boycotts.

The first major women's demonstration 'that can be said to have launched the campaign' against dowry took place in June 1979[26] (Gandhi and Shah 1992: 54). It was to protest against the murder of Tarvinder Kaur, a 24-year old newly married Sikh bride of Model Town (Delhi), for her failure to bring enough dowry to finance her husband's business. In her dying declaration, Tarvinder clearly stated that her mother-in-law and sister-in-law had set her on fire. Despite this, the police registered her case as a suicide. Several women's groups joined together with the Stree Sangharsh—an association which was formed only six months earlier, and the local residents including not only neighbours but also sweepers, domestic workers, and passerbyes. They marched to Tarvinder's in-law's house and demanded punishment for her murderers. Placards bearing such slogans as 'Do not Give or Take

Dowry', 'Stop Killing Women', 'Insist on Marriage by Registration', etc., were displayed (Kumar 1993: 119).

These women's groups also placed a memorandum before the Home Ministry demanding redressal. A meeting called by the Delhi State Women's Federation soon followed. It demanded urgent reforms in dowry legislation. Their demands included: (1) dowry be made an unbailable offence; (2) if death of a girl takes place within seven years of marriage, post-mortem be compulsorily performed; and (3) cases that evidently appear as suicide be fully investigated (Das 1979: 15). Tarvinder's case can be regarded as a typical case of women's organized protest against 'dowry death'.[27]

In an earlier incident, a thumb impressioned statement by one Hardeep Kaur, ironically a friend of Tarvinder cited above, about burning herself while cooking allowed the culprits to go scot free. As the girl belonged to a rich and educated family this was an obvious case of fraud. Such calculated oversight by the police angered women who demonstrated against the verdict. This facilitated formation of a women's group called the Stree Sangharsh in Delhi to fight against such atrocities [Kumar 1993: 117-18; *Manushi* 1979 (1)]. As the campaign progressed and more 'cases' were brought to public notice, further efforts were made to raise women's consciousness to take action against the culprits.

Demonstrations against dowry deaths were organized in several parts of India.The police was forced to take up full investigations in many cases[28] in Delhi as well as in other cities all over India. The police however justified their inaction by linking these cases to 'family quarrel'. Women's groups none the less followed up cases in the courts.[29] Organizations like the Mahila Utpidan Virodhi Manch in Ranchi (1985) were formed as a reaction to local cases of murder for dowry and took up cases of the death of brides in mysterious circumstances.[30] Sustained efforts were made to humiliate culprit at their workplaces and homes.[31] Street corner meetings, public demonstrations, signature campaigns and poster exhibitions were organized to publicize cases of dowry related atrocities.

These demonstrations were motivated by a number of factors—to bring the cases to public notice, to shame the husband and his family, to keep the case alive by making it difficult for police to bury it, and most importantly, to emphasize that issues such as dowry and related violence were not private issues but were the concerns of the state too. The demonstration for Tarvinder's case, for instance, prevented many parents of girls from negotiations with families who demanded dowry for fear of a similar outcome. In some cases demonstrations even took place outside a prospective groom's house whose parents were demanding dowry.[32]

Anti-dowry demonstrations by women's groups and the consequent increase in social awareness facilitated emergence of neighbourhood action committees, women's wings and front organizations of several political parties and activities such as *padyātrās* meetings as well as direct methods of communication such as performance of plays, counselling through women's centres and aid through the Police's Anti Dowry Cell.[33] The entire effort was geared towards making the struggle visible by mobilizing large number of women. The focus placed by women's groups on dowry-related harassment murders widened the awareness of the changed manifestation of dowry as well as its linkages with many socio-economic and structural issues.

Women's activism also included personalized commitment to oppose dowry. The journal *Manushi* took the pledge to boycott dowry marriage as a bid to generate awareness against the evil practice and to demonstrate women's collective struggle against it. The pledge [*Manushi* May-June 1980(5): 3], affirmed that:

1. We will not attend or in any way participate in a marriage where dowry is either given or taken in, however, veiled a form (as gifts, trousseau, money deposited in bank in the girl's name at the time of marriage)' even if the marriage be that of a close relative or a dear friend. We will openly make known our reasons for boycotting such marriages, rather than just quietly staying from the ceremony. We will also boycott all rituals wherein dowry continues to be given after marriage such as customary gifts to the son-in-law's relatives at festivals and child birth.
2. That we will henceforth not confine protest actions to dowry murders but will also protest when dowry is given at extravagant marriage ceremonies.
3. That we will not attend marriages in which the woman has no active choice—in deciding whether she wants to get married at all or in choosing the person to whom she is to be married.

In 1982, a forum of about thirty women's groups and covered

by five national women's organization, was set-up as the Dahej Virodhi Chetna Manch (DVCM). In its August 1982 memorandum, the DVCM linked dowry 'with the entire gamut of inferior female conditions'. It said that the increasing incidence of dowry 'is symptomatic of the continuing erosion of women's status and devaluation of female life in independent India. It is equally related to the worsening socio-economic crisis within which structural inequalities have accentuated and black money power have grown to fuel greater human oppression' (see Palriwala, 1986, 1989; *Manushi*; Kelkar 1985 and 1985a). Anger and resentment against dowry were thus expressed through numerous forms.

The comprehension of dowry as a reflection of the 'whole gamut' of women's subordinate conditions brought about manifold solutions. These included overhauling of legal machinery, registration of marriage and marriage gifts, raising consciousness through media and school textbooks, establishment of vigilance committees comprising of women's groups, appointment of dowry prohibition officers, demand for a national commission on women, and equal and actual inheritance rights for daughters. The Manch, set-up to protest against dowry and raise consciousness against it, reached its momentum in a huge 'largest ever' rally of women to the Parliament on 3 August 1982 (Palriwala 1986: 38).

Despite its internal differences, most women's groups believed that the DVCM presented an united forum and a sustained campaign against dowry on an individual basis as well as in wider campaigns. Cases were investigated but stumbling blocks appeared in the form of reluctance on the part of the girl to indict her husband and his family (Kumar 1993: 117). The police version usually remained the only available evidence [ibid: 122; *Manushi* 1979 (3): 3]. Finally, with the support of the legislative and police machinery, special cells within the state structure were established.[34] Similar special cells for women were opened in other large cities also. Support centres by women's groups too surfaced. The demand for family courts for speedy disposal of cases resulted in the Family Court Act of 1984. The pressure for legislative changes yielded results when a Joint Select Committee of Parliament was constituted in 1981 to review the problem of dowry and its related laws. This was followed by an enquiry conducted by the Law Commission in 1983 into dowry deaths which suggested drastic legislative measures and changes in the Evidence Act to make persecution easier (Sharma n.d.: 23).

The momentum of the visible campaign however gradually decreased. Palriwala (1986: 39) attributes it to 'the very complexity of the dowry problem which is so integrally linked to the entire question of a woman's subordination in Indian society'. The women's groups were quick to realize that the ideological and cultural hold that marriage entails for a girl and her family was a difficult variable to reckon with. With marriage comes *kanyādāna*, hypergamy, different determinants for defining the eligibility of a girl, and other rituals—all of which perpetuate subordination of women in society. The long lasting effects of the socialization process which requires a woman to adjust at every step was also realized. That was evident in the bride's attempt to not to bring shame or disgrace to her husband or her in-laws who may harass her or to her natal family for failure to meet dowry demands. Moreover, the media which was the first to expose 'dowry deaths' also promoted consumerist culture diluting the issue of dowry. The state's cumbersome legal and administrative procedures acted as deterrent for those who wished to attain justice.

Women's lack of response in legal matters was yet another issue highlighted by the women's groups. Despite the 1956 Act providing for equal rights in property, few women actually received equal shares. They either waived away their portions in favour of their brothers or were not provided with any. The cultural ideal of a woman with little or no interest in property was well-projected by the media and internalized by women too (Sharma 1984: 64 and Kishwar 1989d; 6-7).

Moreover, despite the initial favourable and widespread response, women campaigners soon realized that the

> attempts at boycotting or ostracizing culprits were never powerful enough to affect them in any significant way; while attempts to secure convictions largely failed, for a certain degree of police corruption together with inefficiency, the difficulty of procuring evidence, the pressure on the courts and resulting slow pace of the proceedings, all conspired to this end and continue to do so to the implementation of all administrative improvement and legislation in India. (Kumar 1989: 22)

Demonstrations were, however, vital to the growth of women's movement. Even though many differences in the perspective on dowry and on the aims of the movement were apparent yet a united front was perceived by the state and the people. Consequently, dowry was recognized as a social problem of immense magnitude. Vina Mazumdar (1983: 34) states that

> the spontaneous explosion of resentment against 'dowry deaths' of women received support from both the national and international media and the Government was forced to recognize the complexity and seriousness of the problem. A Human Rights Organization of U.S.A. even threatened to launch a campaign within the U.N. Human Rights Commission about the Indian Government's failure to protect women's right to life.

Further, commenting on the historiography of the women's movement, Govind Kelkar (1984: 129) writes that 'the sporadic and spontaneous protests . . . [were] real and worthwhile, an effective means of social agitation. One would err if one fails to recognize the degree of consciousness in these apparently recognized and spontaneous movement of the masses of women.' These attempts 'created legal and political space for the women's movement.' Moreover, the demonstrations brought into open what had till then been the domestic sphere permitting no outside interference. . . . A culture of 'speak bitterness'—empowering harassed wives and victims to speak out their ordeal was the direct result of efforts by women's groups. Yet, the need to combine, what Karlekar (1983: 14) writes, 'direct action with a sustained movement for consciousness raising, through . . . correcting and creating information' led to a further sustained effort to analyze empirically and theoretically the issue of dowry to bring about changes in the society.

From the Phase of Activism to Women's Rethinking and Analysis of Dowry for Strategies for a Movement

(a) *Contemporary Studies on Dowry*

The slackening of movement against dowry persuaded women's groups to search for information and statistics necessary to deal comprehensively with the issue of dowry. Many studies were undertaken for comparison and analysis of dowry in its modern form. For example, a survey conducted by members of the Joint Women's Program of Bangalore revealed the spread of dowry to communities that did not practice it earlier. It also exposed the attitudinal block that was widely rampant that it was easier to cater to the groom's family demands than to rehabilitate a girl who came back to her natal family (see *Manushi* 1983 (15-16)).

Traditional family values, societal apathy and absence of legal literacy among women were also found to be contributing to the growing practice of dowry.[35] The research wing of the Working Women's Forum undertook a study to gauge 'Dowry Practices among Slum Women of Madras City' (Azad 1983: 1-26). It discovered dowry to be prevalent among those who performed marriage rites in the Brahmanical fashion. These included the higher non-Brahmin caste, such as Mudaliars, Chettiars, and the Scheduled Castes who, in a bid to gain social mobility, emulated upper caste norms, what has been referred by Srinivas as the process of Sanskritization. The study also observed that where such marriage forms as intercaste, temple, common-law and registered marriage were the practising norms, little or minimal expenditures were required. Dowry, on the other hand, was an irrelevant item of expenditure for the subsistence level families due to their concept of 'shared poverty'. The female oriented family structures too negated the rationale for the practice of dowry. Dowry, thus existed as 'an ideal achievement concept' rather than the norm among these slum inhabitants.

In contrast, a study conducted among the lower income group in Delhi (Luthra 1983: 1-17) noted the steady shift from bride-price to dowry. Women of these groups were mostly engaged as labour, vendors, household help, etc. The marriage expenses among these groups were borne by the girl's side including gifts for the groom and his kin, whereas the gifts given from the boy's family were mainly for the girl's own use which she carried with her to her husband's home. Asymmetry in payments, public display of gifts given by the bride's family (while any bride-price given was not accepted publicly), centrality of *kanyādāna*, hypergamy, and the integration of 'accepted' rituals such as demanding some item before the completion of some ritual as was prevalent among the Yadavas, Thakurs, Ahirs, Jaduvanshis, etc., were found to have become features of marriage ceremonies even among the tribal and the lower caste migrants. The women among the migrants having lost their productive roles, as they were not equipped for jobs that are not land based, bring the dowry as their contribution to the household. Only when their domestic role was considered productive or they were able to take up remunerative work, were they able to withstand such demands.

The All India Anti-Dowry Movement (Nagpur) presented a report at the IV NCWS (at Visakhapatnam, 28-31 December 1988), which traced dowry to the unjust system catering to the social side of marriage with its emphasis on show of status and to increasing urbanization and industrialization. Earlier Stree Kriti Samiti, Bombay, explained the 'historical process of dowry's consolidation and the factors that have contributed to its institutionalization'. The report concluded that dowry must be seen 'as a reflection of the continuing subordination and exploitation of women in different forms, but within the prevailing dominant feudal ideology. The question of dowry, as the question of women, cannot be separated from the overall socio-economic condition' and a 'qualitative and fundamental change in the familial authority structure and marriage system that maintains prevailing property relations . . . and in the patriarchal system of production and reproduction that subordinates, subjugates, and undervalues women' (II NCWS Report 1984: 9). Such all encompassing view of dowry within the context of women's subordination was typical only of the contemporary women's groups in contrast to the relatively limited perspective of the earlier phase.

However, recently, tendencies to underplay the dowry issue have been noticed in contrast to the earlier surge of documentation on dowry demands and harassment (Fernandes 1992: 30-3). The research-based activities of women's groups, as exemplified above, provided the backdrop for the approach to deal with the dowry cases. The Nari Nirjatan Pratirodh Manch of Calcutta, for instance, came to realize that the pursuit of individual cases would limit the scope of its activities. It, therefore, decided to attend only such cases that could generate widespread action. The Stree Mukti Sangharsh Chalval Kasegaon (Sangli district) and the Stree Jagriti Samiti of Bombay supported concentration on such basic issues of women as poverty and work rather than on issues relating to family such as dowry, rape, etc. It declared that 'if the groups do not connect the struggle in individual woman's lives with wider issues, there is a danger of lapsing into "charity" work'. On the other hand, the Stree Shakti Sangathan of Hyderabad stated that the major achievement of women's mobilization on the problem of dowry could be seen in its shift from private to a public matter. A more rigorous analysis of the problem of dowry was necessary in order to declare it as 'basic' as other issues such as work, etc. *Saheli* of Delhi emphasized changes within the family structure to prevent it from becoming 'an instrument for extending state ideology'. To combat dowry, it suggested a struggle against state patriarchy (FAOW 1985: 5-53). One thus finds diversities and complexities among the women's groups on the subject of dowry—as more data and information flowed in.

(b) *Rethinking Strategies*

Throughout the eighties, dowry regularly featured among the major themes of discussion in women's conferences. The first national women's movement conference in 1980 was 'a sort of a climax to the anti-dowry and anti-rape agitation of the late 70s'. It was the first occasion in which the grass root level women activists and other groups came together under one forum, as the summary report points out, 'on their own initiative to discuss the growing atrocities on women' (see FAOW 1985: 5). The second conference in 1985 was attended by 85 women's groups and many individuals from different parts of the country. It explored seemingly contradictory relationship between the agitation for individual cases and widespread campaigns for consciousness raising. It led to debates on whether the focus should be on specific issues such as dowry or women's issues within the framework of the larger movements (ibid: 6-7). By the third national conference (the Nari Mukti Sangharsh Sammelan (NMSS) in Patna, 5-7 February 1988) a shift from the agitational approach against individual issues to a more consistent attack on the prevailing structural inequalities is discernible. This marked a major shift of focus to comprehend the women's problems in totality. One of the resolutions undertaken thus states:

> Women face specific forms of violence: rape and other forms of sexual abuse, female foeticide, witch killing, sati, dowry murders, wife beating etc. Such violence and the continued sense of insecurity that is instilled in women as a result keeps them bound to the home, economically exploited and socially suppressed. In the ongoing struggle against violence in the family, society and the state, we recognize that the state is one of the main source of violence and stands behind the violence committed by men against women in the family, the workplace and the neighbourhood. For these reasons a mass women's movement should focus on the struggle against state violence while building the strength of

women to confront all those who use violence against them in the home or out of it. [Resolution 12 passed at the Plenary Session (NMSS 1988: 2)].

It can be noticed that the concerns of the contemporary women's movement when viewed in the context of dowry, are different from the 'traditional concerns' with legislation, education and political participation which were a part of the agenda of the earlier women's organizations. The widening of the debate to the more complex nature of women's question is significant for its implications in the understanding of dowry.[36] The present concern with 'gender' in its social, cultural, economic and political manifestations is central to the women's movement.

Accordingly, the women activists' current theoretical premises, that evolved out of their campaigns against dowry, now revolve around the larger issue of subordination of women and its reasons. In contemporary debates, dowry has been explained in the context of the asymmetrical relation between bride-givers and bride-takers as well as women's resourcelessness and lack of inheritance rights on the one hand (Kishwar 1986, 1988 and 1989), and on the other, the changing caste structure within a capitalist economy, and structure of material production (Omvedt 1987 and 1988, Parliwala 1986 and 1989, Kelkar 1985 and 1985a, etc.). These view-points reflect the current major positions on the issue of dowry.

For Kishwar, dowry is an expression of the asymmetrical relations between bride-givers and bride-takers (Kishwar 1986). The dependent status of a girl requires dowry to be paid to increase her worthiness. But, while her parents recover their status at the marriage of a son, the daughter's position remains devalued throughout life. Thus the familial power relationships and social hierarchy are being continuously affected and determined by dowry. A girl's status as a dependent person is the result of such religious and social pressure on marriage as an ideal for a girl, the social mobility of the new rich classes, and education as enhancing the boy's 'market rate' but with no such implication for girls, etc. Her continued dependent status contributes to the growth of dowry as a practice.

In a series of articles in 1989,[37] Kishwar called for a rethinking of the Dowry Boycotts. She criticized the anti-dowry rhetoric and sloganeering by the women's movement in the late 70s and early 80s as ineffective measures. Instead, she made a plea to bring the anti-dowry movement to a 'practical level of implementation'. A struggle for the abolition of dowry was to tackle the problem from the wrong end, for, in spite of a large number of people professing to be against dowry, it had continued unabated. With the onus of resistance to dowry marriage placed on women, their 'resourcelessness' denies them necessary power to refuse marriage with or without dowry. According to her, the anti-dowry campaign will be of little consequence as 'rights, autonomy and power' rest with men. A dowryless marriage by itself is not likely to alter this imbalance. In fact, even if 'dowry were somehow to go out of fashion', women's oppression would continue.

Dowry, Kishwar further elaborated, is an additional instrument to carry out women's oppression. It is used as a means to 'disinherit, objectify and dispose off a woman'. Yet, dowry is today the only available choice of support for women. The need, therefore, is to fight for empowerment of women through effective inheritance rights by combating 'the culture of disinheritance, moral and material, of daughters' (1989: 587 and 1989c: 2739). This would strike at the roots of the problem for dowry and devaluation of daughters which began with the propertied classes and then gradually percolated down to the lower classes. For 'when we talk of dowry we are not primarily talking of the destitute poor but of those who have some economic assets or creditworthiness to encash' (1989: 587). Once inheritance rights become a reality, dowry in its present form is almost certain to disappear. Kishwar (1989: 588) thus suggests following measures:

1. Any will which disinherits daughters should be considered invalid.
2. All land, property and succession related laws including land ceiling laws, should be amended to ensure equal rights to women, particularly over immovable property such as housing and land.
3. Any document whereby a woman surrenders her right in favour of her brothers, husband or in-laws, should be considered invalid.
4. A woman should not be able to pass on to her husband or in-laws any property inherited from her parents. If she dies childless or under suspicious circumstances, the property should revert to her natal family. This will ensure that her inheritance does not become an incentive for her husband and in-laws to kill her. Her inherited property should be inherited by her adult children or, if she is childless and dies a natural death many years after marriage, it may be inherited by her under the same circumstances. . . .

She concludes:

We should work to equip women with the resources and abilities to define control and guard their own interests and their own lives. Whether or not they are given dowry will then become irrelevant to their essential well-being.

Kishwar's plea for 'rethinking' on dowry problem raised hornet's nests among women's activists and groups. They expressed their disagreement with her analysis and strategies on primarily two grounds. First, dowry was not just 'a phoney symbol' of women's subordination as suggested by Kishwar, but co-existed with other forms of women's oppression. Secondly, the boycott against dowry and support of real inheritance right for women were to be simultaneous fights and not one without the other.

Opposing Kishwar's view on dowry and strategies for anti-dowry movement, C.S. Lakshmi (1989. 189-90 and 1989a: 1065), for instance, argued that dowry co-existed hand in hand with other cultural values that perpetuate the devalued and dependent status of a woman and premium placed on man within the family and society. To make inheritance the chief concern for the empowerment of women and to treat dowry as inheritance would be 'reductionist' in approach. Palriwala (1989) presented dowry as a reflection of the larger socio-economic forces that work at the systematic subordination of women. She writes that, 'the intensification of homicidal violence against wives was a consequence of changes in dowry practices due to social and economic changes resulting from the colonial and post-colonial capitalist development in India' (ibid: 942). This wide spectrum from which dowry derives its strength cannot be tackled by any single approach.

Dowry, according to Palriwala, was rampant among the landed castes and the upward mobile castes of the colonial period. The ideology of hypergamy with its 'inherent tendency of continuous inflation' in the amount of dowry contributed to its growth. It spread to other castes beyond the higher ones. Moreover, monetization and the elimination of a large number of women from their traditional occupation to an economically dependent status further exacerbated its practice. As a consequence of the contemporary 'consumerist culture', demands for dowry increased and its form altered. Given the cultural and religious importance of marriage, there is no other option but to marry off the girl at all costs.

Dowry's linkages with the caste-class nexus was also emphasized by Omvedt (1988: 3-4) in her study, *Women and Violence.* According to her, the upper caste 'purdah' norms for women, exemplified by a 'non-working' house-keeping wife, protect women from outside violence. It however exposed her to threats within the home. Dowry deaths thus are most rampant among 'upper-caste, upper class, urban organized sector women', while the lower castes are subjected to 'social violence' such as rape, molestation, etc.

Kelkar (1985: 1-13) attributes increase in dowry to the structural violence inherent in the political, economic and familial arrangements. She argues that the family approach legitimizes the subordination of women in policy-making and the organization of economy. The sexual division of labour forms the basis of the family which is the principal institution underlying the sex-gender system. The familial authority which shapes property relations provides an adequate explanation for the dowry system. The exclusion of women from property determines the organization of marriage and family and also perpetuates the gender specific division of labour. In the maintenance of such unequal relationships, the patriarchal state naturally willingly cooperates. The significance of women's resourcelessness and 'deempowerment' in her continued dependent status within the familial and kinship organization and in practices like dowry cannot be denied.

What is apparent from the above debates on dowry is that beginning with the report of the Committee on the Status of Women (TE 1974) which marked the 'major turning point' to the new and complex set of questions thrown up in the eighties, the contemporary women's movement is burgeoning with activism, introspection and demand for policy intervention. This is apparent from the course taken up by women's groups in tackling the issue of dowry. Has the exercise brought us closer to understanding the problem of dowry?

It must be acknowledged that the dowry campaign has brought to light several pertinent factors. For one, issues that had been so far considered outside the purview of politics and relegated to public-private dichotomy have been brought into the open. The concept of the public and the private had dictated the course taken by the social reformers and the colonial rulers in the nineteenth and early twentieth centuries. Most activists of the contemporary movement now question the patriarchal compulsions of the state in the upkeep of the public/private divide, the power relationships within the family and its repercussion on women. This is different from the limited attention paid to these phenomena in the earlier phase of the women's movement. The sanctity of concepts such as family and marriage, their centrality within the socio-religious and economic system, and the multitudinal dimensions of women's oppression are now consistently co-related in the context of dowry. Strategies of the women's movement suggest breaking the equation of dowry with women. This has led to the expansion of the movement's focus from a struggle for women's actual inheritance rights and access to family resources, attitudinal changes through education, consciousness raising, etc., to immediate measures such as legal, administrative and social aid. Dowry as a critical complex of factors was sought to be fully appreciated in order to ensure a sustained movement against it. Krishnaraj (1988: 88) thus aptly writes that 'unless we come closer to an explanation of the origin of women's subordination and the social mechanism through which it is perpetuated, new strategies may fail'. This brings us to investigate how the state perceived the problem of dowry and what strategies did it employ to combat its practice and expansion.

NOTES

1. For example, see works of Colebrooke (1805) and Max Muller (1823-1900).
2. The idealized notion of 'great' or 'superior' Indian women was often propagated through regional newspapers and journals. For an interesting exposition of this fabricated, and in most cases ambivalent, stand on women's question, see the voluminous 'Special Issue on Women' in the Hindi journal *Kalyan* which was first collated in 1948 and has since then already been reproduced four times in its original version. It presents the glorification of patriarchal order in which the sufferings and hard work of women since the 'golden' ancient days to appease men either as husband, father, or son have been exemplified as exalted virtues.
3. The women's movement thus presented an ideology and programme which, firstly, emphasized women's upliftment through education and removal of certain traditional practices, and, secondly, espoused the theme of equal rights in all spheres with men. The first was linked to the revival of Indian glory with the restoration of the ideals of womanhood through education and

participation in public life. Equal rights was the main goal expressed in the AIWC presidential addresses in 1932-51 period. See Everett (1981) for details.

4. Beginning with the movement for education for women in the early nineteenth century (first started by the Atmiya Sabha founded by Raja Rammohun Roy in Bengal in 1815) and the abolition of *satī*, the early reform campaigns were largely the work of an 'eagerly developing intelligentsia imbued with English education and western ideas of rationalism, evolutionism and utilitarianism' (Kumar 1993: 8). On the other hand, according to Vina Mazumdar (1976a: 47-8), the impact of Western education has been overrated. Its benefits reached only a few. Products of the English education, in fact, included the detractors as well as reformers. Often, the most dedicated reformers had little or no connection with Western education, e.g. Ishwar Chandra Vidyasagar (1820-91), Mahatma Jyoti Rao Phule (1827-90), and Lokahitawadi Gopal Hari Deshmukh (1823-92).
5. Ten years had been recognized as the age of consent for all girls since the adoption of Indian Penal Code in 1860.
6. Prior to this at the instance of Mritunjay Vidyalankara, the chief Pandit of the Supreme Court, that *sati* had no *shāstric* sanction, Bentinck had prohibited it in Bengal in 1818. Thereafter, as a result of the protests from the orthodox Hindus in Calcutta, an Amendment in 1840s to distinguish between 'voluntary' and forcible *satī*, and permitting the act if voluntary (Sangari and Vaid 1989: 16).
7. For a detailed discussion see Omvedt 1976 and 1987; Everett 1981; Mazumdar 1976a; Jayawardena 1986; Liddle and Joshi 1989.
8. For example, three offshoots of the Brahmo Samaj were the Brahmika Samaj (1865), which imparted teaching of Brahmo religion, handicrafts and social skills; the Arya Nari Samaj (1878) stressed upon the ancient Hindu ideals of womanhood, and the Banga Mahila Samaj emphasized women's education and interaction with men. During the Swadeshi period (1904-11), more women's organizations sprang mostly from the Brahmo community. They took care not to be 'inconsistent with religion and the social system'. Yet, upto the first decade of the twentieth century no organized radical onslaught on patriarchal bases of Indian culture is discernible. Instead the emphasis was placed on complementary roles of men and women. It was elitist and reflected the 'male-dominated' ideology (Everett 1981: 53-64).
9. In 1882, for instance, a Mahila Samaj at Poona was founded by Pandita Ramabai which was followed by another in Bombay. Rameshwari Nehru organized a 'Kumari Sabha' in Allahabad to mobilize young girls to political activity. In 1886, Swarnakumari

Devi formed the 'Sakhi Samiti' with the aim to raise consciousness among women. It organized annual handicraft *mela* and also trained widows to become self-reliant. Ramabai Ranade's Hindu Ladies Social and Literary Club was started in 1902. Besides this, numerous women's journals also appeared in the first decade of the twentieth century especially in Calcutta, Madras, Mysore, Allahabad and cities of Gujarat (Basu 1976: 22; Chakraborty 1963: 127-8). Another notable organization was the Bharat Stree Mahamandal (1910) founded by Sarla Devi Chaudharani with branches in Calcutta, Allahabad, and other cities (Everett 1981: 68).

10. The ambit of the WIA included women's suffrage rights and educational and social reforms. It organized orphanages, rescue home, montessori school and published a journal entitled the *Stri Dharma*. Everett (1981: 72) provides the full description of its aims and achievements. The NCWI (1928-9) supported the Child Marriage Restraint Bill and the organization of rescue homes. It also emphasized increased women's representation in government bodies. The AIWC began as an educational and social conference. By 1932, its numerous sub-committees had begun to campaign for literacy, rural reconstruction, labour, indigenous industries, harijan welfare, etc. The issues of birth control and contraception were supported in the thirties. By 1930s, there were 137 branches of AIWC as listed in 1934-5 proceedings (Sharma 1981: 107-23). For a comprehensive description of the roles, aims and achievements of the AIWC see Basu and Ray (1990).
11. See the resolutions to the first AIWC conference at Poona and other subsequent recommendation in the AIWC conferences. For the detail description of women's demands, also see Basu and Ray (1990).
12. See the Indian Women's Charter of Rights and Duties (1946) formulated by AIWC in Basu and Ray (1990: 47-52). On the question of the equal rights for women, Everett comments that 'an equal right perspective had emerged as the dominant women's movement ideology since the 1930s' which infused all their demands for education, changes in legislation regarding marriage and inheritance' (Everett 1981: 180).
13. See Mies (1980: 121); Liddle and Joshi (1985 and 1989: 38)
14. See for example reports of the AIWC Presidents in Everett (1981: 83).
15. For example, the issue was first raised at the All India Women's Social Conference held, in conjunction with the meeting of Indian National Congress, at Calcutta in 1928. Then the chairperson, Her Highness the Junior Maharani of Travancore attacked the

'humiliating custom of dowry' among other problems affecting women. Similarly, after the Sarda Act 1929, the Fourth AIWC held in Bombay in 1930 sought to secure new legislation against the practice of dowry through protest meetings and propaganda (Forbes 1984: 36-8). It was also taken up by Mrs. Nazir Hussain at Madras in 1932. She pointed out that 'the most essential and the most difficult thing to settle in a marriage is the question of dowry and not the personal qualities of the girl. . . . It is a great pity that even educated people have not yet done away with this pernicious practice' making a girl's marriage an 'intolerable burden' (Basu and Ray 1990: 95).

16. See also *Stree Darpan* September 1928 (3).
17. More than six decades later, the impact of education on the escalation of dowry demands remains the same. In *Towards Equality* (1974: 74), the Committee on the Status of Women in India stated that 'it is disconcerting to find that education has hardly had any liberalizing influence on the minds of the people in respect of dowry. On the contrary, education increased dowry both in rural as well as in urban areas'. Also, 'the educated youth is grossly insensitive to the evil and unashamedly contributes to its perpetuation' (ibid: 115).
18. The groom-to-be (a lawyer) was demanding Rs. 2000 as dowry. Her father had no option but to meet the demand by mortgaging his house. Snehlata could not bear to see this and burnt herself to death.
19. *Stree Darpan* [October 1928 (4)] also highlights another case of suicide by Veenapani Devi who was Matric pass.
20. For example, caste Sabhas like the Vaishya Mahasabha, Kanaujia Brahman Sabha, Vishwakarma Brahman Mahasabha including Lohars, babarchis, Beldars, etc., advocated decreased expenditure in marriages (Turner 1933: 551).
21. Mathur Kayasthas appear as a shinning example of a north Indian community not practicing dowry in the CSWI report (TE 1974: 75) published six decades later.
22. *Shobhana*, a periodical published from Midnapore in Bengal in the early twentieth century exhorted the youth to fight against dowry and other evils in order to bring about healthy changes in the society. *Gambhira*, another periodical published from Malda gave an extremely vivid reason for a girl declaring her preference for remaining a spinster rather than marry a man submitting meekly to his father who demanded exorbitant dowry. She also considered performing 'jahabrata', courting death voluntarily or waiting till a rationally disposed man offered for her hand in marriage. The *Gourprabha*, a paper published from Howrah in 1925 made frantic

appeal to the youth to take a vow against dowry (Bhaumik 1986: 393-5).

23. The Hindu Missionary Society was formed in Bombay in 1830s to readmit Hindu converts to Christianity or Islam.
24. According to Desai and Patel, the rise of the autonomous women's groups has been a singularly important achievement of the 1970s and 1980s. These groups, as they write, 'have been fighting for women's issues . . . by articulating the roots of women's oppression. . . . The leadership of the present women's movement is in the hands of the young, dedicated, courageous and theoretically oriented, educated middle class women, some of them have opted out of mass based organizations because their experience showed that though such organizations were sensitive to the problems of poor, denounced casteism and communalism, talked of fighting oppression and exploitation of the toiling masses, but were totally insensitive to the oppression of women and were perpetuating patriarchal norms and forms in both the political and the personal spheres' (Desai and Patel 1985: 62-5).
25. Most women activists and scholars, however, feel that the rise in numbers of dowry related death or suicide does not reflect the actual rate of increase as a substantial number of cases go unreported. Govind Kelkar surmises that a figure of nearly one death a day in Delhi can be ascertained (Kelkar 1985: 1).
26. Prior to this, first protests in the contemporary women's movement were by the POW of Hyderabad in 1975. About 2000 people took part, but it did not develop into a full-fledged campaign (Kumar 1993: 117).
27. Similar protest movements against dowry deaths accompanied by pressure for legislative changes, memorandum, etc., were reported in *Manushi* [May-June 1980 (5)]. Since then the journal *Manushi* has regularly recorded incidents of dowry harassment in its issues.
28. For example, the well publicized case of Kanchan Chopra. See Kumar (1993: 120) for detailed description.
29. Debjani Bhaumik's (Calcutta, 1983) case, among others.
30. Nivedita Dutta (Arora's case of June 1982, in Kumar 1993: 123).
31. Protest outside the house of the prospective groom making demands or of the man charged with his wife's murder for dowry (Manjushree Sharda's in Pune in 1982). The aim was to humiliate and ostracize the culprits, i.e. the husband's family (Bharati Narula's case, 1982, in Kumar 1993: 122) to mobilize public support and raise consciousness against such acts and for social boycott of the family in a sustained manner. Seminars, debates, plays and competitions were other means employed to raise public consciousness.

32. See Das [*Manushi* 1979 (3): 15-16], for Premlata's case.
33. Particularly the Stree Sangharsh's Om-Swaha, anti-dowry street play performed by Delhi University students in the village where an university employee's daughter had been killed (Madhuri et al. 1983: 1-9).
34. For example, the Anti-Dowry Cell in New Delhi in 1983.
35. See, the Ahmedabad Women's Action Group Report 1986.
36. It is equally notable that the resolutions adopted unanimously as an outcome of the major conferences of women's studies always included the condemnation of dowry. The IInd National Conference on Women's Studies held in Trivandrum on 9-12 April 1984 by the Indian Association for Women's Studies resolved that: The number of dowry deaths and atrocities on women are increasing and taking a serious form in recent years. Women's organizations all over India have been struggling against it jointly in various forms like mobilising public opinion, demonstrations, deputations, courting arrests, etc., to bring about change in the laws concerning women. As a result of this a Joint Select Committee of Parliament must be formed to look into the matter and suggest amendments to the existing law.

    The Committee put forward its report before the Parliament in August 1982 but the Government failed to bring it for discussion, despite the pressure from the joint forum of women's organizations at various levels.

    The IInd National Conference on Women's Studies condemned the delay in bringing forth the legislation, and urged the government to take immediate steps to pass needed amendments to the Dowry Prohibition Act.

    A panel discussion was held on 'Dowry and Bride Price' in Vth NCWS organized in Calcutta in January 1991. It discussed the significance of these concepts in different contexts, and analysed how both change their character in the process of economic development. For instance with increasing commercialization and increase of male income, dowry becomes a major issue. On the other hand, in a labour scarce situation, bride-price becomes a way of enslaving women as unpaid labor.

    The panel traced the roots of women's economic deprivation and exploitation to the obsessive significance given to the institution of marriage. The restrictions on women's access to employment and productive assets dictate that marriage alone can possibly provide women with a secure and comfortable life—a carefully constructed patriarchal myth that has to be shattered by the women's movement.

37. For example see Kishwar 1989; 1989a; 1989b; 1989c; 1989d; 1989e. A nimber of newspapers also carried out comments and friendly debares on Kishwar's articles. See for instance, *Sunday Observer* (25 Dec. 1988); *Sunday Free Press Journal* (29 Jan. 1989); *Indian Express* (15 Jan. 1989), *Mass Line* (March 1989).

CHAPTER FIVE

Dowry and the State: The Nature of Anti-Dowry Legislation

No discussion of dowry and its manifold dimensions is fully comprehensible without bringing into focus the role of the state and its law. The state, conceived as a normative order, symbolizes and represents rules and laws. The legal order and political beliefs are the basic determinants of the state apparatus. One of the major characteristics of the modern state is thus its greater trust in law to effect social changes. 'The task of social reconstruction, development and nation building all call for major changes in the social order, to achieve which legislation is one of the main instruments. It can act directly, as a norm setter, or indirectly, providing institution which accelerate social change by making it more acceptable' (TE 1974: 102).

The gender implications of the role of the state are diverse and complex and yet to be fully ascertained. It is evident that the ideology of patriarchy permeates most policies of the modern state and affects adversely a woman's access to resources, her earnings and her work. It is reflected as well as reinforced and reinterpreted in varying intensities by the institutions through which the state operates, i.e. the family, media, and the community on the one hand, and legal, educational, cultural and religious institutions on the other. The state, the community and the household are thus, as Bina Agarwal asserts, interacting structures 'dominated by patriarchal interests and typically, the contradictions as they have played themselves out, have tended to work to the detriment of women' (Agarwal 1988a: 2). If these institutions can be seen as determinants of interest and power of the political actors, a study of state legislation in the context of dowry facilitates not only a comprehension of the state's perception on dowry but also the nature of constraints imposed from above and its viability in curbing the practice of dowry. This chapter is thus concerned with state legislation with respect to dowry during the colonial and post-colonial periods.

The potential of law to create awareness, facilitate social change, and assist in the struggle against women's oppression and dowry in particular, can hardly be questioned. Since ancient times, dowry or marriage payment has been a source of consternation for the state. Manu, the first law maker, condemned receiving or demanding any payment or price for marriage. Payment, only as an act of voluntary gift-giving accompanying the ritual of *kanyādāna* was approved of. The medieval state, as is evident from the scant references available, attempted from time to time to curb exorbitant demands for payment of dowry. The number of legal enactments that followed the struggle for reform from the late nineteenth to the late twentieth centuries manifest colonial and post-colonial state's concern for the problem of dowry. The modern state, moreover, in theory, views men and women as equals, and aims at securing a just political, social, and economic order. The Indian Constitution, for example, grants all citizens equal rights. Its Preamble underscores equality of status and opportunity, and aims for social, economic and political justice for all.[1]

Yet, to the extent that the colonial and post-colonial state's concerns with the problem of dowry eventuated from its patriarchal structure and ideology, its legal enactments and enforcement programmes and policies were cast within the latter mould only and served to preserve the patriarchal social order. This is evident in the Assembly/Parliamentary Debates preceding the Hindu Code Bill of the mid-1930s and the Dowry Prohibition Act from mid-1950s onwards. Dowry, as discussed in earlier chapters, is an expression of the subordinate position of women within the family and its structural components. It relates to the relationship of women and men in the context of their respective rights in the family in terms of marriage, property, access to household resources, etc. That such concerns were integral to dowry is revealed in the focus on these issues in the intensive parliamentary debates preceding the above legislative measures. The proposals in the bills which sought to radically transform the status quo were, however, vehemently opposed in the name of stability within the society and the family. The nature of the opposition to the provision of equal property rights for women in the Hindu Code Bill as well as the Dowry Prohibition Acts by political leaders reveals ambivalence and inherent contradictions within the governmental attitudes regarding women's status. Both the Debates amply demonstrate the reservations as well as the intellectual processes that underline the structure of the modern Indian state and society.

It is thus necessary to recapitulate the Debates in the context of the changes proposed, opinions expressed, reasons forwarded and the consequent enactment of the two major state legislations, the Hindu Code Bill and the Dowry Prohibition Act, 1961, both of which were aimed at the empowerment of women and had direct bearings on dowry. In the larger framework, these state legislations raise questions such as: Has the law served as a vehicle of great social transformation? Or, is it only a means to divert and disperse public attention from a particular issue? Can a stricter dowry legislation bring about abolition of the practice? Has the aim of the law to alter and improve women's status achieved success? Is the law against dowry based on an understanding of the system in all its multi-dimensions—social, political and economic? In the above context, the present chapter focuses first on the Hindu Code Bill, only insofar as its provisions for property rights to women which can be linked to marriage and dowry, and secondly, on the Dowry Prohibition Act.

The Hindu Code Bill

The Hindu Code Bill, which was introduced for discussion between 1930s and 1940s, was the first major attempt to reform and codify Hindu Personal Law. Prior to that and till 1864, some temporal but highly consequential efforts were made by the British to reform Hindu personal laws through selective promulgation of Acts.[2] These social legislations, however, did not concern themselves with the 'basics' of Hindu personal law but only its outward distortions and as such opposition for these on the whole remained limited to some castes in some pockets only. Even then, as discussed in chapter three, these were introduced after gaining *shastric* sanctions. The Revolt of 1857, however, dampened the British zeal to interfere in personal laws as large-scale opposition from the population was feared. It was only when anglicized liberal Indian lawyers as well as modern social reformers—both men and women, campaigned for extending the process of codification, which had earlier begun with criminal and commercial laws, to Hindu personal laws that the British entertained a long lasting discussion leading ultimately to the piecemeal introduction of several social legislations during 1950s.

Two of the major features of the Hindu Code Bill had crucial bearings on the problem of dowry. These dealt with intestate succession and marriage and sought to provide equal rights of property to women. The state viewed that such rights would improve women's status and effectively curtail the growing menace of 'social evils' like dowry. We have discussed earlier that as determinants of power and sphere of control, both property and inheritance rights constitute part of the structural framework of institutions that govern gender relations. Most ancient treatises contain vast exposition of property rights in general and of women in particular. The imperatives of a patrilineal order, however, limited women's rights in property to rights over her *strīdhana* as well as gifts given at the time of marriage. If unmarried, a woman had the right to maintenance.[3] It is important to note that even in modern times *strīdhana* or women's property consisting of gifts given at the time of marriage constitutes women's property rights. Property for women is thus even now linked to her marriage despite the constitutional dictum of equal rights for men and women in all aspects. Why is there a need to uphold the notion of a separate property for women? In the changed circumstances of present times, the upkeep of *strīdhana* as women's separate property appears redundant and with little justification. The reformulations and rearticulations of tradition and beliefs that these Acts upheld ultimately has had far-reaching consequences on the institution of modern dowry.

The demand for a uniform codification of Hindu personal laws was voiced by women's groups in the 1930s and was pursued in a sustained manner till the enactment of the Hindu Code Bill. Its needs as well as some of its proposals had been a matter of discussion for several years. For example, in the 1920s, the Western educated Indian lawyers expressed interest in the state's codification of Hindu Law, but while some wanted to reform the law, others desired mere rationalization. About the same time, a group of members of the Central Legislative Assembly too mobilized the issue of Hindu women's rights through a number of bills. This included persons like H.S. Gour, H.B. Sarda and G.V. Deshmukh among others. However, the opposition to these steps ranged from the bills going 'too far', or as being unrepresentative of the public opinion. It was believed that such issues would create dissensions whereas unity was required to ward off the colonial rule (Everett 1981: 145).

Confronted thus, the Central Legislative Assembly provided through the Hindu Women's Right to Property Act, 1937, life interest in husband's property to the Hindu widow and a share equal to the son's without the right to alienate it. It took the state eight years to move the Bill through the legislature. Even then, it opted for this less offensive position to appease the orthodox elements and supported the Bill only when it was confined to the Hindu widow and excluded the daughter or any other female heir. Moreover, its application was limited only to non-agricultural land as the agricultural land lay under the jurisdiction of provincial legislatures (ibid: 152). This Act of 1937, as Ambedkar pointed out, was significant in the sense that it made inroads necessary for the later enactment of the Hindu Code Bill (The Hindu Code Debates (CAI 1948): 3650). The opposition to the Act's provision is vital too as it facilitates comprehension of sentiments and attitudes of political actors involved in legislation.

In the light of the Act of 1937, the first move to consider women's inheritance rights was made by constituting an expert committee in January 1941 under B.N. Rau, a leading lawyer. This committee recommended codification of Hindu law and an increase in women's legal rights in marriage and succession. The committee was, however, reconstituted by the government in January 1944. In its Report a draft Hindu Code was published advocating provisions in consistence with the Constituent Assembly's Declaration of Fundamental Rights. Widows were to receive a share equal to that of a son in the husband's property while the daughter was to be entitled to half a son's share. While women's organisations pointed to the lack of equal inheritance and equal right for both sons and daughters, a favourable response was received from some leaders of the Congress party, legal reformers as well as government officials (Rao 1948: 75).

At the same time, serious objections were raised in the Constituent Assembly to the question of equality in property.[4] D.N. Mitter asserted that 'Only a microscopic minority . . . favour codification (Hindu Law Committee Report 1947: 113 in Everett 1981: 157). Members expressed their doubts about the ability of Hindu women to manage property. They also added that a daughter in a Hindu household enjoyed preferential treatment because she was an object of worship. So the question of discrimination did not arise. They criticized educated Hindu women clamouring for such reforms as 'social butterflies'.[5] Members also warned that the proposed code would destroy the integrity of the Hindu family through the fragmentation of family assets (ibid: 165; Kumar 1993).

These reactions appear in sharp contrast to the ease with which ideas of political and economic equality of the sexes were accepted as Constitutional provisions. There was no voice of dissent when the chapter on Fundamental Rights was written, providing men and women with equal status. But, while all members accepted in principle the concept of equality at the time of framing of the Constitution, many found the logical consequences of the extension of equality to property inconvenient. This is evident in the dissent expressed in the debates relating to the Hindu Code Bill. In 1948, Renuka Ray, a Constituent Assembly member, urged for a 'explicit proviso' in the Constitution to prohibit discriminatory marriage and inheritance laws. However, the Assembly did not act on this, for fear of hurting religious sensibilities made the leadership hesitant in pursuing the concept of equality in the spheres of marriage and inheritance (Everett 1981: 162). This is reminiscent of the British government's unwillingness to interfere with the socio-religious structure of the society for fear of destabilizing the empire.

The issue of equal inheritance and marriage laws took centre-stage in the decade immediately following Independence. The Hindu Code Bill acquired more radical dimensions under B.R. Ambedkar, then the Law Minister. On 9 April 1948 a revised Hindu Code was introduced in the Constituent Assembly (Legislative). Its main provisions regarding women's right to property and inheritance consisted of the following changes (CAI (Legislative) 9 April 1948: 3629-31].[6] (1) The proposed law of inheritance deferred the *Mitākshara* coparcenary and adopted the *Dāyabhāga* rule which accorded absolute ownership rights to the heir, male or female. (2) Succession was to be based on blood relationship to the deceased rather than on cognatic or agnatic relationship. (3) The widow of a deceased Hindu, the daughter and the widow of a pre-deceased son were to be accorded the same rank as a son in the matter of inheritance. The daughter was to be provided half of the son's share in parental property. (4) A larger number of female heirs were introduced than either under the *Dāyabhāga* or the *Mitākshara.* (5) Abolition of all conditionalities in the inheritance of female heirs in practice earlier such as their marital or economic status. They were to inherit by virtue of being heirs.

Besides the above, the Bill also proposed significant changes in the intestate succession to female property, i.e. *strīdhana* and 'Women's Estate'. It aimed, as Ambedkar pointed out, at consolidating the different categories of *strīdhana* into one category governable by one rule of succession. A son was to be entitled to half of a daughter's share in the *strīdhana*. The 'Women's Estate'[7] was to be converted to *strīdhana*, and from 'limited estate' to an 'absolute' one. After the widow's death, it was no longer to be claimed by the reversioners of her deceased husband.

The Bill also made a special reference to the property given at the time of marriage to the daughter as dowry. This property or amount was to be treated as 'trust property' to be claimed and used by the girl on reaching the age of eighteen years. This would prevent her husband or his relations to use or appropriate it 'leaving her helpless for the rest of her life'. This line of thought, as expressed by Ambedkar, reconfirmed linkages between property transfer and marriage as well as the importance of such a transfer in a girl's life. Its rearticulation at different points of history is significant for the comprehension of the issue of dowry.

Besides inheritance, the Bill legitimized civil marriage in addition to sacramental marriage. It also recognized a marriage as valid irrespective of the caste or the sub-caste of the parties entering into the relationship. In addition, it contained significant provisions for maintenance, adoption, divorce and prescribed monogamy.

Such far-reaching changes suggested in the normative structure of the society expectedly drew sharp criticism from the members of the Constituent Assembly. The debates that preceded the handing over of the Bill to a Select Committee for revision on 9 April 1948 manifest this. After the Law Minister had introduced the Bill, the provisions relating to property rights for women were subjected to intense condemnation.

The members' censure of the Bill ranged from criticism of its potential to destroy the religious structure of the Hindus to the 'sheer impracticabilty' of giving a share to the daughter in immovable property. B. Pattabhi Sitaramayya, for example, pointed out that 'when 80% of pattadars are able to pay only Rs. 10 as tax on 2.5 acres of wet land or 4-5 acres of dry land, where on earth is there a chance for them to give a share to the daughter, which she can carry with her or which she can enjoy' (CAI: 3636). However, interestingly, the member approved of the provision which gave sons a share in *strīdhana* as it 'equalises things' for those who were concerned about 'depriving all the sons of the share to which they are legitimately entitled if the daughter also comes in for her share'.

For some members, the proposed legislation would not curb but precipitate dowry demands. Rohini Kumar Choudhuri, a member from Assam, therefore suggested that the Bill be subjected to 'serious consideration' (CAI: 3649-50). According to him, people would now look for propertied girls for their sons. As a result, the ordinary person who could provide for her marriage by mortgaging his property would not be sought after. The rich who could give dowry and their daughters who inherited property could easily find a suitable match.

This line of argument finds expression in the 1980s too as is evident from the Report of the Joint Committee of the Houses (1982). In its evaluation of dowry and the Dowry Prohibition Act of 1961, the report termed dowry as an 'unintentional' contribution of the Hindu Succession Act, 1956 (in Diwan 1987: 312-13) as the groom's family often insisted on the bride's share in patrimony to be given at the time of marriage. A continuity in the beliefs and attitudes of the state's law-makers can be perceived here. The empowerment of a daughter through property was viewed as defeating the very purpose of the Bill.

There was even a communal reaction to the Bill, contained in the 'Volume of Opinion' section in the Report of the Hindu Law Community which was brought to the notice of the House by Naziruddin Ahmad, a member from West Bengal. The Report mentioned that 'the principles of the Bill are opposed by the entire Hindu community' (CAI: 3640). It also expressed apprehension about the Bill being considered by 'a mixed legislature consisting of members of various communities,' thus dismantling 'the very structure, the very religious basis, and the very religious structure of the Hindus' in one 'sweeping stroke'. The provision seeking to grant share in property to women would lead to excessive fragmentation and destruction of the joint family system as had happened in the case of the Muslims. Moreover, it was alleged that the Bill represented the view of only the 'educated' and the 'ultra-modern section' of the population and not that of the common masses (CAI: 3642).

The Bill's provision for equal property rights for daughters and sons was considered by some agitated members as promoting discrimination against men. Ram Sahai of Gwalior State strongly opined that the Bill would bring about 'the reversal of justice' and the discrimination against men in future with women inheriting from their patrimony as well as from their marital families. A husband, moreover, could not lay his hand on his wife's inherited property—as that was her *strīdhana* over which she had complete control. Men would thus be losers if women's equal property rights were made a reality. The member cautioned the Law Minister to be realistic and not be guided by the Western culture or any other such 'excitement' (CAI: 3647). Instead, he urged the Minister to follow 'the fundamental principles' propounded in the ancient Dharmashāstras and thus retain the basis of Hindu traditions.

In the face of such opposition, the unmitigated support by two women members of the House must have been especially welcomed by the Minister. Both Hansa Mehta of Bombay and Begum Aizaz Rasul of Uttar Pradesh supported the Bill and its provisions wholeheartedly. Hansa Mehta called it a 'great landmark in the social history of the Hindus'(CAI: 3642). She urged that as the new Constitution was to be based on the fundamental principles of equality to all individuals, the daughter must also be given an equal share with the son in the patrimony and in the property of the mother. Sons too forced the division of property and thus the argument that the daughter's share in the landed property would bring about more fragmentation was untenable. The member even suggested some measures to prevent fragmentation of land (CAI: 3643).[8] Begum Aizaz Rasul similarly implored 'courageous minds' to combat the orthodox opinion and make the provisions of the Bill a reality (CAI: 3648).

Ambedkar strongly defended the provisions of the Bill as being 'in perfect consonance with the conscience of the community' (CAI: 3653). It was aimed, he asserted, at the revolutionary overthrow of the structure of the Hindu society. Yet, one can discern some reservations on the part of Ambedkar himself regarding the impending changes. For example, he justified the provision of a share for the son in the *strīdhana* by remarking that:

> members will realise that in formulating this Bill and making changes in rules of succession, it is provided that while the daughter is getting half the share in the father's property, the son is also getting half the share in the mother's property so that in a certain sense the Bill seeks to maintain an equality of position between the son and the daughter'. (CAI: 3630)

Similarly, when a member suggested the implementation of the provision regarding the 'absolute estate' of the widow with retrospective effect, Ambedkar did not agree. He apprehended that it would disturb the earlier 'vested rights' created in that estate before the enforcement of the Bill, and 'it would not be right and proper to divert them however much our sympathy may be with the widow' (CAI: 3652). Expressing his reservations about drastic radical changes, Ambedkar similarly defended the exclusion of agricultural land from the purview of the Bill and the consequent partial nature of codification. He observed that there was 'no necessity that a uniform law of inheritance should apply to all sorts of property' (even though he supported a uniform law of inheritance). Property, he said,

> varies in its nature, varies in its importance in the social life of the community and consequently it may be a matter of no mean advantage for society to have one set of law of inheritance for agricultural property and another set of law for non-agricultural property. It may be that on a better consideration of the situation, Indian or Hindu society may come to the conclusion that land which is the foundation of its economic life had better be governed by the law of primogeniture so that neither the junior sons nor females may take part in the inheritance. (CAI: 3651)

Notwithstanding the above reservations, some of the favourable suggestions in regard to women's inheritance rights were incorporated in the Report of the Select Committee[9] submitted in August 1948. It provided for (*i*) transformation of *Mitākshara* coparcenaries into tenancies in common; (*ii*) extension of uniform succession laws to areas of South India previously unaffected; (*iii*) fixing of a daughter's share as equal to a son's share; (*iv*) determination of order of succession based on 'natural love and affection' (in Everett 1981: 171). Immediately thereafter, seven members of the Select Committee itself dissented and called for the postponement of the issue till the general election of 1952. Their major objections particularly pertained to the abolition of coparcenaries giving equal shares to daughters as well as discarding of religious directive in the succession principle. The Congress leadership remained divided on the issue with several prominent members opposed to the provisions of the Bill. These included Rajendra Prasad, V.B. Patel, B. Pattabhi Sitaramayya, Purushottamdas Tandon, Pt. Madan Mohan Malviya, and S.P. Mukherjee to mention a few. Ambedkar poignantly remarked:

> My ideals are derived from the Constitution we have laid down. The very Preamble to our Constitution speaks of liberty, equality and fraternity. We are, therefore bound to examine every social institution that exists in this

country, whether that institution satisfies the principles laid down in the Constitution (cited in Ahir 1990: 134).[10]

Supporters of the Bill such as Renuka Ray, Sucheta Kripalani and Durgabai however insisted that political, economic and social equality were synonymous and were meaningless in isolation. They respectively drew attention to the 'Declaration of Fundamental Rights' and the principles of equality embodied in the Constitution. The Bill was recirculated and reconsidered during 1949-51. But, in spite of the incorporation of suggestions regarding the reintroduction of *Mitākshara* joint family among other measures, the Bill failed to appease the orthodox groups and was finally dropped by the Government on 26 September 1951. Ambedkar resigned in protest. The Bill was passed only in a piecemeal fashion after a few years with its radical edges rounded off to render it less offensive to its opponents. The half-hearted approach revealed the patriarchal state's compulsions, ambivalence and the lack of will to make social justice a reality.

It is undoubtedly only hypothetical to suggest that the acceptance and passage of equal inheritance rights code in itself would have brought about gender equality and social justice. The Bill, even though referred to as the 'Hindu Women's Code' by one of the members of the Constituent Assembly, did not lead to an in-depth study of, and consequent necessary measures for women's rights. *Towards Equality* (TE) observes that 'the hold of tradition, however, was so strong that even while introducing sweeping changes, the legislators compromised and retained in some respects the inferior position of women' (1974: 135). It would have been quite 'feasible' at that time 'to abolish the ancient legal formula of acquisition of rights by birth and devolution by survivorship' and bring about uniformity in the law in all parts of India (Mulla 1960: 916 in TE: 136). The Select Committee had suggested abolition of the right by birth while amending the Code Bill but this was compromised with in the final Act. In addition, the devolution of tenancy right was excluded from the scope of the Act and the rules relating to it in the state legislation were protected [Sec. 4 (2)]. The daughter was also denied a share in the dwelling house, and only a right of residence to the unmarried or in-distress daughter was provided for. Powers of testation were also kept unlimited (TE 1974: 138).[11] The Law Minister, Pataskar, confidently expressed faith in the security of the family system and on familial relationships based on love and affection. He said that 'I believe that a normal father will never do any such thing [as deprive a daughter of her rights due to his unlimited power of testation], and if at all he has to do it for any reason, he will surely make a provision for his daughter when he is going to deprive her of her share by will' (The Fifth Lok Sabha Debates 1955: 8379). Such simplistic assumptions obfuscate the harsh reality of circumventing of female succession through the powers vested in the head of the family. The widows of Benaras deprived of all familial support stand testimony to this (TE 1974: 138).

The orthodox opinion was thus placated and compromised with through the support of a set-up which upheld unequal sharing of power based on property and which sustained the virtue of a submissive and dependent woman.[12] As Lotika Sarkar observed 'The volte face (on the part of those who had supported equal rights in the constitution) is understandable; lip service to the concept of equality was one thing, its implementation was another' (1976: 92). Female inheritance rights were the real object of attack as these rights in property provide the basis on which intra-household power structure rested. The state was not ready to go far enough. Instead, it chose to accommodate the Hindu coparcenary of the *Mitākshara* which applied to male family members only while declaring in principle equal inheritance for men and women and simultaneously upholding *strīdhana* as a separate property for women. The patriarchal ideology of law thus remained largely unchanged.

Linkages between these attempts at change and the previous efforts undertaken during the late nineteenth and early twentieth centuries can be discerned. The earlier social reformers, not unlike the present ones, too hesitated to bring about structural reforms in family and society. The reform movement of the late nineteenth century, as M.G. Ranade expressed, was to be carried out in the great Hindu tradition of reform—which always sought out ancient principles in order to restate them (Heimsath 1964:184). The reformist efforts by such associations as the Brahmo Samaj and the Prarthna Samaj, and the revivalist campaigns initiated by the Arya Samaj and the Ramakrishna Mission were also directed by similar motives (Mazumdar 1976a: 43). The colonial state too began to block reform measures to appease communal reaction as soon as it apprehended threat to its stability.[13] Likewise, the Hindu Succession Act, as it was finally passed in 1956, ushered in significant changes yet, at the same time, reinforced and reformulated the traditional attitudes and beliefs regarding patriliny and inheritance for women. Its express purpose of providing for equal rights in inheritance in accordance with the Constitutional guarantee of non-discrimination between sexes before the law was achieved only in a limited way.

The Dowry Prohibition Act, 1961

The Dowry Prohibition Act of 1961 too symbolizes the failure of the state, as is evident in its dithering on the Hindu Code Bill, to bring about transformation in women's status. As noted earlier, the obdurate attitude of the state regarding women's rights witnessed further expansion of the practice of dowry in post-Independence Indian society. The Act, promulgated as an acknowledgement of dowry as a major social evil, was an attempt to deal with the problem separately from other issues pertaining to women.

The lack of the state's commitment to the principle of equal inheritance rights for women provides, to a large extent, the contextual background and perspective for the problem of dowry. The most notable and perceptible effort in this respect, as we shall see, is to strengthen women's *strīdhana* as her property through dowry. Even in the modern context, in upholding the concept of *strīdhana* as an integral part of the patrilineal system, the state's approach and objectives have been largely to leave it undisturbed. It thereby assumes that a woman loses the membership of her parental family after marriage. It reiterates the traditional linkages of property, patriliny and marriage. The inherent contradiction in the state's posture is thus evident. It, on the one hand, seeks to dispense equal inheritance rights—although limited in scope, and on the other, it promotes the concept of *strīdhana* as a separate property. This concept was central to the arguments that favoured gift-giving to the bride at the time of marriage in debates in the Lok Sabha preceding the Dowry Prohibition Act of 1961.

These debates divulge disparate opinions on dowry—its definition, nature, and remedial measures. The consensus was on abolition of the 'social evil which we have to fight in the name of transforming our society' (LSD 1959: 4436). Speeches of the Members of Parliament manifest that dowry was an all-pervasive phenomenon. The scenario appears similar to the one seen now three and a half decades later, that speaks of spate of suicides, last minute dowry demands resulting in cancellation of a marriage, the trauma faced by the bride and her parents in not being able to fulfil demands, and above all the imperative of arranging a marriage of a girl at all costs.

(a) *The Historical Background to the Dowry Prohibition Act*

The initial effort to deal with the problem of dowry, as we have indicated above, was the reinforcement of the concept of *strīdhana* as dowry. The historical process of codification of legal enactment on the *strīdhana* began in the 1930s resulting in Hindu women's absolute legal right over it in Baroda through an Act in 1937 and in Mysore through the Hindu Women's Rights Regulation in 1933 (Everett 1981: 146). But such misconceived perception linking dowry exclusively to *strīdhana* were bound to fail from the outset in restricting the growing phenomenon of dowry.

Consequently, the colonial state hesitatingly took the case of dowry separately to curb its practice through legislation. The Sindh Leti Deti Act of 1939 and the impending introduction of a similar act in Bihar in the 1930s were sporadic attempts in this direction. Most of the initial initiatives, however, originated not from the state but the caste councils which passed resolutions against the rampant growth of dowry and consciousness raised against it through the vernacular literature at the local level. They often expressed concern for extravagance in marriage, dowry and its burden on families. For the colonial state and the social reformers of the late nineteenth and early twentieth centuries, the practice of dowry did not perhaps appear as a social evil of dimensions as large as those of *satī*, female infanticide, widow remarriage. It was easier to deal with the latter, which did not touch Hindu society so pervasively and so intimately as dowry. Moreover, as is evident in the statement of objects and reasons for the Act of 1961, the colonial and post-colonial state's lack of attention to the problem of dowry arose from the assumption that changes in marriage and property rights would by themselves curb the evil. It is also probable that the British familiarity with the institution of dowry in their own cultures stilled any outcry against it from the colonial rulers. Despite demands for laws against dowry at the regional level and also at the national level, the colonial state responded only sporadically and the post-colonial state did not promulgate a national Act to put a legislative curb on the practice till 1961.

The Sindh Leti Deti Act, 1939, was the first state measure to contain dowry. It sought to prohibit payments made, or agreed to be made, as a part of the contract of betrothal or marriage in the province of Sindh. The provisions of the Act were not applicable to Muhammadans, Parsis, Christians and Jews. Payment, according to this Act meant

> a payment by or to a parent or any other relation or guardian of such person made or agreed to be made in connection with, or in consequence of, the betrothal or marriage and includes the giving of a gift or present in kind on any festival or auspicious day or on account of the birth of a child or any ceremony in the families of the parents or relations of the bride or bridegroom.

No person was to accept and give, or agree to accept or give, any payment as a part of the contract to any betrothal of marriage. A list of presents, describing their nature and number as well as the occasion, and the giver's name, was to be maintained by a Panchayat, or failing that by the Provincial Government. In the case of the Panchayat, the gifts were to be within Rs. 500 in the first two years, Rs. 50 per year for the next three years and Rs. 25 per year in the years following. Where the list was made by the Provincial Government, the prescribed limit was Rs. 200 for the first two years, Rs. 20 per year for the next three years, and Rs. 10 per year thereafter. The convicted person was to be sentenced for one month imprisonment with/or a fine up to Rs.1000 or the contracted value of the payment. Interestingly, no woman was to be sentenced for dowry-related crimes. An accused woman could dispense with personal appearance in the court. Likewise, in Bihar, another Bill was proposed to abolish large dowries in the mid-thirties (Forbes 1984: 40).

Following Independence, only two states enacted legislation for restraining the taking or giving of dowry in marriage. One was the Bihar Dowry Restraint Act, 1950 and the other was the Andhra Pradesh Dowry Prohibition Act, 1958.[14] The definition of dowry in the Bihar Act was quite elaborate. It meant anything paid or delivered as consideration of a contract of any betrothal or marriage and included: (*i*) *tilak* and *chhenka* where the amount given exceeded Rs. 251; and (*ii*) *dahej* in ceremonies including *dvārapūjā, milan* or *zadrah* exceeding Rs. 251 in cash or kind or both. It however excluded (*i*) *kanyānirakshan* or *mathjhakka,* (*ii*) *stridhana* or any other religious obligations in the Hindu law or any Personal law, and (*iii*) voluntary marriage gifts—ornaments or clothes given after marriage. The punishment of taking dowry was to include imprisonment up to six months with/or a fine up to the value of dowry. The giver and abetter of taking or giving was to be fined Rs. 1000 or a term of one month or both.

The Andhra Pradesh Dowry Prohibition Act, 1958, applied to all persons domiciled or married in Andhra Pradesh except those who followed Muslim law. Here, dowry included any property or valuable security agreed to be given as consideration for any betrothal or marriage before, after or at such marriage. The punishment was not to exceed a six months' prison term or a fine up to Rs. 1000 or both to the giver, abetter, and taker of dowry. A first class Magistrate was to try the offence under the Act on a complaint made within one year of the marriage payment transaction.

These state enactments, according to the Report of the Joint Committee of the Houses (1982), failed to achieve their objectives for two reasons. First, it was difficult to prove cash or property 'as consideration' of marriage and secondly, since the parents of the bride would not come forward to complain, the lack of any agency authorized to initiate action also brought about very few complaints.

(b) *Anti-Dowry Bills in the Parliament*

As incidence of dowry escalated, private members' bills were introduced from time to time in the Parliament and the creation and adoption of a national bill was urged.[15]

The Law Minister assured to prepare a bill on dowry in consultations with the state governments. The proposed bill was however held in abeyance till the enactment of the Hindu Succession Act of 1956 because it was believed that a separate legislation to prohibit dowry would not be required. Yet in view of the persistence of the problem and pressure both at the social and political levels, the Government finally consented to process the legislation against dowry. The Dowry Prohibition Bill, 1959 was introduced in the Lok Sabha on 24 April 1959. Its express objective was to eradicate the evils of the dowry system as existing in several parts of the country. The Statement of Objects and Reasons for the Act also mentioned that 'this problem [of dowry], which is essentially a social one', had been expected to be tackled by the Hindu Succession Act, 1956. The expectations were however short lived. A law was thus required to make the practice punishable and at the same time to ensure that any dowry given was to be for the benefit of the bride. This would go 'a long way to educating public opinion and to the eradication of this evil' [Gazette of India 1959 (II. 2): 397]. In order to make the law 'workable', only gifts worth Rs. 2000 and customary in nature in marriage rituals were to be permitted.

The Bill was referred to a Joint Committee of both Houses of Parliament in September 1959 for examination and report. On 3 December 1959, the 'Bill to prohibit the giving or taking of dowry, as reported by the Joint Committee' was moved in the Parliament. Among the amendments suggested, the most notable pertained to the definition of dowry.

The original Bill favoured a gradual approach and suggested its piecemeal introduction in different states. The Joint Committee however recommended its simultaneous enforcement in all the states (Clause 1). To cover all the plausible act of 'dowry' giving, the phrase 'whether directly or indirectly' was introduced. Changes in the original Bill included more stringent punishment with fine and imprisonment both to be inflicted on the convicted (Clause 3). It was, however, with respect to the definition of dowry in Clause 2 that the Joint Committee proposed the most important modification. In the original Bill, a dowry up to Rs. 2000 and in the form of ornaments, clothes and other articles was 'permissible'. But the Joint Committee removed this exception so that even a payment worth Re. 1 offered in consideration of marriage would become an offence making the accused liable for punishment with both imprisonment and fine.

Consequently, the ensuing debate (hereafter referred as Lok Sabha Debates) on the Bill predominantly focused on the definition of dowry as proposed by the Joint Committee. Most of the legislators vehemently opposed the modification for they viewed dowry as the essential traditional means to provide for a daughter who would otherwise be rendered helpless. Their conviction was that dowry was an evil only if extorted. The final Act of 1961, when approved, thus incorporated as definition of dowry 'any presents made at the time of a marriage to either party to the marriage in the form of cash, ornaments, clothes or other articles, shall not be deemed to be dowry within the meaning of this section, unless they are made as consideration for the marriage of the said parties' (Explanation I). This compromise assumes significance as it explains dowry's continued prevalence and throws light on the pre-dominant popular perception on its meaning. In this context, the Parliamentary Debates preceding the Act of 1961 illuminates our comprehension of dowry within the framework of the state's ideology and its legal enactments. The following section thus analyses the debates in detail as these provide an insight into the justification, aims and objectives of the legislators on this issue. They also help us comprehend the state's cognizance of the problem which in turn influenced the solutions offered.

(c) *The Debates on the Bill Presented Prior to the Dowry Prohibition Act, 1961*

(i) JUSTIFICATIONS FOR THE BILL

The purpose of the legislation to prohibit dowry was spelt out by the then Law Minister, A.K. Sen. He emphasized that 'we are all agreed that the evil should be eradicated wholly by law, nevertheless the law is necessary, if not for anything else, at least for declaring to the whole country the social consciousness of the nation, expressed by the voice of the House. That itself has an effect in weakening the impact and the incidence of the evil.' He further added that:

> No drafting, no device which we may think of here, is going to improve the situation. It is only the consciousness of the evil, armed with the powers granted under the Act, which alone can eradicate the evil altogether. . . . We can only think of introducing such improvement as may be necessary in order, first of all, to understand for ourselves, and for also carrying that understanding to the country as a whole, what the evil is, and how this House sought to tackle it . . . and as an expression of the unanimous will of this House. (XXXVI Lok Sabha Debates 1959: 4009)

Armed with the above formidable purposes, it is not surprising that most of the debates preceding the DPA (1961) in the Lok Sabha, centered around the justification for the bill and definition of dowry. One member even termed it as the 'soul' of the Bill. The understanding of the 'evil' varied and consequently the solutions also differed. That the 'evil' had become all pervasive is reflected in the speeches of the members belonging to different states.

Most of the members in the debate accepted the fact that dowry had pervaded in almost all sections of the society and was no longer limited to only the upper classes or some particular states of the country. They also agreed that the bride and her natal family were being increasingly victimized by the rampant growth of the dowry practice. Narayanankutty Menon of Mukundapuram asserted that 'the giving or taking dowry is taken as a matter of fact in every society' in spite of the fact that everybody considers it as 'an anti-social evil' (LSD: 3237). Dowry was also seen as not being an urban phenomenon only. Satyabhama Devi of Navada, Bihar, indicated its practice among all castes and classes in both rural and urban areas of Bihar. So much so that the girls in the villages of Bihar were unable to find suitable grooms (LSD: 3709). Its prevalence in many Indian villages, was also testified by Sri Jadhav (LSD: 3730).

Linkages of dowry with growing complexities in Hindu marriages as well as with violence on the girl/bride was thus completely recognized. Ila Palchoudhury (LSD: 3437) noted the growing complexities in the performance of Hindu marriages. Instances of the bridegroom leaving the marriage pandal on account of some of his demands not being honoured had become quite 'common'. These demands often included financing a foreign trip for the groom to enhance his educational qualifications. As a result, she added, suicides had become quite widespread among girls who could not bear to see their parents suffer on account of heavy dowry demands. Prakash Vir Shastri of Gurgaon (LSD: 3478) and Parvati Krishnan (LSD: 3696) both mentioned cases of young girls either committing suicide or being discarded by their husbands who remarried for additional dowry. Subhadra Joshi of Ambala cited the case of a girl from Punjab pleading her father to send a radio demanded by her in-laws if he valued her life (LSD: 3705). Similar cases of the untold misery of the daughters and the bankruptcy of the father occur throughout the Debates.

In fact, the Parliament members pointed out various dimensions of dowry as practised all over India. It could be seen as an extravagant marriage expenditure, as Pandit Thakur Das Bhargava of Hissar provided an example of a marriage in which demands included hospitality for the groom's party (*baraat*) at an expensive hotel, the reservation of a room costing Rs. 250 per day for the groom, the presentation of silver plates, bowls and glasses to all the *baraatis*, and fireworks worth thousands of rupees to accompany the procession (LSD: 3446). The bankruptcy of the father of the bride was inevitable in such circumstances.

Dowry also provided an occasion for demand for gold or other precious items. Renu Chakravarty informed that the offer of gold was especially 'prevalent' in the villages where utensils and furniture were becoming less common among the average middle class families. She said that 'they extort gold, because gold is the medium of wealth. They demand it in the form of jewellery for the daughter' thus placing a large number of middle and lower middle class girls 'to a lot of suffering' (LSD: 3712-16). Demands for gold and ornaments, as Parvati Krishnan pointed out, arose out of a need to establish the grooms' families 'social status' thus causing the demand for the diamond ear-rings for the bride and 'many sovereigns worth gold jewellery and so on' (LSD: 3991). Even working women with B.A. and B.T. degrees had to pay such dowry to get suitable choice in grooms (LSD: 3715-16).

Linkages of hypergamous marriages with dowry were also unmasked. Jadhav, for example, noted that while the upper class families were able to meet dowry demands with offers of money, car, furniture, etc., to the groom at the time of marriage, its impact on the middle classes, the peasants, and the labour class was significant. These classes too tried to encash their son's marriage, especially the one with some educational attainments (LSD: 3728-9). For some, it was a pure and simple exploitation of the urgent need of a father to find a suitable husband for his daughter. Those who attained a certain status during the colonial period or earlier as Zamindars, Amins or Patils extracted dowry on account of their social status. Similar commanding position was being enjoyed by newly appointed MP's, MLA's and other influential members of the ruling party. Dowry thus increased with enhancement of one's position or status in society (LSD: 3740-2). Elaborating further, Lakshmi Bai of Vikarabad said that ministers in Andhra Pradesh demanded between Rs. 50,000-70,000 before marriage. The villagers tended to emulate these important public men (LSD: 3760). In fact, 'the well-educated persons who take medical degrees, engineering degrees—law graduates are not very much wanted now—demand the highest prize' (Achar in LSD: 3753). Both at the individual and caste levels, e.g. activities of such caste-based association as the Kayastha Sabha and the Brahmin Sabha, attempts to curb dowry evils had been unsuccessful primarily because members and office-bearers themselves broke the rules in their personal lives (LSD: 3769).

(ii) DISCUSSION ON DEFINITION OF DOWRY

The Joint Committee's Report on dowry that was placed before the House on 3 December 1959 contained the following clause:

In the opinion of the committee, the fixing of a limit of Rs. 2000 for presents, ornaments, clothes etc. made at the time of marriage to either party thereto may have the effect of legalising dowry upto that amount and encouraging the giving or taking of dowry into that limit. This would be defeating the very object of the Act, namely, to do away with the system of dowry. They, therefore, feel that item (II) may be omitted. Presents worth Re.1 would also constitute an offence.

This attempt to de-link gift-giving with marriage, thereby cutting at the roots of dowry, elicited vehement opposition from most members. In fact, the proposal of the Joint Committee to make all gift-giving an offence was spurned by '99 per cent of the participating MPs' (LSD: 3441).Their response provide valuable insights into their understanding of dowry and its implications on the finalization of the Act. This also illuminates: Which facets of the system of dowry did the legislators wish to retain and which did they consider objectionable? What was their understanding of the 'evil' of dowry?

Emphasizing the widespread criticisms that the proposed Bill by the Joint Committee on dowry received, Menon quoted the initial reactions to the Bill from a Bombay journal that described it as 'social reforms running amuck'. The journal pointed out that if a father-in-law gave even a coat to his son-in-law at the time of marriage he could be hauled up before a court of law and the magistrate would have to pass a sentence of imprisonment on him. Thus such a Bill on dowry would bring about 'many a difficulty and also outrage upon the well-settled conscience of certain sections of society' (LSD: 3239). Menon, however, deliberated that since this piece of legislation was one step forward into a new type of society such 'a sort of anachronism, difficulties and even outrages upon the conscience are inevitable' and it thereby 'expresses the earnest desire of the country to check this pernicious system'.

The 'plight' and the 'untold misery' of young girls, some members observed, underlined and justified the need for gift-giving or dowry which protected the interests of girls all over the country. In fact, Pandit Thakur Das Bhargava of Hissar (LSD: 3441) demanded the abolition of the Bill if its intentions were to abolish the system of dowry itself. Other members[16] regarded dowry as 'an ancient custom' which had provided 'security' and 'protection' to women. As such it was a mark of affection for the daughter. Thus it was 'not always an unmitigated evil'. What made this custom objectionable was the recently introduced 'new phenomenon' of dowry demands. The Speaker of the House excluded the *strīdhana* which was given out of love and affection to the daughter from dowry 'the evil'. What was demanded or given as 'consideration of marriage' was dowry, the 'evil'. If the daughter, having no other provision, was not provided with the dowry as *strīdhana,* it would cut at 'the root of even such provision for daughters' (LSD: 3446). While a son was provided education, property rights and family acquisitions, the daughter if not given dowry would be totally deprived, for her marriage severed her connections with her parental family. Dowry as such was not an evil till the demands went 'beyond the reasonable financial competence of the other party or any other person on behalf of such other party' (LSD: 3445-51). The 'unreasonability' of the demands thus depended upon the financial competence of the bride's family. No radical reform was apparently acceptable to the members.

Recurring references to the moral stance as well as natural love and affection emerge as the justification of providing for a girl who has no other means of support. Marriage, which is 'the starting point' for a girl's life, must thus be accompanied by gift-giving (LSD: 3454). The *shāstric* recommendation of the high spiritual merit of *kanyādāna* in a Hindu marriage which required the bride to be properly ornamented and clad in riches was also brought in the discussion to justify dowry (LSD: 3451). Thus, 'voluntary gifts to any extent, in any form, are outside the scope of the Bill. It is only when the money is extorted, or any property is extorted as a consideration', then it would come under the purview of the Bill.[17] Definitions of dowry which thus emerged followed the above line of thinking. For instance, Hem Barua defined dowry as 'a gift or a present which is not a voluntary present or a gift, but a present that is extorted under compulsion' (LSD: 3474). Manjula Devi (Gopalpara) defended the voluntary gift of *strīdhana*/dowry at the time of marriage on the ground of its ensuring the daughter's 'economic independence and security in life' (LSD: 3702).

But the predicament of a distinction between conditionality in payment and giving out of love and affection was pointed out too especially by the women members. Parvati Krishnan cautioned that such endorsement of gift-giving at the time of marriage perpetuated dowry as 'one of the most abominable social evils in this country (LSD: 3695). She questioned the very need for giving—whether due to social sanction or love and affection—at the time of marriage. 'If the parents wish to give their daughter something they can do it at any time from birth till the time of her death' (LSD: 3698). She criticized the suggestion of one of the members that dowry could be based on the affordability of the person concerned as an 'extraordinary' attempt 'to legalize dowry on the same slab system as the income-tax and we will have the same sort of evasion here also' (LSD: 3699).

Subhadra Joshi too demanded the de-linking of marriage with gift-giving in order to end the exploitation of women. To support dowry in order to uphold a certain tradition which was no longer favourable would only amount to accepting 'a chronic illness for oneself without attempting to cure it'. Such a tradition, she asserted, should be destroyed from its roots (LSD: 3708-9). As a result, whatever has to be given to the girl must be done outside the framework of the marriage ceremonies as it was difficult to ascertain the nature of gift-giving at that time (LSD: 3706-7). Renu Chakravarty justified this on the grounds that 'in a majority of cases, when a young bride goes to the house of the bridegroom most of the property—money cash, jewellery, etc., is actually in the control of the father-in-law or somebody else in the husband's family. Often times, the daughter-in-law is not even able to see the jewellery later on, if she needs it' (LSD: 3710-11). Therefore, the concept that at the time of the marriage of a daughter Rs. 25,000 or Rs. 50,000 will be settled to lend her security be changed drastically. In fact, setting any limit for gift-giving would only 'legalize' dowry (LSD: 3712). Women members thus questioned the daughter/woman's power to control dowry offered to her as gift or *strīdhana*, a point discussed later as a theoretical issue in Ursula Sharma's study on dowry (Sharma 1984). They thus also exposed the futility of the discussion of dowry within the framework of gift-giving.

(iii) DISCUSSIONS ON THE SCOPE OF DOWRY

Another aspect of the discussion preceding the DPA (1961) was that most members focused on the scope of dowry or on what was permissible. In spite of some, and especially women members' objections, the definition of dowry elicited broad acceptance of its equation with gift-giving. What was then needed was not to totally declare dowry as an illegal custom but to determine the extent of its scope. Thus, there were many suggestions to limit the value of 'customary presentations' made at the time of marriage to the bride and the groom.

Such limits proposed for dowry ranged from a gift of *mangalasūtra* and clothes for bride and the groom worth Rs. 100 (Jadhav in LSD: 3724); or Rs. 500 (Bhakt Darshan in LSD: 3728); or a security or property up to Rs. 2000 (Patel in LSD: 3724), to property, gifts or ornaments, and entertainment expenses to any extent provided these were not given for the purpose of procuring a consideration for marriage and not 'beyond the reasonable financial competence' of the party concerned (Bhargava in LSD: 3725-6). More specifically, Manabendra Shah (of Tehri Garhwal) suggested that the aggregate value of presents must not exceed: '(a) in the case of persons paying income tax upto 2% of their wealth; and (b) in other cases upto five hundred rupees'[18] (LSD: 3727).

Clearly, the debate centred around 'extortion' of dowry and the unfairness of dowry demands except for a few arguments to the contrary. To distinguish between gifts given voluntarily and those in consideration of marriage, limits were prescribed. But if dowry provided security to the girl as she stepped into her new life, why was there the need for such drastic limits?

The state's position on the scope of dowry was represented in Clause 2, as moved by Hajarnavis, Deputy Minister of Law, on 7 December 1959. After defining dowry, it explained that:

> For the removal of doubts, it is hereby declared that any presents made at the time of a marriage to either party to the marriage in the form of cash, ornaments, clothes or other articles, which by custom or usage are made at the time of a marriage by any person to either party to the marriage, shall not be deemed to be dowry within the meaning of this section, unless they are made as consideration for the betrothal or marriage of the said parties. (LSD: 3731-2)

The validity accorded to custom in defining the scope of dowry was an implicit acceptance of the system itself. Menon thus correctly forewarned that nothing would be 'prevented by this legislation'. He doubted whether the minister was really keen 'to check this pernicious system of dowry' (3964). To permit gift-giving according to custom would only legalize dowry. 'In exercise of the right of this custom', the grooms and their families would demand dowry with impunity. With its teeth extracted, the Bill was an innocuous document and Menon suggested it to be withdrawn from consideration.

The Speaker as well as A.K. Sen, the Law Minister, on the other hand, endorsed the giving of customary ornaments or gifts as 'absolutely obligatory' gift- giving and not 'dowry' (LSD: 3966-7). The

Speaker insisted that the intention of the Bill was to restrict and avoid anything being given by way of extortion, at the same time, excluding the smaller ones which, by custom and habit, will form a necessary part of the marriage ceremony (LSD: 3968).

While one member suggested that a schedule be prepared of the customary gifts of different regions (cf. Jadhav), Menon cautioned against the use of the word 'custom' as it was difficult to prove what it sanctioned (LSD: 3968). He pointed out the inherent danger in keeping presents up to Rs. 2000 as the limit of exemption from the penal provision of the Bill. 'In almost all middle class families the system of dowry will continue' (3970) and the government's above quoted explanation would provide 'a blanket moratorium to pay dowry, to get dowry and to ask for dowry' (LSD: 3971). Nathwani felt that the explanation was unnecessary as 'custom or usage may be interpreted or construed as dowry which is also customary, which also obtains as a practice in many parts' (LSD: 3972). Krishnan denounced the efforts on the part of some members of the House to take advantage of the sentiments of people through talk of 'spirit of joyousness' at the time of marriage, that people were happy and be allowed to give 'presents' that they naturally wanted to give. But this, according to her, would be used in 'an invidious way to avoid the very spirit' of the measure and would make the Bill 'a dead letter' even before it became an Act (LSD: 3993). Chakravarty also warned that 'custom and usage' will allow all sorts of 'blackmail dowry' to go through (LSD: 3993) and could be easily manipulated.

Summing up the argument regarding the definition of dowry, T.D. Bhargava distinguished between dowry and *strīdhana*. The latter must be permitted because it was traditionally offered to the daughter at the time of marriage and was never given as a consideration for marriage. 'Dowry' is only 'what the father of the bridegroom gets in order to induce his son to marry. And it is there that we want to eliminate the element of extortion. We do not want to eliminate all sorts of gifts. We only want to see that at the time of marriage, persons do not come with bloated faces, almost in sorrow, without any happiness and without any sort of gifts' (LSD: 3981).

To demarcate the line between customary gift and 'conditional' payment he suggested that (*i*) The court must ascertain the 'reasonable financial competence' of the person concerned; and (*ii*) It should also verify the presents' customary nature. He further explained that if a marriage is eancelled on account of the question of presents then it is payment *as consideration*, but if it is performed without consideration of presents then these amount to only 'incidental' or customary gifts (LSD: 3983-4). He also pleaded for exemption of gifts given from husband to wife or *vice-versa* from the purview of the Act (LSD: 3984-5 and 3987). Hajarnavis also reiterated that voluntary gifts to any extent, whatever may be the reason for the offer—it may be affection, it may be because the parents feel that they are bound by custom or it may be because usage dictates so, are not dowry. The term 'extortion' implies that 'but for a promise to pay that sum the marriage would not come of'. Obviously no shades of grey were evident to these honourable members. It was a case of love or affection on the part of parents vs. extortion which may stall the marriage.

Questions then naturally arose on the line of demarcation between voluntary gift-giving or legalized customary presents and dowry given out of consideration.[19] To guard against exploitation on grounds of custom, members suggested placing limits on the value of gifts in order to make the Bill more practical and 'workable'.[20] C.K. Bhattacharya explained that the sacramental customary nature of the Hindu marriage necessitated giving of gift to the daughter and the groom. The ritual of *kanyādāna* in which the Hindu father sits 'with all the things that he considers holy in life—first, the holy water, the god head represented by Saligram and other things' and says 'I give away my daughter to you properly ornamented and in the name of God' and the ritual of *vara dakshiṇā* to the groom, were some of the customs that had to be considered (LSD: 4004). Besides, no father would like to call gifts given to his daughter as compulsory, it will always be treated as voluntary. So a more realistic solution would be to limit the gift of presents and other things at the time of marriage to a certain valuation (also Shah in LSD: 4006).

The Law Minister, A.K. Sen justified gift-giving to the bride at the time of her marriage as the only way by which 'our women used to acquire *strīdhana*'. Although the Hindu Succession Act granted women the right to property, it could be defected by a will or by testamentary or non-testamentary desposition. The 'surest way' in which women can still acquire property was what was given to them by their parents and relatives at the time of marriage (LSD: 4011). Therefore, he asserted, there was no 'evil' in dowry unless extorted. It was a 'pure transaction' (LSD: 4012-13).

Finally, the Clause 2, i.e. the definition of dowry—as present in the DPA (1961), was passed with 183 members approving and 40 voting against it. According to the definition, any property or valuable security given directly or indirectly, before or during or after marriage as consideration for the marriage was to be considered 'dowry'. In Explanation I, it was declared that presents in the form of cash, ornaments, clothes or other articles were not 'dowry, the evil' unless given as consideration of marriage. Thus, gift-giving up to any amount was legalized by this act if given voluntarily. Despite the warning by members that such a definition of dowry would legalize it, the legislators paid little attention to it and bowed down to the traditional approach of the 'necessity' of gift-giving. Some members had also warned against difficulty in distinguishing between voluntary giving and extortion yet the Clause remained. As later developments were to show, it was practically impossible to prove that any 'gift' was given in consideration of marriage. This proved to be the major lacuna in the Act. Members especially opposed Explanation I as 'throwing the door wide open' (Menon); 'all dowry is legalized' (Chakravarty); and some even sarcastically commented that the word 'prohibition' be dropped from the title of the Bill (LSD: 4016). Renu Chakravarty and other Members left the House in protest at what they called the 'nullification' of the whole object of the Bill (LSD: 4209).

(iv) DISCUSSION ON OTHER CLAUSES OF THE DOWRY PROHIBITION BILL

Parliamentary discussions on other sections of the Bill did not receive as much attention as the one dealing with the definition of dowry. An overview of these discussions point out once again to the state's stance to maintain the low profile of the Prohibition Act and prevent any radical change. With dowry being in a sense legalized by legitimization of the custom, and by anachronistic interpretation of customary norms and practices, it is not surprising to observe similar effort to keep other clauses as ineffective and vague as possible. As noted earlier, the state's major aim and objectives in the presentation of the Dowry Prohibition Act was not the complete abolition of the practice but to maintain it within tolerable limits in the patriarchal social structure, of which the state itself was an integral part.

The debate on Clause 8 to consider whether or not the dowry offence be considered cognizable provoked much response. A large number of members opposed the move to make the offence of demanding or giving dowry cognizable. Their apprehensions included fear of police entering 'every aspect of our private lives' and disturbing 'the sanctity, sacramental quality and beauty' of marriage as well as simply a lack of faith in the police force.[21] Ila Palchoudhury also opposed cognizance and, instead, emphasized changing of public conscience as a corrective measure (LSD: 4246). Several members on the other hand pressed to make the offence cognizable in order to increase its effectiveness.[22] They held that an old custom like dowry could not be abolished by mild legislative measures. The gravity of the offence committed under the Dowry Act exceeded the act of murder and it should thus be made 'cognizable and non-bailable' (LSD: 4241). Without the state taking responsibility of implementation of the Act through high level police officials, the Act would remain a dead letter and would abet dowry rather than curb it. The raising of social consciousness against dowry would not alone solve the problem (LSD: 4247). The Deputy Minister of Law, however, echoed the sentiments of the majority and ruled out the need for making the Act cognizable.[23] He contended that wider powers to the police would only 'entail invasion of liberty of an individual', without any 'corresponding gain to the state' (LSD: 4248). Clause 8 was finally adopted as part of the Bill. It left the dowry offence as non-cognizable, bailable and non-compoundable.

The above debate indicates that the legislators, many of whom were prominent lawyers, always stopped short of assuaging or arousing public disapproval in spite of the DPA's professed aim of providing advantage to the public by making it more practical. It was therefore alleged that the government, while having accepted changes in the Bill as proposed by the Select Committee, adopted a different course and continuously shifted its attitudes.[24] To pass the onus of inefficiency on the police was to skirt the real issue, i.e. how far was it willing to make the legislation an effective one? Moreover, as pointed out earlier, making the offence cognizable was an evidence of the realization that the problem was grave and required urgent and effective reform. Unwilling to interfere in the patriarchal family 'privacy', the government obviously thought otherwise despite strong protests.

The discussion on Clause 3 pertained to the penalty for giving and taking of dowry. Both the Minister and the Deputy Minister of Law proposed that the giver, the taker, and the abetter of dowry be declared guilty and punished in order to make the Bill a healthy measure.[25] Most members agreed to this. Yet, they disagreed on the amount of fine. It was felt that since dowry was a 'social evil' compulsory jail sentence would turn it into a criminal offence. A heavy fine was enough as exemplary punishment.[26] Bhakt Darshan (LSD: 3744) especially pleaded for avoiding force or stringent punishment as it would ward off complainants and would also be difficult to enforce. The emphasis was instead placed on moulding the public opinion against dowry.[27] Some members forewarned that such moves would render the legislation 'lame', 'toothless', and 'ineffective'. One member for instance, pointed out that there was no distinction between a social and any other crime and accordingly no leverage was required for the former in terms of punishment or seeking evidence (LSD: 3745).

In all, 11 members spoke on Clause 3. The government, as pointed out by A.K. Sen, was in favour of including the giver of dowry within the ambit of the offence so as not to make the bill 'shorn of its value'. Only 39 members voted for excluding the giver of dowry while 141 voted for inclusion of all—the giver, abetter and the taker of dowry in the ambit of punishment (LSD: 3960). The punishment recommended by the Joint Committee (i.e. a fine of Rs. 5000 and/or the imprisonment up to six months) was not accepted. Those who voted for either imprisonment or fine or both according to the decision of the magistrate based on the gravity and significance of the offence numbered 153 while 22 members voted against (LSD: 3956) stringent punishment. The Clause 3 was thus adopted in the Bill. On the one hand, the giver, abetter, and the taker of dowry were all brought within the ambit of punishment, on the other, members were hesitant to impose compulsory imprisonment along with fine on those committing the offence. The nature of punishment was to be concurrent with how significant was the dowry exchanged. This inferred that some level of dowry was acceptable which required little or no punishment. The magistrate was to evaluate the level exceeded.

Clauses 4, 5 and 6 did not elicit lengthy discussion and were approved almost as presented. They respectively concerned with the penalty for demanding dowry, illegality of any agreement on dowry, and benefit of dowry to wife and her heirs. The penalty for demanding dowry was fixed to be a fine of Rs. 5000 and/or imprisonment up to 6 months. It was similar to the one accepted for the giver, taker and abetter of dowry as in Clause 3 (LSD: 4210). Clause 5 affirmed that the state did not provide recognition to any agreement made for the exchange of dowry. The next Clause fixed same punishment as the two earlier Clauses for the person who failed to transfer the dowry to the bride within one year of marriage. If the woman died before receiving the amount, her heirs would be the claimants to such property. According to Paras Diwan, this section has made even extorted dowry into *strīdhana* thereby changing the nature of *strīdhana* which customarily consisted only of voluntarily given gifts (Diwan 1987: 171).

Clause 7 pertained to the cognizance of dowry offence and the discussion revolved around the best method to implement the Act and to make it really effective. Patel's amendment suggested that a person convicted of dowry offence be not allowed to continue in his service or to improve his status because the ascending social status was linked to the escalation of dowry demands (LSD: 4215-17). Such exemplary punishment would convey to the people that dowry is a social evil and whoever demands it shall have no special status. This amendment was vehemently opposed by several members including the Law Minister for being too severe. Pattabhi Raman commented that this would turn 'most marriages, Hindu marriages in particular, into funeral occasions by terrorizing family members on a festive occasion. People would take advantage of this measure to settle scores out of spite' (LSD: 4224). The Law Minister dismissed the suggested amendment as an 'outmoded' one similar to the 'attitude of the law-makers in the medieval ages and also of the seventeenth and eighteenth centuries when they thought that crime can best be met by making the law rigorous so that if the punishment is very extreme it is the best deterrent against crime. It would be similar to taking a dowry-taker to his death sentence'. A wide social conscience was a more viable remedy than rigorous punishment through law. It was the system that encouraged dowry which required tackling and not 'individual delinquents'. He further said that 'I do not claim—none of us can claim—that just by passing this law we are going to completely eradicate dowry. We are not; I am perfectly sure we are not' (LSD: 4237-8). Patel's amendment was thus defeated.

Another amendment called for permission to only 'the aggrieved person' or a social organization to report dowry related offences in order to forestall false complaints and harassment due to caste or family feuds.[28] The Law Minister, in spite of the members' objections, encouraged the approach of depending upon the boldness of an individual who will voluntarily go to a court to lay a complaint when he thinks that a crime has been committed against the society (LSD: 4240). In this case, Sen felt it appropriate to discount the factor of social reality even though many members pointed out that the 'social conscience' or 'selfless motive' of people had not reached such a stage that a person could report about a crime committed against society.[29]

Clause 7 when adopted thus accordingly provided that the Courts of Metropolitan or First Class Judicial Magistrates could alone take cognizance of the offence under the Act. The complaint had to be made within one year from the date of the offence. No specifications were provided as to who were authorized to lodge the complaint. It was left to the aggrieved party to do so which was unpractical and unrealistic. They were unwilling to lodge a complaint for fear of it affecting their daughter adversely.

Clauses 9 and 10 were added to the Bill without discussion and these provided for the central and the state governments to make rules for the purposes of the Act. There was a sense of hurriedness and urgency in completing the proceedings related to the Bill. The Government was not interested in adopting the suggestions of the Joint Committee on vital issues like the definition of dowry or the nature of punishment. The aim of the Bill, as the government accepted, was 'to create public opinion' (LSD: 3748-54).[30] The Bill was finally considered at the Joint Sitting of both the Houses of Parliament held on 6 and 9 May 1961 and was passed. The said Act, namely, the Dowry Prohibition Act, 1961 came into force from 1 July 1961 (Diwan 1987: 315). Members had mixed opinion about the Act. Ila Palchoudhury, for instance, felt that such a legislation focused public attention on the dowry issue as well as provided 'a channel through which one could protest when necessary'. Others, however, believed in the need for a 'powerful movement', 'a resurgent or a generating force', 'arousal of social conscience through education' before the legislative measure could become effective. The task of moulding public opinion could be undertaken either by political parties or through social organization. Little faith was expressed in government machinery. 'The keepers of the law are mainly the breakers of the law, i.e. the police. Nobody, trusts them', Renu Chakravarty said (LSD: 3715). Instead, 'an awakened social conscience and a strong public opinion' could prevent the law from becoming 'infructuous'. Yet, on the whole, despite the large number of legal enactments being executed most members expressed little faith in the Bill. 'No amount of legislation', Patel remarked, 'will cure this disease'. It would only serve as 'balm to the uneasy conscience' of some social reformers as 'the remedy is worse than the disease' (LSD: 3742, 3748, 4249).

EPILOGUE: THE CONTEMPORARY STATE AND THE RECONSIDERATION OF ANTI-DOWRY LEGISLATION

The despondency and distrust of some members of the Parliament, who debated the Dowry Prohibition Act (1961), was not misplaced. Provisions of the 1961 Act were porous and lacked effective measures to deal with dowry cases. It singularly failed to achieve its objectives. Dowry took on wider proportions and newer dimensions than ever before. Dowry demands and 'dowry deaths' remained not only unabated but frightfully expanded forcing the state to review its anti-dowry legislation.

In this context, the CSWI committee reported that 'we are compelled to record our finding that the Dowry Prohibition Act, 1961, passed with the ostensible purpose of curbing this evil, if not of eradicating it, has signally failed to achieve its purpose. In spite of the rapid growth of this practice, there are practically no cases reported under the Act' (TE: 115). In late 1970s, the widespread agitation against the institution of dowry and for the amendment of anti-dowry legislation became the important struggles of the women's movement. However, the 'soft-peddling' attitude of the government made it prevaricate for several years before it considered amendments in the 1961 Act to combat dowry's wide social range and manifestations. The media too highlighted cases of dowry oppression and 'even a section of the judiciary and the legal profession which had earlier never displayed any concern for this problem, has now become active contributor to the debate on the dowry problem and the role of the state in controlling it' [see Editor's note in *Samya Shakti* 1984 (1:2): IX].

Finally, a motion adopted in Lok Sabha on 19 December 1980 and the Rajya Sabha on 24 December 1980 to assess the working of the Dowry Prohibition Act, 1961, led to the appointment of a Joint Committee. It was to suggest measures to deal effectively with the evils of the dowry system. After a massive study and long deliberations, a report was submitted on 6 August 1982.[31] The report traced the origin of dowry as well as the legal enactments to eradicate the evil and suggested both specific and general measures to lend teeth to the existing anti-dowry legislation.

(a) *Report and Recommendation of the Joint Committee of Parliament on the Problem of Dowry*

The Joint Committee report briefly outlined the origin of the dowry system which provides insights into the changes recommended. The Committee traced dowry to the *vara dakshinā* that accompanied the act of *kanyādāna*. The *vara dakshiṇā* was given away as *strīdhana*, which was the property of the bride and consisted of ornaments and clothes to provide her financial protection. With the 'degradation of the status of women in society' the voluntary element disappeared and what was 'originally intended to be a token *dakshiṇā* for the bride-groom has now assumed enormous proportions and as a price for the alliance'.

The report also mentioned that the 'change caused by modernization, urbanization and industrialization has fostered the frankensteinian growth of the dowry system instead of uprooting it'. The ostentation and display of accounted and unaccounted wealth at marriages by the high strata of society was emulated by the less well to-do sections.

Finally, the report reviewed several legal enactments passed by both the central and state governments in their efforts to restrain dowry. Following the Dowry Prohibition Act, 1961, several states had ordained amendments according to their local needs.[32] The amending Acts either extended the scope of the offence to include ostentatious expenses in rituals and in such arrangements as the number of *baraatis*. But the abject failure of the Act of 1961 to even 'curb the evil not to speak of its eradication' was the Joint Com-mittee's central concern. Two reasons were pointed out as causing the failure. First, it did not specify how to prove presents as dowry given as consideration for the marriage; and second, it lacked power to enforce because the complaint had to be lodged within one year of the offence to be taken cognizance of by the court. Both the aggrieved party or any invitee to the wedding would be reluctant to report the matter for fear of adversely affecting the interests of the bride.

In light of the above, the Joint Committee presented specific recommendations. It brought all the gifts under the purview of dowry by omitting the cliche 'as consideration for the marriage'. To protect the interests of the girl, dowry in the form of cash, ornaments, clothes or other articles not exceeding in value 20 per cent of the income in the preceding year of the person bearing the marriage expenses, or Rs. 15,000, whichever was less, and Rs. 2,000 or 3 per cent in value of the said income for the groom given voluntarily, was permitted.[33] This was in accordance with the committee's stated purpose of dowry providing financial protection to the bride. Also, a list and registration of all gifts for the bride in her name with adequate safeguards against its appropriation by others was suggested. Marriage expenses were also to be limited to seven percent of the income of the person bearing it or to Rs. 3,000, whichever was less.

In addition, the Report recommended that the giver of dowry, who is 'a victim of circumstances', should not be penalized. For abetters, taker or those demanding dowry, more stringent punishment was suggested. It recommended measures for speedy disposal of dowry cases and lowered the time period for the return of dowry to the bride to three months. To combat 'dowry deaths' and cases of cruelty on the non-payment or insufficient dowry, it recommended imprisonment up to a year or fine of Rs. 10,000 or both. In case a woman died an unnatural death within seven years of marriage, her dowry was transferred to her parents or children. Recommendations were also made for the setting up of family courts, reduction of time limits for lodging complaints, authorization to social organizations to report dowry offences, appointment of Dowry Prohibition Officers, and formation of a National Commission for Women. The offence of dowry was made cognizable and compoundable. Besides this, the Report emphasized as a long-term measure the minimum marriage rituals, compulsory registration of marriage, encouragement of intercaste marriages, penalization of the government servants demanding or taking dowry, and restrictions on the number of *baraatis* and ostentatious display. More employment opportunities for women and equal inheritance rights were suggested to combat the growth of dowry.

(b) *Recommendations from Other State Agencies*

In 1983, the Law Commission on its own initiative conducted an enquiry into dowry deaths and prepared a report. It redefined dowry to include 'money, or other thing estimable in terms of money demanded from the wife or her parents or other relatives by the husband or his parents or other relatives, where such a demand is not properly referable to any legally recognized claim and is relatable only to the wife having married into husband's family'.[34] It also suggested changes in the Evidence Act to facilitate prosecutions against the person committing the dowry murder, often within the safe precincts of a residential house making availability of evidence scant (see Sarkar 1988: 77-82).

The shortcomings of the Dowry Prohibition Act, 1961, finally resulted in amendments through the Criminal law and the Indian Evidence Act, 1872. To provide for punishment for violence against a married woman by her husband and in-laws, 'cruelty' was defined to include harassment and coercion to bring more dowry or leading the bride to attempt or commit suicide. Moreover, enquiry and post-mortem was made compulsory in all cases where a woman died within seven years of her marriage. In addition, the court could presume abetment to suicide by her husband or his relative if a woman died an unnatural death within seven years of marriage and if proved that she was being subject to cruelty. These measures dealt with dowry as a criminal offence and were largely in response to the phenomena of 'dowry deaths'.

(c) *The Dowry Prohibition (Amendment) Act, 1984, 1986 and Related Amendments*

The Report of the Joint Committee and the Law Commission Report finally resulted in the state's promulgation of the Dowry Prohibition (Amendment) Act of 1984. This Act came into force on 2 October 1985. Yet, it largely ignored the recommendations of the Law Commission as well as of the Joint Committee. Several women's organizations termed it to have defeated the 'basic objective of the amendment and [ignored] the active and informed social movement which has preceded the introduction of this amendment before Parliament' [*Samya Shakti* 1984 (1-2): 134] .

The Amending Act of 1984 substituted the words 'as consideration for the marriage' of the DPA (1961) by an equally vague 'in connection with the marriage' for the property transferred to be treated as 'dowry'. The Explanation 1 which had permitted giving of cash, ornaments or clothes unless given as consideration for the marriage, was omitted. The penalty for giving or taking dowry was further enhanced. The imprisonment term was to be not less than of six months but was extendable up to two years and the fine enlarged to Rs. 10,000 or the amount of the value of dowry, whichever was more. However, the court's discretion to reduce the term to less than six months was also included. The voluntary presents given to the bride and the bridegroom were to be listed. Presents made by or on behalf of the bride or her relatives in accordance with their financial status were made permissible as long as they were of customary nature and voluntarily given.

The penalty for demanding dowry was also made the same as that for giving or taking dowry. The clause which permitted the transfer of dowry to the wife or her heirs was also amended. The transfer of dowry if received by any other person than the bride was now to be accomplished within three months from the date of marriage, or on reaching 18 years of age if the bride was a minor. Failure to do so was made punishable.

The trial of offences under the Act was to be held by a court not inferior to that of a metropolitan or a judicial magistrate of the first class. No court was to take cognizance of an offence under the Act except on the basis of a police report or its own knowledge, or on a complaint made by an aggrieved person or by any recognized welfare institution or organization. The one year stipulated period for making complaints was removed. Moreover, arrests were to be made only on warrant or on an order of a magistrate. The offence, however, remained bailable and non-compoundable.

In 1985, the central government framed rules for the listing of presents to the bride and bridegroom in exercise of the powers conferred by Section 9 of the DPA, 1961 According to these rules, a list of presents, their approximate value, description and the signature of the recipients were to be maintained by the bride or the groom. The list was to be prepared in writing at the time of the marriage or as soon as possible after the marriage. Government servants taking or demanding dowry were to be punished through an amendment of the Indian Services (Conduct) Rule, 1968.

Yet, the amendments of 1984 were only an insignificant improvement of the DPA (1961). Consequently, several women and civil rights organizations prepared a memorandum detailing the shortcomings of the amendments which led to the Amendment of September 1986.[35] The definition of dowry was widened to include even the gifts given 'after the marriage or any time after the marriage'. The minimum punishment for taking or abetting dowry as well as other stipulated dowry related crimes was raised to five years and the fine enlarged to Rs. 15,000. Moreover, the onus of proving innocence was placed on the person prosecuted for taking or abetting dowry. A new section was inserted making it punishable any offer of property, share or money as consideration of marriage through journal, periodical or any other media. The scope of cases coming under the 'dowry deaths' was defined and stringent punishment was included for the accused. The 'dowry death' thus found a place in the legal statutes. Cases which had been written off as suicides earlier were now being investigated. Most of these were welcome amendments.[36]

In spite of stricter amendments, the problem of dowry however remained unabated. The state initiatives continued to be directed only at anti-dowry legislation and amendments of enactments which treated dowry as a criminal offence dealing with suicides or deaths, while the problem transcended mere legislation. The patriarchal state's miscomprehension of the roots of dowry and its dimensions both in its origins and its present manifestations thus failed to curb this evil practice.

This failure is most demonstrated in the legal interpretation of the provisions of the Act. In spite of changes in the Indian Evidence Act for the approbation of circumstantial evidence, and the Supreme Court's observation regarding the rare availability of direct evidences in dowry cases given the cultural and social constraints on a young married woman, 'insufficient evidence' was the reason given for the acquittal of many of the prosecuted.[37] Added to this, the police as the vigilant arm of the state often neglects recording the First Information Report in collecting evidence or in handling the post-mortem of an unnatural death. It often registers a case only after all attempts at reconciliation fail.[38] The low rate of conviction of dowry cases, and the long wait for cases to be decided have made retribution sought by the aggrieved party extremely difficult to attain. The National Commission for Women constituted 15 months after the National Commission on Women Act, 1990, even recommended that the Act of 1961 be scrapped as it was only a 'toothless tiger'. While the activists were particularly concerned about the Commission making its recommendation without consulting anti-dowry campaigners, it was pointed out that the urgent need was for 'plugging loopholes in the existing law' (*TOI* 26 April 1992)

(d) *State and the Problem of Marriage and Dowry* vs. *Property and Inheritance*

Concluding this chapter, we observe that the state and its legal apparatus continue to accord respectability to dowry by terming it as property to be transferred to the bride if given to a person other than the bride herself. The time period within which such a transfer has to take place was reduced from one year (1961 Act) to three months (1984 Amendment) and the punishment for failure to do so was greatly enhanced. Other measures were also suggested to safeguard this property to prevent its appropriation by the in-laws. In case of a woman's death in unnatural circumstances within seven years of marriage the dowry amount was to be given to her children or in their absence to her parents. As a final measure, the Supreme Court in its judgement in Pratibha Rani *vs.* Suraj Kumar (*AIR* 1985, Vol. 72, Part I SC 628) held that whatever was given at the time or subsequent to marriage to the bride and the in-laws was her *strīdhana* and failure to return these articles on the demand of the wife was guilty of criminal breach of trust under Sections 405 and 406, IPC (S. Murtaza Fazl Ali and Sabhyasachi Mukherji, J.J. with A. Varadarajan J. dissenting).

According to this judgement, the concept of *strīdhana* still holds good despite the Hindu Succession Act and the Hindu Marriage Act. Fazl Ali, representing the majority view described the case as revealing:

> the sad story of a helpless married woman who, having been turned out by her husband without returning her ornaments, money and clothes despite repeated demands and dishonestly misappropriating the same to her utter dismay and disappointment. When she moved the High Court she was forced like a dumb-driven cattle to seek the dilatory remedy of a civil suit. Such was the strange and harsh approach of the High Court. It may be stated that even the old classic Hindu law jurists and celebrated sages conceded certain substantial rights to the woman, one of which was what is called *Saudāyika or Strīdhana* with which we concern here.

Saudāyika included 'gifts' of affectionate kindred over which a woman has absolute control. The judges concurred with the definition of *strīdhana* as spelt out by the ancient law givers such as Manu and Katyayana. They further held that

> we are clearly of the opinion that the concept of *strīdhana* property of a married woman becoming a joint property of both the spouses as soon as she enters her matrimonial home and continues to be so until she remains there or even if there is a break in the matrimonial alliance, is in direct

contravention of Hindu law of *saudāyika* which has been administered since more than a century by High Courts, Privy Council as also this court.

The importance of the property given to a woman at the time of marriage, i.e. *strīdhana*, was recognized by the Court. Dowry in the case of Pratibha Rani was worth Rs. 60,000 which largely included jewellery, clothes and items of her immediate use as well as furniture and utensils. The court held that 'the jewellery, clothes, blouses, nighties and gowns' could be used by the wife alone and so were her *strīdhana*. Failure to return these amounted to an offence of criminal breach of trust. The furniture and utensils though belonged to the woman could be by-passed as they were of common use of the family.

In this way, *strīdhana* dowry was sought to be ensured for the woman in the same way as in the pre-1956 Hindu law. The equation of *strīdhana* with dowry and women's control over the former were major themes of the debates preceding the Hindu Code Bill, the Dowry Prohibition Act and in the provisions of the legal enactments against dowry. The former Law Minister and the Father of the Indian Constitution B.R. Ambedkar had recommended that property given as dowry be made 'trust property' for the woman to control and use, 'so that neither her husband nor the relations of her husband will have any interest in that property; nor will they have any opportunity to waste that property and make her helpless for the rest of her life' [CAI Debates (Legislative) 1948: 3631]. The term 'property' in Section 14 of the Hindu Succession Act, 1956, accordingly included the gifts given at the time of her marriage. Property was defined as

> both movable and immovable property acquired by a Hindu female by inheritance or devise, or at a partition or in lieu of maintenance or arrear of maintenance, or by gift from any person, whether a relative or not, before, at or after her marriage, or by her own skill or exertion, or by purchase or by prescription, or in any other manner whatsoever, and also any such property held by her as *strīdhana* immediately before the commencement of the Act.

Unfortunately, in most cases, dowry given at the time of marriage, if under the bride's control, constitutes the main possessions of an average Hindu girl. This is evident from references to 'helpless wife' and 'dumb driven cattle' for a woman deprived of her dowry despite such elaborate enumeration of property rights. The legitimacy lent to gift-giving by the Act of 1961 and its amendments have served to strengthen this. The Supreme Court judgement cited above has provided an exclusive and absolute right to the woman over property and gift given at the time of her marriage and thus furthered the linkages between marriage and property.

Even during the ancient times, *strīdhana*, whatever its amount, comprised primarily of gifts or property given at or about the time of a daughter's marriage. The Smritis, the Commentaries and Digests recognized the concept of *strīdhana* for a woman although their definitions varied. Its purpose in the context of the economic and social conditions as well as the cultural imperatives of those times, no longer holds true for modern times. The constitutional provision of equality between the sexes and the right to hold property granted under the Hindu Succession Act of 1956 leave little justification for a separate property for woman payable mostly at the time of her marriage. The dowry part of *strīdhana* not only recognizes the need for giving at the time of marriage on the part of the bride's family but also provides an easy avenue for the in-laws' family to appropriate it. This is credulous in the context of the arranged nature of marriage system where a girl, a stranger in the new household, is hardly in a position to secure her possessions whether given voluntarily out of love and affection or a result of extortion.

The continued recognition of *strīdhana* as an essential part of marriage and a woman's well-being and support, therefore, only perpetuates the patriarchal ideology. This acknowledges the male as the successor and inheritor of the family line and severes the female's relationship with her parental family with marriage. This thrust can be viewed as the rearticulation of the 'traditional' family structure and relationship as well as its organization of marriage and family. The linkages between the concept of women's property rights with marriage, with all its ideological underpinnings, thus gets reinstituted. Of course, we must not allow our discussion to get subsumed under an all-embracing attack on the state. The complex social reality which underlies patriarchy needs to be focused on and attacked along with the state apparatus that helps to sustain it. However, by focusing on policies and their ideological imperatives that have continued discrimination against women, the collusion between the state and the familial patriarchy gets concretized and exposed. The working of law, judiciary and the police system is one example of the role of state in controlling and enforcing various dimensions of women's oppression. Dowry or family violence can no longer be looked upon as being domestic in nature, even though the pervading ideology regards it as such.

To be sure, marriage and property rights were not issues in isolation in the ancient times. The state's policy and the dominant ideology have not allowed separation of the two issues in modern times either. In September 1979, for example, a Bill was introduced in the state of Haryana to deprive women from inheritance rights on the plea that they received their due share through dowry. '*The Organizer*', a local newspaper, supported the Bill as 'No Second Dowry'. It was argued that fragmentation of land holdings would be the adverse effect of women's inheritance. However, persistent efforts by women's groups and lawyers prevented the Bill from being approved [*Manushi* 1979-80 (December-January: 4)]. Similar move had been attempted in Punjab in the sixties to jeopardize women's succession right over agricultural land. The attempt had to be shelved due to agitation by women's groups. The above examples are evidences of the reluctance on the part of the state to make legal and social equality a reality.

However, no single factor solution is evident, for the changes that have emerged are complex and the result of a variety of interacting forces. The state has, however, largely viewed the practice of dowry in itself and not in its larger context of women's subordination or their deteriorating status. It has not envisaged the problem fully thus addressing only to the symptoms or the peripheral aspects rather than the cause of the phenomenon. The tightening of the criminal law relating to dowry is an example of this.

Another example of sustaining the structures and ideology of women's oppression is the state's support of a specific form of marriage and family. It assumes that a woman's marriage results in the severance of relationship with her parental household. There is thus an emphasis on the concept of *strīdhana* which, it believes, will provide her with support in her married life. This belief has resulted in the permission to gift-giving through law with a view to make the daughter secure in the 'new life' that she starts after marriage. While attempts on the one hand were made to make the gifts a bride's possession, through several provisions including terming it as part of her *strīdhana*, efforts on the other were also directed to place limits on the gifts. How to define 'limits' which can ensure her security and well-being?

This inherent contradiction is self-explanatory in the ambivalent and paradoxical nature of the state's intentions. Similarly, in the debates that preceded the enactment of Hindu Code Bill, its opponents insisted that the Hindu woman was revered in the family; and that Western concept of individual rights was not applicable to the Hindu joint family where the needs of each member were adequately looked after. Thakur Das Bhargava declared that 'those who want to deal with Hindu Law and the place of woman in Hindu society should look at the questions not through Western glasses but through the glasses of our own civilisation' (CAI Debates (III): 2278). It was apprehended that the grant of right to women to inherit property would lead to its fragmentation and also upset the familial traditions with women remaining single in preference to marriage or even neglecting the family with their new found independence. To counter this, leaders such as J.B. Kripalani assured that their wives as women leaders, 'lacked none of the ancient virtues of Indian womanhood' and even performed 'housework' (Everett 1981: 179). Such reassertion of the norms about the 'traditional' structure of family and marriage and women's place within it prevailed. Consequently, the Hindu Code provided only limited inheritance rights for the daughter in her parental property, and its transfer to her at the time of marriage was secured through dowry as her *strīdhana*.

Thus, the concept of women's property cannot be de-linked from marriage. The state's legal enactments and policies, although quantitatively numerous, have served to perpetuate these linkages. This, in the final analysis, is a pointer to the state's abject failure to even curb the dowry system, what to say of its eradication. Unless modernization and women's movement do not secure an equal position for women in the Indian society, the problem of dowry is likely to remain unabated within the framework of a patriarchal state and society.

NOTES

1. For example, Articles 14 and 15 guarantee equality before law and guard against discrimination in specific public places on the basis of sex. Article 15 also provides for special provisions for women and children without violating right to equality. Article 23 prohibits 'traffic in human beings' as well as 'forced labour.' Similar sentiments are to be found among the Directive Principles of State Policy [Articles 39(d), 39(e), 42], and in some of the amendments that have been effected from time to time.

2. These legislations were usually connected with some of the brutal practices and atrocities heaped on women, e.g. prohibition of infanticide in 1795, abolition of *satī* in 1829, legalization of widow remarriage in 1856, and the Age of Consent Act in 1891.
3. See chapter two for detailed discussion.
4. The Table 14, in Everett (1981: 157), gives an account of those who voted for and against the proposal.
5. For them, the ideal Hindu woman was one who was dependent, required protection, and was worshipped rather than one who demanded equal rights and freedom. They were in fact endorsing, to a great extent, such picture of Hindu women as was presented and perpetuated by the middle class. It is not surprising that even progressive writers like Premchand weaved stories and novels underscoring the above 'ideal' image.
6. See the Constituent Assembly of India (Legislative) 9 April 1948: 3628-53, hereafter referred as CAI.
7. The Women's Estate, as Diwan (1987: 111-12) writes, meant property acquired by a female through inheritance or on partition designated so by the British Privy Council. It was, however, only a limited right.
8. In fact, both Hansa Mehta, and another member of the Assembly, B.V. Keskar surmised that the Bill had only limited scope and it appeared revolutionary only because the 'Hindu society had not been allowed to evolve' for the last thousand years (CAI: 3647).
9. The Committee comprised of 21 members including three women with B.R. Ambedkar as the chairperson.
10. The Hindu Code, however, met with stiff opposition from the orthodox elements and had to be dropped. Prominent leaders too both within and outside the Parliament opposed the Bill. For example, Shyama Prasad Mukherjee said that 'the Hindu Code Bill would shatter the magnificent structure of Hindu culture and stultify a dynamic and catholic way of life that had wonderfully adapted itself to change for centuries.' Pandit Malaviya too warned the government 'not to destroy the fabric of respect for law' (in Ahir 1990).
11. Prior to 1956 only the Bombay and the Madras Schools of *Mitākshara* permitted testamentary rights to dispose of undivided coparcenary interest. Such a right was conferred upon all *Mitākshara* coparceners by the Act (Carroll 1991: 801).
12. It is interesting to note that several leaders, women as well as men, attempted to strengthen the case for equal property rights for women by asserting that such a move would not divert the latter from fulfilling their familial duties. See, for example, J.B. Kripalani's remarks about his wife, Sucheta.

13. See, the Constituent Assembly of India (Legislative) (9 April 1948: 3634) for the British motives. Similarly, Rajendra Prasad's statement on the Hindu Code Bill, which urged the Prime Minister to withdraw it on the grounds that the changes suggested would 'cause disruption in every family' is another example of the dominant ideology (cited by Sarkar 1976: 94) and is reminiscent of not only the earlier colonial state's attitude but also of all pervading sentiments of reformers three decades later which look askance at the question of women's rights with similar serious apprehensions. The grant of total legal equality would have provided a logical finale to the newly enshrined principles of equality of sexes in the Constitution. The equal property rights was only a step towards directly altering the power relationship that characterized the male domination and women's subordination. The opposition, as indicated above, was fierce and it viewed it as an attempt at the 'demolition of the entire structure and fabric of Hindu society. The very foundation not only of one pillar but of all the pillars on which the Hindu society rests are shaken' [CAI Debates, Vol. VII(II) December 1949: 784 cited in Sarkar 1976: 92].
14. For full texts of these Acts, see Diwan (1987).
15. For example, the Restraint of Dowry Bill, 1952, was sponsored by Renu Chakravarty who was later appointed the chairperson of the Joint Committee constituted to evaluate the Bill introduced in the Lok Sabha in 1959. A non-official Bill was presented by Uma Nehru, M.P., in the Lok Sabha on 27 November 1953.
16. Like Ila Palchoudhury (LSD: 3437), Lakshmi Bai of Vikarabad (LSD: 3758-9), Manjula Devi of Gopalpara (LSD: 3701-2), etc.
17. Cf. the speech by Hajarnavis, Deputy Minister of Law (LSD: 3447). This definition of dowry was reiterated by several members including Prakash Vir Shastri of Gurgaon (3480); Uma Nehru (3461); and Hem Barua. Similarly, P.R. Patel of Mehsana and Naushir Bharucha of East Khandesh condemned only that part of dowry which was given in 'consideration' of the marriage. They added that large amounts of gold or any other property offered by the father to his daughter should be outside the purview of dowry (LSD: 3713). Likewise, the Deputy Minister of Law asserted that 'where voluntary gifts are made either by the parents or relations in any form in any extent, they are not dowry. What we intend to prohibit is extortion of property out of unwilling hands of the parents. Who ever wants and is willing to give is free to give. Which one of us, on the occasion when girls from our families are married, would not like to give as a token of our affection something which we can give, which we are in a position to give?' (LSD: 3720). He went on to reaffirm, 'unless the money or property passed as consideration for the marriage, the mere passing of money is not within the section at all' (LSD: 3721).

18. Currently too, the government is setting up 'limits' on gifts—for example, up to Rs. 1 lakh in its Annual Budget of 1994.
19. See debates on this question especially by Subiman Ghosh (LSD: 3983); N. Menon (LSD: 3969); Raghubir Sahai (LSD: 3990); Renu Chakravarty (LSD: 3993).
20. Raghubir Sahai (LSD: 3989) suggested a 'practical' limit of Rs. 2000; P.R. Patel (LSD: 3999) favoured measures to presume dowry if the value of property or valuable security exceeded Rs. 2000; and M.S. Aney (LSD: 4001) and C.K. Bhattacharya (LSD: 4002) wanted to penalize payment of dowry at the demand stage.
21. See Ila Palchoudhury (LSD: 3437); Uma Nehru and Shri Narayan Das (LSD: 3770). Hajarnavis, for instance, felt that the line between a cognizable and non-cognizable offence was 'very thin'. Under the Criminal Procedure Code, he maintained, when a complaint is made to a magistrate he has to examine the complaint on oath and then either issue a summons or a warrant to the accused. He can also instead send it to the police for investigation which is carried out under the control and supervision of a court 'a very salutary protection' (LSD: 3721-3).
22. Parvathi Krishnan (3701) Manjula Devi (3703); Subhadra Joshi; Jadhav; Balmiki (3752), and Jogendra Sen (3765).
23. See, Nathwani and Renuka Ray's comments (LSD: 4231). Members also suggested that the courts' powers be widened to take cognizance of the offence committed under the Act. No police officer below the rank of a DSP could have power of investigation. This would lessen harassment of the aggrieved party as well as make the Bill more practical. The need for providing authorization to social organizations to complain on behalf of the aggrieved party was also emphasized.
24. See Brajraj Singh and Subiman Ghosh (LSD: 4242-5). Ghosh also pointed out that if the state was interested in reforms as it professed it would not hesitate to take the initiative in investigating the fifty or more cases that have come up to the court uptil 9 December 1959.
25. D.C. Sharma also wanted all to be included (3746) in the punishment of the severest form. The giver, abetter and taker were 'social miscreants' (3746). P.R. Patel (3738) and Bhakt Darshan (3739) suggested omitting the giver of dowry from the punishment in order to enable him to complain. P.R. Patel also said that due to the social custom of the imperative of finding a suitable groom for the daughter, the giver is obliged to pay dowry. Thus he was a victim of the social circumstances and an exploited person who could hardly be punished (3740). This view was upheld by Achar (3753) and Narayan Das (3773) and Bhargava (3755).

26. The fine suggested ranged from twenty times the amount demanded (Patel, 3738); five times the value of dowry or Rs. 2,000 whichever was higher and the fine recovered was to be used to help compensate the aggrieved party for the loss incurred in dowry as well as in fighting the case and also as a reward for complaint (Bhargava, 3738, 3757); or fine as the cash equivalent of dowry taken (Shah, 3740), to simply a fine of Rs. 2,000 (Balmiki, Bulandshahr, 3739). The imprisonment clause also ranged from one month in 'grave' cases (Bhargava) to three months (Balmiki) to six months (Shah, 3740 and Sharma, 3746) to no jail sentence at all (Bhakt Darshan, 3739; Patel, 3738, Achar, 3754).
27. For example, instead of imprisonment, Bhargava (3756-7) suggested other measures to mould public opinion (1) government servants, if the offence of taking or giving dowry is proven, must be penalized, (2) University Graduates when taking degrees should be asked not to take or give dowry, (3) Congress and other political party members must in their oath pledge against dowry, (4) Social organizations must be encouraged by cash incentives to produce evidence of offenses.
28. Cf. speeches of Bhakt Darshan, T.D. Bhargava and Nathwani (LSD: 4216), Sinhasan Singh (LSD: 4221), Renuka Ray (LSD: 4232). They favoured increased power of the court to take action on complaint filed and involvement of a police officer not below the DSP rank.
29. See Nathwani, Braj Raj Singh, Subiman Ghosh, etc. (LSD: 4239-40, 4245).
30. When asked about the efficacy of the Bill, A.K. Sen, the Law Minister, commented 'I have my grave doubts' (LSD: 4238).
31. Through 41 sittings the Committee deliberated with state governments, public bodies, women's groups, voluntary organizations, etc., with the aid of questionnaires inviting suggestions and comments, through study visits to some selected places in the country as well as oral evidence. Oral evidence was given by 617 witnesses representing various organizations before the Committee (in Diwan 1987: 310).
32. Six state governments passed amendments in the Act of 1961 between the years 1975 and 1976. These were the states of Bihar (1975), West Bengal (1975), Haryana, Himachal Pradesh, Punjab, and Orissa (all in 1976) and a second amendment in Himachal Pradesh in 1978. Except West Bengal, Haryana and Orissa, these made the offence at least partially cognizable and Bihar was the only state to make it non-bailable. For details of the state statutes, see Appendix II, Diwan (1987: 263-92).
33. Pramila Dandavate, a member, however suggested lowering the value of the bride's gift to 10 per cent of the income or Rs. 15,000. She also emphasized giving a share in parental property to the daughter even after marriage (Diwan 1987: 346).

34. This was hailed by women's organization as 'a concrete and a legally clear definition' [*Samya Shakti* 1984 (1:2): 132].
35. Two meetings were held in July 1984, attended by eight organizations in the first and eleven in the second. The consensus arrived at in the discussions pointed out that the Bill had largely ignored the recommendations of the Joint Committee and the Law Commission which represented a more genuine and realistic attempt to grapple with the problem of dowry with all its social, economic and political implications' [*Samya Shakti* 1984 (1:2): 134].
36. For details on this issue see a summary of the consensus in *Samya Shakti* [1984 (1:2): 132-4].
37. For example, see 'Torture is Abetment to Suicide—Supreme Court sets new precedent' (Luthra and Anand 1989). Yet, acquittals on the ground of insufficient evidence can be observed in the Court's decision of even such nation-wide reported cases as of Tripta Sharma, Sudha Goel, Vibha Shukla, Manjushree Sarda to name a few. See also Chatterjee 1980; Haksar 1985; and Rama Devi 1986 for a detailed evaluation of the judiciary's role.
38. See, 'Can Police Reform Husbands? The Crimes against Women Cell', *Manushi* 1987 (40).

CHAPTER SIX

Conclusion

Raising their banner, participants of the women's movement declared:

> We Do Not Want Dowry!
> Give Us Right of Inheritance!!
>
> * * *
>
> Neither Bride-price, Nor Dowry!
> Marriage Is Not A Transaction!!
>
> * * *
>
> Don't Burn the Bride!
> Burn the Custom!!

The centrality of dowry to the question of women's subordination and oppression cannot be undermined. The present study focuses on dowry in order to bring it to the forefront to comprehend not only one of the most pressing problems affecting women but also the larger question of women's status in Indian society. In doing so, it has drawn upon a long and wide canvas and traversed from the ancient to modern times in an attempt to examine dowry and its various dimensions. Not taking dowry in the sense of a static custom or practice, the study examined it in a historical context of the prevailing socio-cultural, political, and economic structure. This facilitates comprehension of its changing nature as well as its linkages with the state, society, and economy.

The origin and growth of the practice or custom of dowry, the study confirms, cannot be comprehended in isolation from marriage, property, and inheritance. Our forays into the historical background reveal two distinct patterns. First, neither dowry nor bride-price (i.e. marriage payments) was part of the marriage form prior to the gradual establishment of settled agricultural society and plough cultivation economy. The earliest sections of *Mahābhārata* therefore not surprisingly, exalted the virtue of what later became known as the *Rākshasa*, *Gandharva* and *Paishācha* forms of marriage for warriors of tribal communities.

Second, the shift from communal/egalitarian to stratified society led to the sway of patriarchy and the establishment of private property. This is characterized by, on the one hand, a growing entrenchment of Brahmanical power and authority over the society and, on the other, the concomitant reconfiguration of women's status. Women's sexuality was increasingly controlled and their independent economic role also gradually diminished. Caste purity and patrilineal succession both required a control of women through ideological hegemony. Such shifts are most apparent in the emergent marriage forms.

A growing emphasis was placed upon the performance of marriage in *dharmya* forms, consisting of what is referred to as *Brāhma*, *Daiva*, *Prajāpatya*, and *Ārsha* forms of marriage in the Dharmashāstras. All these forms, and especially the ideal most *Brāhma* form, promoted the concept of the gift of daughter or *kanyādāna* by the father to be accompanied by gifts of other valuable items. At the same time, the emerging socio economic pattern witnessed growing exclusion of the woman from the property of her natal family and its inheritance. The compensation provided to the fatherless daughter in lieu of inheritance was the provision of one-fourth of her brother's share in the father's property for marriage expenses and gifts. Where the father performed the *kanyādāna*, it was assumed that the prescription of gift-giving by the Dharmashāstra would be compensatory in the same fashion as the recommended minimum of one-fourth of the son's total share set aside for the daughter's marriage. The practice of gift-giving along with *kanyādāna* as prescribed in the *dharmya* forms of marriage can be linked to the shifts in patterns of property and inheritance. The concept of *dāna* associated with marriage of a daughter is what dowry originated from and meant in ancient India.

Yet as the intent and meaning of *dāna* historically changed so did such symbolism attached with dowry. Nowhere in the Dharmashāstras and the later commentaries one finds reference to dowry in sense other than *dāna*. From the early medieval period onwards, terms like *jahez*, *daeej*, or *dahej* start appearing with connotations much similar to dowry as we understand now. Etymology of these terms have been traced to Sanskrit root word *dā* in the sense of nuptial gifts or *dāya* in the sense of a share in inheritance. Needless to say, more researches by linguists are needed to confirm these hunches. What is however important for our purpose is to note that dowry in the form of both *dāna* and *dahej* was voluntary and was prevalent mostly among the upper castes and classes in the medieval Indian.society. Yet, the use of term other than *dāna* indicates the process of institutionalization of dowry in the forms of marriage prescribed for the predominant castes and classes while the subordinated castes and classes practiced bride-price or other so-called *adharmya* forms of marriage. Moreover, it indicates the continued fluidity in forms of marriage in Indian society.

It may be pointed out that some scholars associate *stridhana* or women's property with dowry. This is often cited as symbolizing women's status. The present study however argues that the concept of *strīdhana* epitomized the institutionalization of permanent dependence of women. That the concept is upheld even in the contemporary period is indicative of its hold and purpose. The *strīdhana* was an essential and inherent part of patrilineal devolution of property. It primarily constituted of items like jewellery, clothing, etc., which were offered to the woman as gifts at the time of marriage and over which she at least normatively had control. Its transmission at the time of marriage and its contents being similar to that of dowry led to its equation with the dowry. However, to equate it with dowry would cloud the multitudinal dimensions of the latter. Moreover, the *strīdhana* included gifts given to the bride alone by her natal as well as marital families while the dowry includes in its ambit a wide range including the groom's family. The equation of the *strīdhana* with dowry thus presents a misconstrued picture of the latter and glosses over the significant bearing of caste, hypergamy, and property upon dowry besides providing it with cultural sanction.

From the end of the medieval period, and especially after the establishment of the colonial rule, the modern form of dowry characterized by forced demands begins to emerge. Such shifts could be traced to the colonial reinvention of tradition and the beginning of the process of Brahmanization that in effect institutionalized and expanded the custom and practice of dowry.

'Invented tradition,' as Hobsbawm (1983: 1) explains, 'is taken to mean a set of practices, normally governed by overtly or tacitly accepted rules and of a ritual or symbolic nature, which seek to inculcate certain values and norms of behaviour by repetition, which automatically implies continuity with the past. In fact, where possible, they normally attempt to establish continuity with a suitable historic past.' The need for the 'invention of tradition' arose from the colonial state's attempt to establish its cultural legitimacy alongside its political legitimacy. The grand project of the codification of Hindu laws was thus a major effort of the colonial state towards this end, and to become, what Cohn (1983) remarks, 'insiders' from 'outsiders'. Being based on the evidences from the written *shāstric* texts compiled predominantly by Brahmins in order to provide normative injunctions for conduct, it ignored the continued and practised customs of the contemporary period and emphasized Brahmanic rule for almost all of the Hindu population through its legal agencies. It led to the beginning of a process of Brahmanization which significantly affected the Indian society.

The beginning of the process of Brahmanization meant more or less uniform imposition of a moral, religious and spiritual code of social conduct derived from one tradition on a society characterized by fluid plural traditions. The Anglo-Indian Courts thus emerged as the most important upholders and mediators of the ancient Brahmanic family law replacing the customary status and authority of both pundits and caste Panchayats in this matter. The result was the rearticulation and reassertion of the *Brāhma* form of *kanyādāna* marriage along with the custom of gift-giving or dowry as legally as well as religiously the most ideal and 'approved' system. The notion of caste purity and pollution was honoured and the inter-caste marriages were discouraged and legally disapproved. The state sponsored reassertion of a selective Brahmanic system further exacerbated caste endogamy and hypergamy—the two most significant factors, according to Srinivas and others, in sustaining and perpetuating the fabric of dowry as an integral part of the marriage custom.

Moreover, the colonial project for codification began concomitantly with the restructuring of social, political and economic order. This witnessed social mobility of castes/classes. Many castes as well as sub-castes improved their class ranks and demanded better caste status in the colonial rearticulated four varna based system of social hierarchy through census and other registration activities. This promoted sub-caste exogamy as well as the replacement of their own customary form of marriage, often characterizing the bride-price, by the Brahmanic *kanyādāna* form of marriage with dowry

Consequently, the practice of the *Brāhma* form of marriage expanded to a larger number of castes and so did the dowry. 'Sanskritization', as Srinivas (1971: 93) has pointed out, 'enabled low castes which had acquired wealth or political power to shed their low ritual status and be included among the high castes . . . while the traditional system allowed individual castes to move up or down, the system itself remained unaltered. In other words, there was only positional change, not structural change.' Thus the state-sponsored shift in the social, political and economic structure of pre-modern India did not lead to the replacement of the dowry-linked marriages by such 'modern' forms which are associated with rise in women's status and authority.

That dowry may have originated from the particular devolution of property between sons and daughters in a patrilineal set-up is in no way a justification for the system. Neither is, or was, the dowry given in proportion to the family property or assets, nor did women appear to have exercised full control over it. Nevertheless, the linkages between property and dowry help us to understand the necessity of gift-giving as also the premium placed on a male child. The cultural values reinforce and perpetuate the maintenance of the patrilineal system with emphasis and approbation of a particular or specific relationship of women with property. That the emphasis on pre-puberty marriage, epitomization of the highest spiritual merit to *kanyādāna*, culturally approved practice of hypergamy, caste purity, *anuloma* and *pratiloma* marriages, and sending off a 'bedecked and bejewelled' bride with gifts may have taken different colouration over the years but the basis of its intrinsic form has remained uncontested. This may be traced to women's subordination arising from the primary difference in the relationship of men and women to property. Consequently, the 'modern' dowry and the ancient custom of *dāna* or gift-giving may appear different in form and content or in degrees but both reflect women's subordinate position in the family and society.

The history of the growth of dowry is also the history of exclusion of women from the process of production. While the present study explores this aspect in brief, it demonstrates that there was a progressive withdrawal of women from the workforce. This indicates on the one hand the emulation of Brahmanic ideals of the upper caste by a larger number of women from low castes and on the other, the impact of expanding market economy on the home industry which was the massive retainer of women workforce. Most importantly this points to the diminishing economic status of women during the colonial period which may have augmented the practice of dowry.

Women's and the state's response to the problem of dowry have been discussed in the fourth and fifth chapters of this study. The centrality of the problem of dowry and rape in the consolidation of women's movement in late 1970s and early 1980s cannot be denied. Yet, during the late nineteenth and early twentieth centuries marked by the beginning of the first stage of women's movement, dowry received less attention than issues such as female education, child marriage, widow remarriage and *satī*. These issues were dealt with separately and treated in isolation by the contemporary social reformers who did not challenge the patriarchal family structure and singularly idealized women's role as wives and mothers. No critique of the gender-based differences within the hierarchical and power-based structure of the family and society was voiced. Their reform attempts were driven partly by the need to make conditions for women less dissatisfactory as well as to provide stability to the family and state structures. The priority to political struggle against the colonial rule later subsumed even these issues. The British 'civilizing mission' was selective in approach and always stopped short of any radical change for fear of destablising their empire.

Nevertheless, the stirring against dowry; mainly at the regional level, was significant. It, as numerous reports and comments on dowry from women's journals of the north Indian Hindi-speaking belt demonstrates, pointed out dimensions of the practice of dowry, its shift to extortionist demands and its impact on women's lives. They also offered vehement and vivid criticisms of traditional values and norms, and enforced rituals and ceremonies by the Brahmanical priesthood. An emphasis was placed on the empowerment of women through the grant of equality in all spheres. Such concerns voiced at the regional level were not articulated in the mainstream women's organization.

The contemporary women's movement originated out of the activities of several autonomous women's groups who came together in the late seventies and early eighties on a joint platform to focus upon the phenomena of 'dowry deaths', 'bride burning', and violence committed against women in the 'safe' portals of family life. Pressures from these women's groups resulted in both legislative changes and introspection on the question of dowry. One discerns a more consistent attack on structural inequalities and an examination of women's status in totality. From 'traditional concerns' with legislation, education, and political participation that marked the first phase of women's movement of the late nineteenth and early twentieth centuries, the new women's movement substantially widened the debate on dowry to the more complex question of 'gender' in its social, cultural, economic, and political manifestations. It offered explanation for women's subordinate status that underlines the dowry in the context of inequalities within caste and class structure in a capitalist economy, women's resourcelessness and lack of access to productive process, and the cultural values and the socio-economic forces that exacerbate systematic devaluation of women.

This movement, the study notes, also helped to bridge the public/private divide through the exposure of dowry related offences. It brought to public sphere the problem of dowry which both the colonial and post-colonial states tended to keep within private/family sphere. The characteristic form of the direct struggle against dowry ranged from demands for actual inheritance rights, access to productive resources within the family and the society, and legal, administrative, and social reforms.

The role of the state and its law in appropriating the problem of dowry has been ambivalent, as the study's analysis of the parliamentary debates and provision of the Hindu Code Bill with reference to property rights and dowry as well as Dowry Prohibition Act indicates. The state responded to the demands of women's movement with legal enactments to combat the evil of dowry. On the question of the structure of power within the family, its outlook was however far from gender neutral. It reinforced patriarchal interests as evident from its treatment of dowry and its perception of the problem. It endorsed gift-giving both in the ancient period—when gifts were voluntarily offered along with the gift of the bride, and in the modern—when attempts were made to transfer even the extorted gifts to the bride through provisions in the Acts against dowry. The state also upheld the tradition of providing for a girl's life-time security in the form of ornaments and other items of movable property when she embarks on a new life after marriage. Dowry or gift-giving was approved if it went to the daughter and was given voluntarily to her. The state thus maintained the patriarchal order with its concurrent and specific patrilineal form of property devolution and reiterated the relationship between property, marriage, and inheritance.

The pre-colonial state accorded considerable significance to the *strīdhana* or the women's property which consisted primarily of gifts and other movables to the bride. The delinking of woman from immovable property was furthered by the colonial state through the recognition of her only limited rights over what was gained through partition or inheritance. The post-colonial state, in spite of providing women with unprecedented rights in property through the 1956 Hindu Succession Act, preserved the earlier structure through the retention of coparcenary interests, designation of agricultural land outside the Act's jurisdiction, and other provisions of similar nature. Thus the newly enshrined principles of the Indian Constitution were circumvented when it came to providing economic and social equality to women and men. Early in the twentieth century, the state had realized the need to reform laws relating to marriage and property for abolition of the evil practice of dowry. It required provisions for adequate compensation to a woman at the time of marriage, which marked her transfer from her own patrilineal descent. But the inheritance of immovables was not approved and permanent dependence of women was thus institutionalized.

Finally, the study argues that the state's interests in the upkeep of patriarchal order has precluded comprehension of the dowry in all its multi-dimensions. The reformulation and rearticulation of tradition and anachronistic beliefs in the context of women's status that the Dowry Prohibition Act and the related rights to property acts characterized had far-reaching repercussion on the question of dowry and the status of women in society. One thus discerns accentuation of 'traditional' family organization and structure in the context of marriage and dowry as the hallmark of the state policies and programmes.

Concluding this, we must admit that the study began from hunches and ended with impressions. These impressions, it is hoped, shed lights on the complex nature of dowry in the long history of Indian society and stimulate further research towards a feminist conceptual framework for delving deeper into the history of the dowry. More historical perspectives on power relations within the family and the community in the context of gender and generation as well as the patriarchal society, ideology, and the nuclear family based on regional and comparative studies would help enrich our comprehension of dowry.

Bibliography

Agarwal, Bina, 1988, 'Who sows? Who reaps? Women and Land Rights in India', in *Journal of Peasant Studies*, Vol. 15, No. 4.

———, ed., 1988a, *Strucures of Patriarchy: State, Community and Household in Modernizing Asia*, Kali for Women, New Delhi.

Ahir, D.C., 1990, *The Legacy of Dr. Ambedkar*, B.R. Publishing Corp., Delhi.

All India Anti-Dowry Movement (Nagpur)—*A Report, 1988*, IAWS, Fourth National Conference on Women's Studies, Visakhapatnam, 28-31 Dec.

Altekar, A.S., 1956, *The Position of Women in Hindu Civilization*, Motilal Banarsidass, Banaras.

Apte, Usha M., 1978, *The Sacrament in Hindu Society: From Vedic Period to Dharmashastras*, Ajanta, Delhi.

Apte, V.M., 1954 (rpt. of 1939), *Social and Religious Life in the Grhya Sutras*, Popular, Bombay.

Ashraf, K.M., 1969, *Life and Conditions of the People of Hindustan*, Munshiram Manoharlal, New Delhi.

Asthana, Pratima, 1974, *Women's Movement in India*, Vikas, New Delhi.

AWAG (Ahmedabad Women's Action Group), 1986, *A Report*, IAWS, Third National Conference on Women's Studies, Chandigarh.

Azad, Nandini, 1983, 'Dowry Practice among Slum Women in Madras City', in Seminar on the Dowry Phenomenon, Indian Social Institute, New Delhi.

Aziz, Abdul, 1983, 'The Economics of Brideprice and Dowry', *Economic and Political Weekly*, 9 April, pp. 603-4.

Bader, Clarisse, 1925, *Women in Ancient India*, tr. by Mary E.R. Martin, (rpt. 1987), Anmol Publications, Delhi.

Bala, Krishna, 1989, 'Marriage and Violence: An Analysis of Cruelty Related to the Practice of Dowry', pp. 80-91, in Sinha, 1989.

Ballhatchet, Kenneth, 1980, *Race, Sex, and Class under the Raj: Imperial Attitudes and Policies and their Critics, 1793-1905*, St. Martin's Press, New York.

Banerjee, Gooroodas, 1896, *Hindu Law of Marriage and Stridhana*, (Tagore Law Lectures, rpt. 1915), Mittal, Delhi.

Banerjee, Nirmala (n.d.), *Interaction between Cultural Patterns, Development Forces and Women's Position*, CWDS Paper.

Banerjee, S.C., 1962, *Dharmasutras—A Study in their Origin and Development*, Punthi Pustak, Calcutta.

Barrett, Michele, 1980, *Women's Oppression Today: Problems in Marxist Feminist Analysis,* Verso, London.

Basham, A.L., 1954, *The Wonder That Was India,* Sidgwick and Jackson, London.

Basu, Aparna, 1976, 'The Role of Women in the Indian Struggle for Freedom', in B.R. Nanda (ed.), *Indian Women: From Purdah to Modernity,* (rpt. 1990).

Basu, Aparna and Bharati Ray, 1990, *Women's Struggle: A History of the All India Women's Conference 1927-1990,* Manohar, New Delhi.

Basu, Rumki, 1985, 'Dowry and Right to Property', *Mainstream,* 13 April.

Bayly, C.A., 1988, *The New Cambridge History of India: Indian Society and the Making of the British Empire,* 2:1, Orient Longman, New Delhi.

———, 1992, *Rulers, Townsmen and Bazaar: Age of British Expansion, 1770-1870,* Oxford, New Delhi.

Bhargava, P.L., 1988, 'Women in the Early Vedic Period', in Tripathi, 1988, pp. 1-7.

Bhattacharji, Sukumari, 1991, 'Economic Rights of Ancient Indian Women', *Economic and Political Weekly,* 2-9 March, pp. 507-12.

Bhattacharyya, N.N., 1988, 'Property Right of Women in Ancient India', in Tripathi, 1988, pp. 62-71.

Bhaumik, Nivedita, 1986. 'Women and Indian Nationalism', IAWS, Third National Conference on Women's Studies, Chandigarh, 1-4 October.

Beteille, Andre, 1969, *Castes Old and New,* Asia Publishing House, Bombay.

Billig, Michael S., 1991, 'The Marriage Squeeze on High-Caste Rajasthani Women', *The Journal of Asian Studies,* Vol. 50, No. 2, pp. 341-60.

Blunt, E.A.H., 1912, *Census of India*—1911, Vol. XV (United Provinces of Agra and Oudh), Pts. I and II, 1987 (rpt. of 1912), Usha Publications, New Delhi.

———, 1931 (rpt.1969), *The Caste System of Northern India,* S. Chand & Co., Delhi.

Bordewich, Fergus, 1988, 'Dowry Deaths: Our National Shame', *Reader's Digest,* 133 (797) September 1988, pp. 35-40.

Boserup, E., 1970, *Women's Role in Economic Development,* St. Martin's Press, New York.

Boulding, Elise, 1976, *The Underside of History: A View of Women Through Time,* Westview Press, Boulder, Colorado.

Bradford, Nicholas J., 1985, 'From Bridewealth to Groom-fee: Transformed Marriage Customs and Socio-economic Polarisation amongst Lingayats', *Contribution to Indian Sociology,* 19 (2) July-December, pp. 267-302.

Breman, Jan C., 1972, *Master and Servant: A Study of Changes in the Relationship between Landlords and Agricultural Laborers in South Gujrat, India,* University of California Press, Berkeley.

Buhler, G., 1886, *The Laws of Manu: Translated with Extracts from Seven Commentaries,* Oxford, London.

Calman, Leslie J., 1989, 'Women and Movement Politics in India', *Asian Survey,* Vol. XXXIX, No. 10, October.

Caplan, L., 1984, 'Bridegroom Price in Urban India: Class, Caste and Dowry Evil among Christians in Madras', *MAN,* 19, 2, 216, London.

Carroll, Lucy, 1978, 'Colonial Perceptions of Indian Society and the Emergence of Caste(s) Association', *Journal of Asian Studies,* 37 (1978), pp. 233-50.

———, 1989, 'Law, Custom and Statutory Social Reform: The Hindu Widow's Remarriage Act of 1856', in Krishnamurthy, 1989.

———, 1991, 'Daughter's Right of Inheritance in India: A Perspective on the Problem of Dowry', *Modern Asian Studies,* 25, 4 (1991), pp. 791-809.

Chakrabarti, Tridib, 1981, 'Dowry System in India: A Study of Bengalee Hindu Community', *Asian Profile* (Hong Kong), Vol. 9, No. 1 (February), pp. 41-56.

Chakraborty, Usha, 1963, *Condition of Bengali Women around the 2nd Half of the 19th Century,* Firma K.L. Mukhopadhyay, Calcutta.

Chakravarthy, Gargi, 1984, 'Dowry: Can law alone fight the feudal outlook?', *Mainstream,* 12 May.

Chakravarty, Uma, 1989, 'Whatever Happened to the Vedic Dasi? Orientalism, Nationalism and a Script for the Past', pp. 27-87, in Sangari and Vaid, New Delhi.

———, 1993, 'Conceptualising Brahmanical Patriarchy in Early India: Gender, Caste, Class and State', *Economic and Political Weekly,* Vol. XXVIII, No. 14, 3 April, pp. 579-85.

Chandran, Geeta, 1986, 'Daughter in Distress', *Mainstream,* 25(14), 20 December, pp. 32-3.

Chatterjee, Shoma A., 1980, *The Indian Women's Search for an Identity,* Ajanta, New Delhi.

Chatterji, Partha, 1989, 'The Nationalist Resolution of the Women's Question', in Sangari and Vaid, 1989, Delhi.

Chattopadhyaya, Kamala Devi, 1939, *The Awakening of Indian Women,* Government of India Publication, Calcutta.

———, 1975, 'The Women's Movement—Then and Now', in Devaki Jain, 1975.

———, 1987, 'Some Real Issues Facing Women', *Economic and Political Weekly,* 22(12), 21 March, pp. 495-6.

Chopra, P.N., 1963, *Some Aspects of Society and Culture during the Mughal Age (1526-1707 A.D.),* Shiv Lal Agarwala and Company, Agra.

Clark, Alice W., 1987, 'Social Demography of Excess Female Mortality in India: New Directions', *Economic and Political Weekly,* 22(17), 25 April.

Cohn, Bernard S., 1955, 'The Changing Status of a Depressed Caste', in Marriott, 1955, pp. 53-77.

———, 1968, 'Notes in the History of the Study of Indian Society and Culture', in Singer and Cohn, 1968, pp. 3-28.

———, 1969, 'Structural Change in Indian Rural Society', in Frykenberg 1969, pp. 53-122.

———, 1983, 'Representing Authority in Victorian India', in Hobsbawm and Ranger, 1983.

Cohn, Bernard S. and N. Dirks, 1988, 'Beyond the Fringe: The Nation-State, Colonialism and the Technologies of Power', *Journal of Historical Sociology*, June (1, 2).

Comaroff, J.L. (ed.) 1980, *The Meaning of Marriage Payments*, Academic Press, London.

Constituent Assembly of India Debates (*Legislative*), 9 April 1948, pp. 3628-53.

Constituent Assembly Debates, 1949, Vols. II, III, IV, VII.

Crooke, W., 1896, *The Tribes and Castes of the North-West Province and Oudh*, Vols. 1-4, Cosmo, Delhi (rpt. 1974).

Das, Manini, 1979, 'Women against Dowry', in *Manushi* (1979).

Das, R.M., 1962, *Women in Manu and His Seven Commentators*, Kanchan Publications, Varanasi.

Das, Veena, 'Marriage among Hindus', in Devaki Jain, 1975.

Dass, Isushree, 1866, *Domestic Manners and Customs of Hindus of Northern India*, Banaras (2nd edn.).

Derrett, J.D.M., 1957, *Religion, Law and the State in India*, Faber & Faber, London.

Desai, A.R., 1985, 'Women's Movement in India', *Economic and Political Weekly*, Vol. XX, No. 23, 8 June.

Desai, Neera, 1982, 'Emergence and Development of Women's Organizations' (mimeo), Research Unit on Women's Studies, SNDT University, Bombay.

Desai, Neera (ed.), 1988, *A Decade of Women's Movement in India*, Himalaya Publication, Bombay.

Desai, N. and V. Patel, 1985, *Indian Women: Change and Challenge in the International Decade, 1975-1985*, Popular, Bombay.

Desai, Ulhas, 1985, 'Streedhan', *Stree*, 56(661), December, p. 45(M).

Deshpande, Indu, 1988, 'Position and Status of Women in the Sutra Literature', in Tripathi, 1988, pp. 55-61.

Devendra, Kiran, 1985, *Status and Position of Women in India*, Shakti Books, New Delhi.

Devi, V.S. Rama, 1986, 'Laws Related to Dowry Prohibition and Offences', in the Report of the National Seminar on Legal Aid for Women—The Role of Voluntary Organisations, New Delhi.

Dietrich, Gabriele, 1988, *Women's Movement in India: Conceptual and Religions Reflections*, Breakthrough Publications, Bangalore.

Diwan, Paras, 1987, *Dowry and Protection to Married Women*, Deep and Deep, New Delhi.

Dodwell, H.H. (ed.) 1932, *Cambridge History of India*, vol. VI, *The Indian Empire* (rpt. 1959), S. Chand & Co., Delhi.

Dubey, Leela, 1983, 'On Dowry', CWDS, New Delhi.

Dumont, Louis, 1959, 'Dowry in Hindu Marriage As a Social Scientist Sees It', *Economic Weekly*, pp. 219-20, 11 April.

———, 1964, 'Marriage in India', in *Contribution to Indian Sociology*, Vol. 7.

Dutt, R.C., 1888 (rpt. 1972), *History of Civilisation in Ancient India*, Vishal, Delhi.

Eisenstein, Zillah R. (ed.), 1979, *Capitalist Patriarchy and the Case for Socialist Feminism*, Monthly Review Press, New York.

Epstein, T.S., 1973, *South India: Yesterday, Today and Tomorrow*, Macmillan, London.

Erikson, E.H., 1964, 'Inner and Outer Space: Reflection on Womanhood', *Daedalus* 93.

Everett, Jana M., 1981, *Women and Social Change in India*, Heritage, New Delhi

FAOW, 'Perspectives for the Autonomous Women's Movement in India', A Report of National Conference, Bombay, 1985.

Fernandes, Audrey, 1992, 'A Burning Silence', in *Women's Equality*, Quarterly Bulletin of AIDWA, Vol. V, Jan.-March.

Flavia, D'Mello, 1987, 'There is More to Violence than Dowry and Death', *Indian Express*, 24 May 1987, p. 6.

Forbes, A.K., 1878 (rpt. 1973), *Rasmala: Hindu Annals of Western India*, Heritage, New Delhi.

Forbes, Geraldine, 1979, 'The Women's Movement in India: Traditional Symbols and New Roles', in Rao, 1979.

———, 1982, 'Caged Tigers: "First Wave" Feminism in India', *Women's Studies International Forum*, 5, 2.

———, 1984, 'In Pursuit of Justice: Women's Organisation and Legal Reform', in *Samya Shakti*, CWDS, Vol. 1, No. 2, New Delhi.

Frykenberg, R.E. (ed.), 1969, *Land Control and Social Structure in Indian History*, Wisconsin University Press, Madison.

Forum Against Oppression of Women (FAOW), A Report, 1985, Summary Report: National Conference, Bombay.

Fruzetti, Lina M., 1990, *The Gift of a Virgin: Women, Marriage and Rituals in a Bengali Society*, Oxford University Press, Delhi.

Gandhi, M.K., 1958, *Women and Social Justice*, Navjivan Publishing House, Ahmedabad.

Gandhi, N., and N. Shah, 1992, *The Issues at Stake: Theory and Practice in the Contemporary Women's Movement in India*, Kali for Women, New Delhi.

Gautam, D.N., and B.V. Trivedi, 1987, Unnatural Deaths of Married Women with Special Reference to Dowry Deaths: A Sample Study of Delhi, *Police Research and Development* (January-March)

Gazette of India, 1959, Pt. II, Sec. 2; 19 August 1985 (Extraordinary) Pt. II Sec. 3, Sub-Section (i) at No. 366.

Ghosh, S.K., 1984, *Women in a Changing Society*, Ashish Publishing House, New Delhi.

Ghosha, Jogesachandra, 1928 (rpt. 1984), *Hindu Women of India*, Bimla Publishing House, New Delhi.

Ghurye, G.S., 1969, *Caste and Race in India*, Popular, Bombay.

Gonsalves, Lina, 1993, *Women and the Law*, Lancer Paperbacks, New Delhi.

Goody, J.R., and S.J. Tambiah, 1973, *Bridewealth and Dowry*, Cambridge University Press, London.

Grihalakshmi, Allahabad.

Gulati, Saroj, 1985, *Women and Society: Northern India in 11th and 12th Centuries*, Milan, New Delhi.

Gupta, Kamala, 1987, *Social Status of Hindu Women in Northern India (1206-1707 A.D.)*, Inter India, New Delhi.

Haksar, Nandita, 1985, 'Women and Public Interest Litigation: A Decade of Struggle', *Samya Shakti*, Vol. 2, No. 1, CWDS, New Delhi.

Heimsath, Charles H., 1964, *Indian Nationalism and Hindu Social Reform*, Princeton University Press, Princeton.

Hirschon R. (ed.), 1984, *Women and Property: Women as Property*, Croom Helm, London.

Hobsbawm, E.J. and Terence Ranger (eds.), 1983 (rpt. 1992), *The Invention of Tradition*, Canto, London.

Hooja, Swarn, 1968, 'Dowry System among the Hindus in Northern India: A Case study', *Indian Journal of Social Work*, January, Vol. XXVIII, No. 4.

———, 1969, *Dowry System in India (A Case Study)*, Asia Press, Delhi.

Huber, J., 1988, 'A Theory of Family, Economic and Gender', *Journal of Family Issues*, 9(1), pp. 9-26.

Ikram, S.M., 1964, *Muslim Civilization in India*, Columbia University Press, New York.

ILR: Indian Law Reports.

India Today, New Delhi.

Indra, 1955, *The Status of Women in Ancient India*, Motilal Banarasidass, Varanasi.

Islam, Riazul, 1950, 'The Age of Firuz Tughluk', *Medieval Indian Quarterly*, Vol. I.

Jain, Devaki (ed.), 1975, *Indian Women*, Govt. of India Publications, New Delhi.

Jain, J.C., 1947, *Life in Ancient India as Depicted in Jain Canons*, New Book, Bombay.

Jain, K.C., 1967, *Baudh Aur Jain Agamon Mein Nari Jeevan*, Sohanlal Jaindharma Pracharak Samiti, Amritsar.

Jain, Shobhita, 1983, 'Dowry, A Structural Perspective', *Economic Times*.

Jaiswal, Suvira, 1979, 'Studies in Early Indian Social History: Trends and Possibilities', *The Indian Historical Review*, VI, 1979-80, pp. 1-63.

———, 1981, 'Women in Early India: Problem and Perspective', *PIHC*, (42nd Session), Bodh Gaya, 1981, pp. 54-69.

Jayal, Shakambari, 1966, *The Status of Women in the Epics*, Motilal Banarsidass, Delhi.

Jayaswal, K.P., 1930, *Manu and Yajnavalkya: A Comparison and Contrast*, Butterworth, Calcutta.

Jayawardena, K., 1986, *Feminism and Nationalism in the Third World*, Kali for Women, New Delhi.

Jolly, J., 1885, *Outlines of an History of the Hindu Law*, Calcutta.

———, 1928, *Hindu Law and Custom*, translated from the German edition of 1896, Calcutta.

Joshi, Vaijayanti G., 1989, 'Hindu Women and Stridhan', *Maharashtra Women's Herald*, 1 (26, 30), 11 Nov.- 19 Dec., p. 2.

Juneja, Monica and Sudesh Vaid, 1980, 'Delhi Women Protest Dowry Deaths', *Alternate News and Features*, January.

Kane, P.V., 1941-6, *History of Dharmashastras*, Vols. II and III, Bhandarkar Oriental Research Institute, Poona.

Kangle, R.P., 1972, *The Kautilya Arthasastra*, 2nd edn, University of Bombay.

Kannan, C.T., 1963, *Intercaste and Inter-Community Marriages in India*, Allied, Bombay.

Kannabiran, Vasanth and Kalpana Kannabiran, 1991, 'Caste and Gender: Understanding Dynamics of Power and Violence', *Economic and Political Weekly*, 14 September, Vol. XXVI, No. 37, pp. 2130-33.

Kapadia K.M., 1966, *Marriage and Family in India*, Oxford University Press, Calcutta.

Kaplan, Marion A., 1985, *The Marriage Bargain: Women and Dowries in European History*, Harrington, New York.

Kapoor, Nina, 1987, 'The Ritual Murder', *Seminar* (331), March, pp. 28-32.

Karlekar, M., 1983, 'Women's Studies in the Eighties—State of the Discipline in the U.S.A. and India', *Samya Shakti*, July, Vol. 1, No. 1.

Kaur, Manmohan, 1968, *Role of Women in the Freedom Movement*, Sterling Publication, Delhi.

Kaushik, S. (ed.), 1986, *Women's Oppression: Patterns & Perspectives*, Shakti Books, New Delhi.

Kelkar, G., 1984, 'Women's Movement Studies: A Critique of the Historiography', *Samya Shakti*, Vol. 1, No. 2.

———, 1985, 'Women and Structural Violence in India', *Occasional Paper*, No. 4, CWDS, New Delhi.

———, 1985a, 'Violence against Women—An Understanding of Responsibility for their Lives', *Samya Shakti*, Vol. 2, No. 1.

Khan, M.S. and R. Ray, 1984, 'Dowry Deaths', *The Indian Journal of Social Work*, XLV (3), pp. 303-15.

Khan, Rashida, 1987, 'Seminar on Burning of Brides', *Roshni*, March, April, May, and June, Diamond Jublee Issue, pp. 32-3.

Kishwar, Madhu, 1986, 'Dowry—To Ensure Her Happiness or To Disinherit Her', *Manushi*, No. 34.

———, 1988, 'Rethinking Dowry Boycott', *Manushi*, No. 48.

———, 1988a, 'The Struggle of the Indian Women', *Philosophy and Social Action*, Vol. 14, No. 4, Dec. 1988, pp. 5-22, New Delhi.

———, 1989, 'Dowry and Inheritance Rights', *Economic and Political Weekly*, Vol. XXIV, No 11, 18 March.

———, 1989a, 'Inheritance, Not Dowry is the Issue', *The Sunday Observer*, 1 January, p. 15.

———, 1989b, 'Deprived of Dignity', *Legal News and Views*, 3(4), April, pp. 7-8.

———, 1989c, 'Dowry Deaths: The Real Murders', *Indian Express Magazine*, April, pp. 1, 6.

———, 1989d, 'Towards More Just Norms for Marriage: Continuing the Dowry Debate', *Manushi*, No. 53.

———, 1989e, 'Continuing the Dowry Debate', *The Economic and Political Weekly*, Vol. XXIV, No. 49, 9 December.

Kishwar, Madhu and R. Vanita (eds.), 1984, *In Search of Answers: Indian Women's Voices from Manushi*, Zed Books, London.

Kishwar, Madhu and R. Vanita, 1990, 'Inheritance Rights for Women', *Manushi*, No. 57.

Kolenda, Pauline, 1987, *Regional Differences in Family Structure in India*, Rawat Publications, Jaipur.

Kosambi, D.D., 1965, *The Culture and Civilisation of Ancient India—An Historical Outline*, Routledge & Kegan Paul, London.

Krishnamurthy, S., 1981, *The Dowry Problem: A Legal and Social Perspective*, IBH Prakashan, Bangalore.

Krishnamurthy, J. (ed.), 1989, *Women in Colonial India (Essays on Survival, Work and the State)*, Oxford University Press, Delhi.

Krishnaraj, M., 1988, 'Relevance of Research on Women', *Economic and Political Weekly*, 16 January.

Kunh, Annette and Ann Marie Wolpe (eds.), 1978, *Feminism and Materialism: Women and Modes of Production*, Routledge, London.

Kumar, Radha, 1989, 'The Women's Movement', *Seminar*, 355, March.

———, 1993, *The History of Doing*, Kali for Women, New Delhi.

Kumar, Virendra, 'An Evaluation of Dowry Prohibition Law', pp. 325-42, in D.N. Saraf (ed.), *Social Policy, Law and Protection of Weaker Sections of Society*: proceedings of the UGC seminar, University of Jammu.

Kumari, Madhu, 1989, 'Patriarchy and Violence against Women in India', pp. 139-47, in Sinha, 1989.

Kumari, Ranjana, 1989, *Brides are not for Burning—Dowry Victims in India*, Radiant, New Delhi.

Lakshmi, C.S., 1989, 'On Kidneys and Dowry', *Economic and Political Weekly*, 28 January, No. 4.

———, 1989a, 'Family as an Area of Power Struggle', *Economic and Political Weekly*, 24(19), 13 May, pp. 10-65.

Lanepoole, Stanley, 1951, *Medieval India under Mohammedan Rule (712-1764 A.D.)*, Calcutta.

Leonard, Karen, 1978, *The Social History of an Indian Caste: Kayasthas of Hyderabad*, University of California Press, Berkeley.

Lerner, Gerda, 1986, *Creation of Patriarchy*, Oxford University Press, N.Y.

Liddle, J. and Rama Joshi, 1985, 'Gender and Imperialism in British India', *Economic and Political Weekly*, pp. WS72-WS78, October.

———, 1989, *Daughters of Independence: Gender, Caste and Class in India*, Rutgers, New Jersey.

Lok Sabha Debates (IXth Session), 1959, Vol. 36, No. 14 (3 December 1959), New Delhi.

Luthra, Arati, 1983, 'Practices and Perception of Dowry in the Lower Income Group in Delhi', in *Seminar on Dowry Phenomenon*, ISI, 27-28 January, New Delhi.

Luthra, G., and P. Anand, 1989, 'Torture Is Abetment to Suicide: Supreme Court Sets New Precedent', *Manushi*, Nos. 54-5.

Mahila Darpan, Allahabad.

Madan, T.N., 1975, 'Structural Implications of Marriage in North India: Wife-Givers and Wife-Takers among the Pandits of Kashmir', *Contribution to Indian Sociology* (n.s.), Vol. 9.

Madhuri, Deepti, and Vrinda, 1983, 'Problem, Perceptions and Forms of Protest: Women Students in Delhi University', IAWS, Third National Conference on Women's Studies, Chandigarh.

Majumdar, R.C., 1954, *The Classical Age*, Bharatiya Vidya Bhavan, Bombay.

Mani, Lata, 1989, 'Contentious Traditions: The Debate On Sati in Colonial India', in Sangari and Vaid, 1989.

Manohar, K.M. (ed.), 1983, *Socio-Economic Status of Indian Women*, Seema, New Delhi.

Manucci, N., 1907 (rpt. 1990), *Storia Do Mogor*, Vol. III (tr. by William Irvine), Low Price Publications, Delhi.

Manushi, A Journal of Women and Society, New Delhi.

Marriot, McKim (ed.), 1955, *Village India: Studies in the Little Community*, University of Chicago Press, Chicago.

Martin, Montgomery, 1838 (rpt. 1976), *The History, Antiquities, Topography and Statistics of Eastern India*, New Delhi.

Mauss, Marcell, 1954, *The Gift: Forms and Functions of Exchange in Archaic Societies*, London.

Mayne, J.D., 1883, *A Treatise on Hindu Law and Usage*, Madras.

Mazumdar, Vina, 1976, 'Whither Women's Movement in India', *Indian and Foreign Review*, Vol. 14, No. 3, 15 November.

———, 1976a, 'The Social Reform Movement in India—From Ranade to Nehru', in B.R. Nanda, 1976.

———, 1983, 'The Role of Research in Women's Development: A Case Study of the ICSSR Programme of Women's Studies', *Samya Shakti*, Vol. 1, New Delhi.

———, 1985, 'Emergence of Women's Question and Role of Women's Studies', CWDS, New Delhi.

Metcalf, T.R., 1969, 'From Raja to Landlord: The Oudh Talukdars 1830-

1870', and 'Small Effects of British Land Policy in Oudh', in Frykenberg, 1969.

Mies, Maria, 1980, *Indian Women and Patriarchy*, Vikas, New Delhi.

Mill, James, 1840, *The History of British India*, with notes by H.H. Wilson, 5th edn., London.

Miller, Barbara D., 1980, 'Female Neglect and Costs of Marriage in Rural India', *Contributions to Indian Sociology*, Jan.-June 1980, pp. 95-129.

Mishra, Rekha, 1967, *Women in Mughal India (1526-1707 A.D.)*, Munshiram Manoharlal, Delhi.

Mukherjee, Ila, 1972, *Social Status of North Indian Women 1526-1707 A.D.*, Shiv Lal Agarwala and Company, Agra.

Mukherji, Partha N., 1986, 'Sex and Social Structure', *Man and Development*, 8(4), December, pp. 120-46.

Mukhopadhya, Arundhati, 'Attitudes towards Religion and Culture in Nineteeth Century Bengal: The Tatvabodhini Sabha', in *Studies in History*, (n.s.), Vol. 3, No. 1, pp. 9-28.

Mukund, Kanaklatha, 1992, 'Turmeric Land, Women's Property Rights in Tamil Society Since Early Medieval Times', *Economic and Political Weekly*, 25 April.

Murti, M. Srimannarayan, 1988, 'Position and Status of Women in the Age of the Liturgical Samhitas, Brahmanas and Upanishads (c.1500-500 B.C.)', in Tripathi, 1988.

Nair, P.T., 1978, *Marriage and Dowry in India*, Minerva Associate Publications, Calcutta.

Nanaiah, Saraswathi N., 1992, *The Position of Women during Vijayanagara Period (1336-1646)*, Saraswathi Publication, Mysore.

Nand, Lokesh Chandra, 1989, *Women in Delhi Sultanat*, Vohra Distributors and Publishers, Allahabad.

Nanda, B.R. (ed.), 1976, *Indian Women: From Purdah to Modernity*, Radiant, New Delhi.

Nangia, J.N., 1984-5, *Dowry*, Pragati Prakashan, New Delhi.

Narang, Bhim Sain, 1990, *Concept of Stridhana in Ancient India*, Parimal Publication, Delhi.

Nari Mukti Sangharsh Sammelan: Resolutions, 1988, pp. 1-3.

Natarajan, Saroj, 1959, *A Century of Social Reform in India*, Asia Publishing House, New Delhi.

Nath, Vijay, 1989-90, 'Ritual Symbolism and Status Conferring Role of Dana', *PIHC*, Golden Jubilee Session, Gorakhpur, pp. 80-7.

National Federation of Indian Women, 1987, 'Know Your Legal Rights: Return of Dowry (Stridhan)', *Bulletin*, May, pp. 3-4.

National Federation of Indian Women, 1987, 'Hindu Women's Right to Property', *Bulletin*, July, pp. 4-6.

Ojha, P.N., 1956, 'Early Marriage, Dowry and Divorce in Northern India under the Great Mughals (1556-1707)', *PIHC*, (19th Session), pp. 263-70, Agra.

Oldenburg, V., 1984, 'Women Against Women or Culture against Women?', paper presented at the New York State Asian Conference, State University of New York, Courtland, October.

Omvedt, Gail, 1975, 'Caste, Class and Women's Liberation in India', in *Bulletin of Concerned Asian Scholars*, 7 Jan.-7 March, pp. 43-8.

———, 1976, *Cultural Revolt in a Colonial Society*, Bombay.

———, 1987, 'Feminism and the Women's Movement in India', mimeo, SNDT Women's University, Bombay.

———, 1988, 'Women and Violence', paper presented at the Fourth NCWS, Vishakhapatnam.

Pal, Radha Binod, 1938, 'History of Hindu Law in the Vedic Age and in Post-Vedic Times Down to the Institutes of Manu', New Delhi.

Palriwala, R., 1986, 'Suicides under Scrutiny—India's Anti-Dowry Campaign', *Inside Asia*, April-May, pp. 38-9.

———, 1989, 'Reaffirming the Anti-Dowry Struggle', *Economic and Political Weekly*, No. 17, 29 April.

Pande, S., 1988, 'Rights of Women in the Arthasastra', in Tripathi, 1988.

Pandey, R.B., 1949, *Hindu Samskaras*, Vikrama Publication, Banaras.

Pandey, U.C., 1967, *Yajnavalkya Smriti (Yajna)* (translated), Chowkhmba Prakashan, Varanasi.

Pandhe, Sunita, 1988, 'Women's Studies and Women's Movement', *Economic and Political Weekly*, 23(40), 1 October, pp. 2049-50.

Panikkar, K.M., 1961, *Hindu Society at Cross Roads*, Asia Publishing House, Bombay.

Parliament Debates, 1951, Vols. VI-XVI (Pt. 2).

Patel, Vibhuti, 1989, 'National Conference on Women, Religion and Family Laws in India—A Report', *The Indian Journal of Social Work*, 50(1), January, pp. 125-8.

———, 'Reaching for Half the Sky', Reflections of Fourth National Conference on Women's Movement in India—A Summary Report, SNDT University, Bombay.

Paul, Madan C., 1986, *Dowry and Position of Women in India*, Inter-India, New Delhi.

PIHC, Proceedings of the Indian History Congress.

Pradhan, Shruti S, 1988, 'The Concept of *Kanya Sulka* in Vedic and Post-Vedic Literature', *Annals of the Bhandarkar Oriental Research Institute*, 69(1-4), pp. 29-49.

Rajaraman, Indira, 1983, 'Economics of Bridewealth and Dowry', *Economic and Political Weekly*, 19 February, pp. 275-80.

Ramu, G.N., 1977, Family and Caste in Urban India, Vikas, Delhi.

Randeria, Shalini and Leela Visaria, 1984, 'Sociology of Bride Price and Dowry', *Economic and Political Weekly*, 14 April.

Rao, Kitty Shiva, 1948, 'The Hindu Code', *Roshni*, Special No., AIWC.

Rao, M.S.A. (ed.), 1979, *Social Movements in India*, Vol. II, Manohar, New Delhi.

Rao, V.V.P, and V.N. Rao, 1982, *Marriage, the Family and Women in India*, South Asian Books, Missouri.

Ravindran, Visa, 1994, 'The Darkness Has Not Lifted for Women', *The Hindu*, 17 April.

Ray, Bibekananda, 1983, 'Dowry to the Daughter', *Amrita Bazar Patrika*, 10 July, p. 6.

Ray, Rajat K., 1975, 'Differential Modernization in the Colonial Society: Bengal under Lt. Governors', *The Indian Historical Review*, Vol. II, No. 1 (July).

Rigveda (RV), 1905, With Sayana's Commentary, edited with notes and translation by P. Petuson, 3rd edn., revised and enlarged by S.R. Bhandarkar, Bombay.

Risley, Herbert, 1915 (rpt. 1969), *The People of India*, Oriental Books, Delhi.

Rowe, William R., 1969, 'Mobility in the 19th Century Caste System', in Singer and Cohn, 1968.

Roy, Kumkum, 1985, 'Legitimation and the Brahmanical Tradition: The Upanayana and the Brahmacharya in the Dharma Sutras', *PIHC*, 46th Session, Amritsar, pp. 136-46.

Ruth Vanita, 1987, 'Can Police Reform Husbands: The Crimes against Women Cell, Delhi', *Manushi*, 40[7(4)]; May-June, pp. 12-18.

Sachau, Edward C. (tr.), 1971, *Alberuni's India* , W.W. Norton and Company, New York.

Saheli, Allahabad.

Sambrani, Rita Bhandari, and Sreekant Sambrani, 1983, 'Economics of Bride-price and Dowry-l', *Economic and Political Weekly*, 9 April, pp. 601-3.

Samya Shakti, A Journal of Women's Studies, CWDS, New Delhi.

Sampurnananda, 1956, *Hindu Vivāh Men Kanyādān kā Sthān*, Bharatiya Jñanpīth Pitha, Varanasi.

Sandhu, M.K., 1988, 'A Study of Dowry among Working and Non Working Women', *The Indian Journal of Social Work*, 49(2), April, pp. 155-64.

Sangari, Kumkum, and Sudesh Vaid (eds.), 1989, *Recasting Women: Essays in Colonial History*, Kali for Women, New Delhi.

Sanyal, Hiteshranjan, 1975, 'Social Mobility in Bengal: Its Sources and Constraints', *The Indian Historical Review*, Vol. II, No. 1.

Saraf, Samarendra, 1973, 'Hindu Marriage and Dowry', *Vivekananda Kendra Patrika*, Aug. 2(2), p. 6.

Sarkar, Lotika, 1976, 'Jawaharlal Nehru and the Hindu Code Bill', in B.R. Nanda, 1976.

———, 1988, 'National Specialised Agencies and Women's Equality', A Report, *Law Commision of India*, CWDS, New Delhi.

Sarkar, S.C., 1928, *Some Aspects of the Earliest Social History of India*, London.

Sastri, H.C., 1972, *The Social Background of the Forms of Marriage in Ancient India*, Vol. I, Sanskrit Pustak Bhandar, Calcutta.

Shamsastry, R. (tr.), 1929, *Kautilya's Arthshastra (AS)*, Wesleyan Mission Press, Mysore.

Sharma, B.N., 1958, 'Varṇāshrama Vyvasthā in the Age of Harsha', *PIHC* (21st Session, Trivandrum), pp. 169-78.

———, (1) 1966, *Social Life in Northern India (AD 600-1000)*, Munshiram Manoharlal, New Delhi.

Sharma, Kumud, n.d., 'Women's Movement in India, Dialectics and Dilemma', CWDS, New Delhi, pp. 1-26.

Sharma, Radha Krishna, 1981, *Nationalism, Social Reform, Indian Women, 1921-37*, Janaki Prakashan, Patna.

Sharma, R.S., 1966, *Light on Early Indian Society and Economy*, Manaktalas, Bombay.

———, 1983, *Perspectives in Social and Economic History of Early India*, Munshiram Manoharlal, New Delhi.

Sharma, Shubhra, 1988, 'Women in the Sutra Period', in Tripathi, 1988.

Sharma, Ursula, 1980, *Women, Work and Property in North-West India*, Tavistock, London.

———, 1984, 'Dowry in North India: Its Consequences for Women', in Hirschon, 1984.

Shastri, Madhu, 1990, *Status of Hindu Women*, RBSA Publications, Jaipur.

Sheel, Ranjana, 1997, 'Institutionalisation and Expansion of Dowry System in Colonial North India', *Economic and Political Weekly*, 6-12 September.

Sheth, Surbhi, 1979, *Religion and Society in the Brahma Purana*, Sterling, New Delhi.

Singer, Milton and Bernard S. Cohn (eds.), 1968, *Structure of Change in Indian Society*, Aldine, Chicago.

Singh, Indu Prakash and Renuka Singh, 1988, 'Dowry: How Many More Deaths?', *JNU News* 9(6), April 1988, pp. 28-31.

Singh, M.P., 1981, *Life in Ancient India*, Vishwavidyalaya Prakashan, Varanasi.

Singh, Sarva Daman, 1959, 'Social Life as Depicted in Medhatithi', in *PIHC* (22nd Session, Gauhati), pp. 119-28.

Singh, Sitaram, 1968, *Nationalism and Social Reform in India*, Ranjit Printers, Delhi.

Sinha, Mrinalini, 1986, 'Colonial Politics and the Ideal of Masculinity', Indian Association of Women's Studies, Third National Conference on Women's Studies, Chandigarh, 1-4 October.

Sinha, Niroj, 1989, *Women and Violence*, Vikas, New Delhi.

Sircar, D.C., 1967, *Studies in the Society and Administration of Ancient and Medieval India*, Vol. I, Firma K.L. Mukhopadhyay, Calcutta.

Siu, Helen, 1990, 'Reconstituting Dowry and Brideprice in South China', in *Family Strategies in Post Mao China*, Debrah Davis and Stevan Harrel, California (forthcoming).

Sontheimer, Gunther-Dietz, 1977, *The Joint Hindu Family: Its Evolution as Legal Institution*, Munshiram Manoharlal, New Delhi.

Srinivas, M.N., 1966 (rpt. 1971), *Social Change in Modern India,* Orient Longman, New Delhi.

———, 1968, 'Mobility in the Caste System', in Singer and Cohn, 1968.

———, 1984, *Some Reflections on Dowry,* CWDS, New Delhi.

Stein, Burton, 1991, 'Towards an Indian Petty Bourgeoise: Outline of an Approach', *Economic and Political Weekly,* 26 January.

Sternbach, L., 1965, *Juridical Studies in Ancient Indian Law,* Pt. II, Motilal Banarsidass, New Delhi.

Stree Darpan, Allahabad.

Stri Kriti Samiti, Bombay, 1984, Report presented in IAWS, Second National Conference on Women's Studies, Trivandrum, 9-12 April.

Supreme Court, *AIR* 1985, Vol. 72, Pt. I.

Talbot, Cynthia, 1980, 'How to Get a Wife: Marriage Strategies in the Mahabharata', Master's Thesis (unpubl.), University of Michigan, Ann Arbor.

Talwar, Vir Bharat, 1989, 'Feminist Consciousness in Women's Journals in Hindi, 1910-20', in Sangari and Vaid, 1989.

Thapar, Romila, 1963, 'History of Female Emancipation in Southern Asia', in Barbara Ward (ed.), *Women in the New Asia,* UNESCO, Paris, 1963.

———, 1975, 'Looking Back in History', in Devaki Jain (ed.).

———, 1978, *Ancient Indian Social History: Some Interpretations,* Orient Longman, New Delhi.

———, 1984, *From Lineage to State,* Oxford University Press, Bombay.

Thomas, P., 1964, *Indian Women through the Ages,* Asia Publishing House, Bombay.

Times of India, New Delhi.

Towards Equality, 1974, Report of the Committee on the Status of Women in India, Government of India.

Tripathi, L.K. (ed.), 1988, *The Position and Status of Women in Ancient India,* Banaras Hindu University, Varanasi.

Trivedi, K.K., 1975, 'Changes in the Caste Composition of the Zamindar Class in Western Uttar Pradesh, 1595-circa 1900', *The Indian Historical Review,* Vol. II, No. 1 (July).

Trautman, T.R., 1981, *Dravidian Kinship,* Cambridge University Press, New York.

Tulsidasa, rpt. 1976, *Shri Ramcharitamanas,* Gita Press, Gorakhpur.

Turner, A.C., 1933, *Census of India, 1931* (United Provinces of Agra and Oudh), Pts. I and II, Usha Publications, New Delhi.

Upadhyaya, B.S., 1941, *Women in Rigveda* (rpt. 1994), Khama Publishers, New Delhi.

Upadhya, Carol Boyack, 1990, 'Dowry and Women's Property in Coastal Andhra Pradesh', *Contributions to Indian Sociology* (n.s.) 24, 1.

Vaidya, C.V., 1933, *Epic India* (1st rpt.) The Bombay Book Depot, Bombay.

Van der Veen, Klas, 1972, *I Give Thee My Daughter—A Study of Marriage and Hierarchy Among the Anavil Brahmins of South Gujarat*, Van Gorcum & Co., N.V., Assen.

Vatuk, Ved Prakash and Sylvia Vatuk, 1976 'The Social Context of Gift Exchange in North India', in Giri Raj Gupta, ed., 1976, *Family and Social Change in India*, New Delhi.

Verghese, Jamila, 1980, *Her Gold and Her Body*, Vikas, New Delhi.

Vishnoi, Savita, 1988, *Economic Status of Women in Ancient India*, Kusumanjali, Meerut.

Vivekananda, Swami, 1958, *Complete Works*, Pts. II and V, Advaita Ashram, Almora.

Watters, T., 1904-5, *On Yuan Chwang's Travels in India AD 629-645*, Royal Asiatic Society, London.

Westermarck, E., 1926, *History of Marriage*, Macmillan, London.

Index